Be Somebody

A Biography of

Marguerite Rawalt

To Sharon Petersen
Marguerite Rawalt

By

Judith Paterson

EAKIN PRESS ★ Austin, Texas

FIRST EDITION

Copyright © 1986
By Judith Paterson

Published in the United States of America
By Eakin Press, P.O. Box 23066, Austin, Texas 78735

ISBN 0-89015-551-8

Library of Congress Cataloging in Publication Data

Paterson, Judith, 1938–
    Be somebody : A biography of Marguerite Rawalt.

    1. Rawalt, Marguerite, 1895–   . 2. Feminists — United States —
Biography. 3. Women lawyers — United States — Biography.   I. Title.
HQ1413.R39P37 1986   305.4'2'0924   85-31151
ISBN 0-89015-551-8

It certainly must have been a relief for the women of the country to realize that one could be a woman and a lady and yet be thoroughly political.

> — Agnes Meyer
> Letter to Eleanor Roosevelt
> July 25, 1952

Contents

Marguerite Rawalt

Foreword

By Liz Carpenter

[Journalist and activist for ERA]

It was a day to remember — New Year's Day of 1986, the first
day of the Sesquicentennial and here was Marguerite Rawalt more
than half as old as Texas, eating the customary black-eyed peas for
good luck. She had flown up that day, alone, from Corpus Christi,
to be the honoree at the New Year's Day gathering at my house.
And as it turned out, she had arisen at five to catch a 6:30 A.M.
plane, which she had to board and unboard to take another plane
when the first turned out to have engine trouble. So she arrived at
10:30, met by her friend and publisher, Ed Eakin, who had chosen
her for one of his Sesquicentennial books. He gallantly offered to
meet her so I could get the brunch ready and keep her promise to
return to her Corpus kinfolks at 3:30 that afternoon. I had tried to
round up people who would have known a piece of Marguerite's life
as a Texan. Marguerite was once secretary to Governor Pat Neff,
early woman lawyer, battler for the Equal Rights Amendment
which kept her before the Congress analyzing the legislation for
forty years, and organizing genius and president of the national and
international women's clubs. She had worked for progressive
causes within the establishment, the Democratic Party, and her
wide influence among thousands of friends.

Marguerite has never been open about her age. She's from a
generation that wasn't, and she still prefers not to mention it. So I
won't either. But what a lot of history she has seen and made happen. Her memory stretched back beyond everyone gathered to
greet her, and none of us were spring chickens.

So there we were on this clear, crisp January day sharing anec-
dotes of time and politics: Lady Bird Johnson, Congressman Jake
Pickle, Chrys Dougherty, a leading American jurist and once pres-

ident of the Texas Bar Association, and a dozen more. She kept us enthralled remembering, joking, laughing about presidents from Herbert Hoover to Ronald Reagan; governors from Pat Neff to Mark White; women leaders from Alice Paul to Ellie Smeal. She had known "Lyndon" when he was a congressional secretary on Capitol Hill, an early job that was forever to make him understand government as no other president. They had both been in Washington in the early 1930s when FDR was lifting the country out of the Depression with the heady whirlwind legislation and Lyndon Johnson was running the office of Congressman Dick Kleberg, "my Congressman," as Marguerite said, for her Texas roots were South Texas, the King Ranch area. She had known the Texas delegation in Congress pre-Lyndon, pre-Pickle, pre-Thornberry — back when James Buchanan was the congressman from Austin's Central Texas district. And she had known the American Bar Association when there was no woman admitted to the House of Delegates. Indeed, she had been the very first woman admitted to it. And she saw that the door remained open for others. She had also known the long string of national figures who made history for women: Eleanor Roosevelt and her coterie of women reformers; and in Texas, the women who were out front for suffrage, Minnie Fisher Cunningham, State Senator Margie Neal, Sarah T. Hughes. Her string of marvelous male admirers included some of Texas' best known powers: Harry Crozier, Louis Bennett who would take her out to dinner when he came to Washington and advise her, "Eat well. Don't diet. Get fat and be somebody," and of course, Pat Neff who went on from the governor's office to the National Mediation Board in Washington and wired back: "You can come to Washington as my secretary and attend a first-rate law school at night." And she did, launching a legal career and political influence that was felt over six decades. But she never lost her Texas citizenship or voting rights.

Indeed, she first knew Texas from riding a covered wagon across the Texas Panhandle with her family.

"I was about eleven. We children didn't think about hardship. We followed the windmills, from ranch to ranch, to find our way from Oklahoma to New Mexico. It was great fun," she told me.

"Windmills were the landmarks that marked our way. My brother and I would ride the wagon awhile and then change to the buggy behind and pull up in front occasionally to see the wide horizons that lay ahead of us. All of our goods were in the wagon, pulled by two mules. We were children going west on an adventure and we loved it."

Actually Marguerite has always been pulling out front, looking for the wide horizons. Fences were overcome. She has spent a lifetime helping remove the fences for women. And she still has the sparkling eyes, the commanding knowledge, the gentle presence, trademarks she carries along her trails of life. There is much to be proud of among her milestones.

"I guess I am proudest of getting women admitted to the ABA," she told me when I pressed her, "creating the first women's tax-exempt foundation when I was president of the federation of Business and Professional Women's Clubs, testifying before congressional committees of both houses, fully analyzing the decisions of the United States Supreme Court which had always denied that the equal protection clause protected women, and shepherding the precedent-setting cases banning sex discrimination under Title VII."

Just a few things like that which had made it easier for women to operate as equals, or almost as equals, since both Marguerite and I know and still fight to get women into the constitution through those sixteen little words of the Equal Rights Amendment: "equality of rights under the law shall not be denied nor abridged on account of sex." We had seen it passed after dragging its feet in Congress for forty-seven years. We had seen thirty-four of the necessary thirty-seven states ratify it, and then we had done battle for Congress to extend the time allowed. And we had won briefly. But the end was still out of reach. I remember May 17, 1978, when I was asked to testify as chairman of ERAmerica before Don Edwards's subcommittee on Civil and Constitutional Rights. There we were in the crowded House Judiciary Committee chamber eyeball to eyeball with the enemy, Phyllis Schlafly and her Stop ERA troops. I was no lawyer. But I asked for the best and got her — Marguerite herself — who knew law and the history of this legislation better than anyone in the country. It made all the difference to have her at my side. She went to the well with me that day, steady, backed up by the ammunition of facts, and ready to fire when we needed it. We extended the time in which ERA could be passed again. In the unbelievably brutal battle to win the last three states, we lost. Five votes in three state legislatures could have changed the outcome. It was a heartbreak, for by now the majority of both men and women were favoring it in all the polls and we know it was only a matter of time. One day it will pass, probably in a whisper, and America will wonder, after it is done, why we were so long in bringing about equal rights just as we now wonder why it took so long with the civil rights legislation.

That is part of the story that makes *Be Somebody* Marguerite's own story. And it is an intriguing story, with the inner struggles told; how hard it was to pull labor behind ERA after their traditional opposition; how often the weak buckled under; how necessary it was to have someone who knew the law and how to use it to keep this alive, and among them, the marriages of Marguerite, two of them, both interesting men as one would expect.

None of us gathered over the black-eyed peas on New Year's Day knew all of Marguerite's story. And she doesn't talk about herself. But what we all knew by the time she left to take the plane back to Corpus alone was that we had been in the presence of somebody who was somebody and that we would soon read her whole story, a story of one woman's efforts for equal rights for herself and others. It is part of the history of human rights.

The story has been culled from the detailed, well-organized journals and diaries which Marguerite kept. Even more so from the voluminous letters she has kept since she first went to work ("I have copies of every letter I ever wrote"). And from the oral histories she has given from her exacting and lucid memory. Unlike so many, she remembers both the date and the flavor of an incident. It has been marvelous that Judith Paterson has had access to all of the papers and to Marguerite. Marvelous for women. Marvelous for Texas. I want Marguerite on hand in my library forever.

Texas can cheer for its 150th birthday better because of the tireless work, cheerful optimism, and courage of this particular woman.

Foreword

By Martha W. Griffiths
[*Lieutenant-Governor, State of Michigan*]

I am delighted that a book has been written about Marguerite Rawalt. Marguerite is a dear friend for whom I have the greatest admiration and respect. Her life is not only the story of a remarkable, courageous, and determined woman, but a chronicle of the women's rights movement in this country.

In the struggle to achieve equal rights for women, Marguerite has been a dynamic force. The triumph of congressional passage of the Equal Rights Amendment in 1972 is tribute to her leadership and commitment to justice. I believe all of us who participated and had a role in that historic moment acknowledge that were it not for Marguerite, victory may have been lost.

Marguerite became a worker for the "cause" long before emergence of any women's rights movement. A child of the last frontier, she firmly believed in the promise of the land in which she was reared and its guarantees of equality and opportunity. Yet, she was as much a product of her times as she was the instigator of change. Like so many of her generation, she learned the hard way that life was not fair and that even an education, law degree, and brilliant mind would not insure success or overcome the many man-made barriers to equal opportunity.

It was following World War II and later that Marguerite put her principles into action with the greatest amount of enthusiasm. She was quick to observe the vast social and economic changes taking place forcing a reevaluation of traditional ways of thinking about women and their role in society. Using the forum of the vast network of professional women's organizations to which she belonged, she called for an end to sex discrimination and for a constitutional amendment to assure women equal protection under the law. Moreover, she began documenting and challenging inequities in the law which were denying women equal access to education, housing, jobs, and full opportunity.

What she accomplished was extraordinary. Working together with legislators, individuals, and innumerable groups of women, Marguerite gradually was able to help mold the national consensus and support for moving the Equal Rights Amendment through the Congress. This was no easy task, particularly given the sharp divisions and diversity of views in the women's ranks.

Unquestionably, there was no one more ably suited to take on this tremendous challenge. Marguerite was a doer, and she knew how to get the job done. An astute observer of the political scene, she understood the workings of Congress and its centers of power. She also was a woman of exceptional abilities, intellect, and incredible stamina. Most of us were staggered by the enormous amounts of time and energies she voluntarily put into this effort at great personal sacrifice.

Marguerite's qualities were second to none. She was a strong but gracious woman of immense loyalties. Although her nature was aggressive, she was sensitive to the feelings of others. She led, but was able to listen and learn. She seemingly was never embittered by defeat or frustrated to the point of inaction.

Her legal expertise made her powerfully persuasive. Even those who disagreed, respected her knowledge and integrity. But, in my judgment, her real effectiveness lay in her vast organizational skills. She believed in organizations and their capacity for strength and education. If one failed her or she became dissatisfied, she simply went on to join or help create another. She knew incredible numbers of people across the country, and they knew her. In the end, it was this resource which she drew upon to mobilize women into a nationwide campaign to pass the ERA. Nothing to this day gives me greater satisfaction than to recall the astonishment of my male colleagues when the ERA reached the House and Senate floors. Not only were they stunned by the intensity of Marguerite's campaign, but they were awakened to a new political force.

I have only the highest words of praise for Marguerite. Her fight as an individual citizen against social and economic injustice touched the lives of millions of women. I am proud to have shared this exciting time in our history with Marguerite and countless others whose contributions were equally important. Although ratification of the ERA was not achieved, its passage was a turning point marking the beginning of the end to decades of discrimination.

I sincerely hope that Marguerite's story will serve as an inspiration for others to carry on making the goal of equality a reality for all women. I further would like to believe that this book will serve to recognize the invaluable contributions of the many spirited women behind the scenes who led this fight.

Preface

If Marguerite Rawalt is there, she is at the center of things. In Washington, she has a reputation: she is someone we should all be grateful to, she was here before the rest of us, we can learn a lot from her. There is something else too. Affection. People don't just admire her, they love her. She is one of them.

As an afterthought, someone will tell how she came here from Texas and worked her way through law school and became one of the first high-level women lawyers in government. Nobody knows much about her personal life. They know she worked for ERA before they ever heard of it.

What is this woman really like? I wondered. How had she gotten to be the way she was during that bleak time between suffrage and "women's liberation." When her friends call her "Miss ERA," I thought it sounded old-fashioned. Yet I knew she had taken the National Organization for Women's first sex discrimination cases to court and won big victories for working women during the 1960s and 1970s. I knew she had gone to court twice in order to keep the name she was born with.

I had no idea what to expect of her personally. Despite the "Miss ERA" I didn't really anticipate the idealistic remoteness of the lingering suffragists who haunted the National Woman's Party headquarters on Constitution Avenue. What then: New woman? Tough feminist lawyer? Little old lady? None of the stereotypes seemed to fit.

I saw Marguerite Rawalt for the first time at a huge luncheon given in 1982 for Sandra Day O'Connor, who had just become the first woman on the United States Supreme Court. She was having her picture made with O'Connor and Sarah McClendon, Washington's most opinionated newswoman. McClendon, like herself, was a Texan.

Rawalt's enthusiasm pulled the others toward her. Wearing a white wool suit and a blue and red silk blouse, she gestured with one hand and held a mixed drink in the other. She was as at home with herself as anybody I had ever seen.

She is small and wiry now, with the compact look of someone put on earth for the long haul. But she had been a big woman, tall and powerful with the long stride of a farm girl. In her lavender blue eyes and smooth, translucent skin you have no trouble imagining the magnetic blonde whose easy style attracted a string of suitors, mentors, friends, and distant admirers. You see the strong jawline, too. But what you carry away with you is the spirit of the woman, her enormous capacity for enjoying other people and herself. How, I wondered, had such ease survived the discipline, the drive, the struggle it must have taken to accomplish what she did?

The answer must lie buried somewhere in the pioneering childhood that carried her across the plains from Illinois to Texas, where her hardworking, nomadic family finally settled when she was in high school. By then she had lived in three young states and two sparsely settled territories, known the demands of following the land and the exhilaration of crossing the frontier in a covered wagon. She had learned to look after herself and to work and play on equal terms with her two brothers. She had felt the power of locking her strong, plump legs against a half-trained Indian pony and riding until both were ready to drop. She had lived among Indian tribes and families both richer and poorer than her own. The itinerant life taught her many things, the meaning of loss, sacrifice, fear, and the importance of friends and family.

Like many successful women, she grew up a Daddy's Girl, learning the physical and mental skills she needed from her taciturn but dependable father. In later years, she recognized the great emotional debt she owed to her enterprising, fun-loving mother. Despite economic hardship, the Rawalts built a sound family for their children, finding, somehow, that precarious balance between freedom and control. They went to endless trouble to keep their daughter in school while they settled and resettled in the Southwest and honored her unprecedented desire to go to college. At bottom, Rawalt's feminism springs from an ingrained sense of her own worth and an ever-increasing sympathy for the grueling, unrewarded labor of women like her mother.

One of a handful of women to graduate from law school during the 1930s, she has been a token woman and a "first woman" more times than she can count. When she went to work in the Office of the Chief Counsel at the Bureau of Internal Revenue in 1933, she was the only woman among thirty newly appointed attorneys. In 1943, she was elected first (and to date, only) woman president of the Federal Bar Association, a nearly all-male national organization. That same year, as president of the influential National Association of Women Lawyers, she became the first woman delegate to be seated in the American Bar Association's House of Delegates.

Beginning as a poor, unhappily married stenographer in Governor Pat Neff's office in the 1920s, she developed a network of Texans on whom she relied for many years and repaid with lifelong devotion. Fifty years of correspondence pays tribute to those friendships.

When, in 1929, Georgetown University refused to admit her to its law school because she was a woman, she came face to face with discrimination for the first time. Later, in order to protect her job at Internal Revenue, she kept her second marriage secret for three years — until a law forbidding the equal employment of married women in the government was repealed.

In 1943, at a White House conference on women sponsored by Eleanor Roosevelt, Rawalt joined the National Federation of Business and Professional Women's Clubs and began her long struggle for women's rights. That same year, she began paying dues to the National Woman's Party, still led by suffragist Alice Paul's single-minded advocacy of the Equal Rights Amendment. Soon she had added memberships in two other ERA-supporting groups, the sprawling General Federation of Women's Clubs and Zonta International, a service club. She would spend the next thirty years weaving an immense network of influence within women's organizations. As if by instinct, she seems to have sensed her role in the changes that were coming for women and began keeping voluminous records of all her activities — both personal and political.

In order to accomplish what she did during those nonfeminist years, Rawalt carved out a brand of leadership that wasn't always popular. Although she became a skillful and compassionate negotiator, her superhuman drive, her uncompromising commitment to "what is right," and her goal-directed, bootstrap style often met stubborn, uncomprehending resistance.

Some will see her — especially when she was young — as radical, harsh, too ambitious. She was, after all, a woman who pushed — and pushed hard — for what she wanted. She was admittedly ambitious in ways that were not then, and still aren't, considered "feminine." She remains true to the puritan ethic on which she was raised, believing always that hard work pays, that there is always a "right thing" to do, and that people must bear the consequences of their own choices.

In one of those midlife shifts that are rarer than we might wish, she turned the energy that had made a Texas farm girl into a nationally known lawyer toward the monumental task of changing the world for women. World War II had held the promise of a brave new future for working women. During the postwar 1940s the mirage dissolved; Rawalt and others like her had to admit they had wrung their accomplishments out of a system that limited how far they could go — and worse — denied even the possibility of achievement to most women.

Marguerite Rawalt had come a long way in her own life before she realized the odds were not even, and that most women held much worse hands than she. Her image of herself and her belief in democracy hinged on her efforts to turn her country from what it was into what she thought it should be. Since the 1940s, she had worked for that goal as if her life depended on it; in a sense, it does.

Without Rawalt and a few others, there would have been no feminist bridge between suffrage and the women's movement of the 1960s. Working doggedly, behind the political scene in established organizations, they built the bedrock on which the new movement was founded.

In the 1960s, after twenty years of laboring in traditional women's organizations, Rawalt finally found a large group of women who shared her political vision. At seventy, she became part of an army that seemed to come out of nowhere to fight the battle she had dreamed of. "The most important thing I did," she says, "was to connect all those women up. By the time the women's movement came along, I knew everybody. I knew the professional women and the lawyers and the people in government. Then I knew the women on the Kennedy Commission on the Status of Women and in NOW and WEAL. They didn't know each other, but I knew them and could get them all together."

More than a generation older than current feminist leaders, she cut her activist teeth during those dry years after World War II. When she saw the women's movement coming in the 1960s, she threw the full weight of her long experience behind it. Her experience was, however, different from that of the new feminists with whom she worked and her prospective remains "conservative." Her fierce commitment to individual liberty and her belief that the free enterprise system is the best way for it to express itself and democracy its best protection have never waivered. Her activism was in part fueled by the naive — perhaps guilty — conviction that if she was having it all, other women should too.

She faced many defeats and then saw victories beyond anything she had imagined. In a way that goes beyond political creeds, she shows us how to take the cards (aces and deuces alike) that fortune deals and play them for all they are worth. Her life has been one of continuous growth — through conflicts, compromises, and reassessments — a steady unfolding toward maturity. At the heart of that maturity lies an unshakeable integrity — a fundamental sense of her own worth. For me her message is not "Be like me," but "Be yourself. And be it in spades."

Acknowledgments

At a time when she had earned the right to sit in the proverbial rocking chair a hundred times over, Marguerite Rawalt agreed to cooperate in the writing of a book that would combine her life's story with an account of the growth of the modern women's movement. What she did went far beyond cooperation and my gratitude to her is immense — both for living the life she lived and for her willingness to help me understand it. Her commitment, in this as to everything she ever did, was absolute. Her tolerance when I was ignorant, her patience and affection when I was impatient and out of sorts, her persistence when my own energies flagged will never be forgotten. I am particularly grateful that, as a student of women's history, I was given this rare opportunity to sit at the feet of experience. Most of all, now, I am grateful for the friendship that grew between us as we worked together to put into words a century of struggle for women's equality.

A grant from the Business and Professional Women's Club of the District of Columbia, Inc., enabled me to devote full time to the book for a year. I wish to thank the club for funding without which the book would simply not have been possible. I am particularly grateful to the efforts and continued support of the members of the Rawalt Book Committee: Vera Emery, chairman, Nancy Halvorson, Patricia Bruce Jeffries, Adair Mitchell, Thelma Pease, Jean Pucher, Irene Thomson, and Frances Ware Moore.

The book and my experience in writing it were greatly enriched by interviews with many of the women who made history during the 1960s and 1970s. I wish to thank: Virginia Allan, Elizabeth Boyer, Elizabeth (Liz) Carpenter, Kathryn Clarenbach, Grace Daniels, Catherine East, Mary Eastwood, Betty Friedan, Martha Griffiths, Elizabeth Koontz, Dr. Pauli Murray, Esther Peterson, Elizabeth (Libby) Sachar, Irene Scott, and Lorena Weeks.

Dr. Kathryn Heath earns my special gratitude for the love that enhances everything she does and for the depths of her generosity in sharing her knowledge of women's history.

My thanks are also due to the staff of the Rawalt Resource Center of the National Federation of Business and Professional Women's Foundation and to the Arthur and Elizabeth Schlesinger Library at Radcliffe College, which houses the papers of many women activists. Director Patricia King and a knowledgeable, cooperative staff made the Schlesinger Library congenial indeed for reading the available papers of Rawalt, Mary Eastwood, and Pauli Murray. I also wish to thank Elizabeth Snapp, director of the Texas Woman's University Library, for research done on Rawalt's Texas network. Anne MacDonald and Mary Anglund provided invaluable research assistance in the archives that remain in Rawalt's home in Arlington, Virginia.

A project as emotionally and intellectually demanding as this one was for me could never have been done without the help of friends. Personally as well as professionally, I am deeply grateful to Elizabeth Benedict, Lynn Brallier, Lynda and Harry Brown, Dr. Pete Daniel, Dr. Guinevere Nance, Jayne Rushin, Daphne Simpkins, and Dr. Leslie Wolfe.

[1]

Setting Out

Detroit's Book–Cadillac Hotel was swarming with women lawyers. Young soldiers covered their ears as they walked past several noisy groups clustered in the lobby. Despite the heat and the wartime hardship of traveling during the summer of 1942, scores of women had made it to the annual meeting of the National Association of Women Lawyers.

When the group chose Marguerite Rawalt both president and vice-president in an electoral fluke, they knew what they were getting. She had gotten where she was the hard way, putting herself through law school at an age when women were already settled into family life. Like many women attorneys in 1942, she worked for the government. The legal profession and the law schools still kept women out whenever they could. Few made it in individual practice and even fewer were asked to join existing law firms. Although Marguerite had lived and worked in the nation's capital for close to fifteen years, her down-home style and telltale accent gave away her Western origins.

She was a tall, good-looking woman whose vitality and self-

confidence drew people to her like a magnet. Her voice had a reso-
nance that stopped other conversations, and she seemed never to
doubt that she deserved the attention she got. Her very nature demanded it. Soon her accomplishments would be featured in major
newspapers across the country, a woman lawyer making it big,
president of two national bar associations in one year.

For a while during World War II, women like Marguerite Rawalt saw old career barriers falling and thought they had it made.
In those days, her message to women went like this: "I made it, so
can you. Now that women have an opportunity to practice law, all
we have to do is measure up." Some of her listeners thought she
made it sound too easy. Only a few knew the price she had paid to
get there. Even fewer suspected the depths of commitment and determination she brought to the job. They had no way of knowing
that by the end of her presidency, their little group would have become the first women's organization ever to be admitted to the
American Bar Association.

Waiting for the previous year's president to hand her the gavel
that night at the Book–Cadillac, she thought about her husband,
Major Harry Secord, who was stationed far away from her in Mississippi, and was warmed by memories — late Sunday breakfasts of
fried chicken and rum apples and long rides along the Chesapeake
shore.

Late in March, a few weeks before he was to report for wartime training, Harry and Marguerite spent a Friday night alone,
dancing, reminiscing, as if to store up for the long separation that
was coming. The next day they drove down the Maryland countryside to the Patuxent River, awaking on Sunday to find the river fro-
zen and covered with snow. In silvery silence, the far side of the
river looked very close.

Her thoughts drifted from Harry to her mother. Harry and
Mom, her pals and her critics. She remembered a letter her mother
had written on her birthday five years before:

> Yes it was a great day and the most fortunate day of our lives. . . .
> You arrived around 5 P.M. and I remember Pop wired Grandma
> Hale and she came down on the evening train and we all rejoiced
> together. Old Dr. Kreider and his daughter Hanna with whom I
> had lived for 7 years were with me.
>
> From that day til this you have been the greatest blessing

and stand by. Just couldn't have done without you and hope I never have to.

When Viola Flake Rawalt recalled her daughter's birth — on October 16, 1895 — she remembered the autumn sun shining on a two-storied white clapboard house in the tiny Illinois farm town of Prairie City. Here, while the whole country battled economic depression, her young husband, Charles, struggled to support their growing family with the income from a small plot of land and a flour mill.

Mingling European–American wanderlust with the pragmatism of the Irish, Viola's family had pushed westward, opening up the frontiers and settling Indiana's fledgling towns. Her great-grandfather William Flake operated a large tannery and represented Dearborn County in the legislature in 1831. Her grandfather, Lewis Flake, established three newspapers in Illinois farm communities before dying at twenty-nine.

Frontier families like the Flakes and Viola's maternal forerunners, the Terrys, were accustomed to separations and knew they did not break the bond of affection between parents and children. Leaving three young daughters behind with their uncle in Methe County, Ireland, Viola's widowed great-grandmother, Mary Jenkins, came to New York as a nurse, or a tutor, gradually saving enough money to send for her daughters one by one.

Margaret, the youngest of the girls, made the trip in 1836, when she was eighteen years old. She wrote about it later to a grandson:

> It took us seven weeks to cross the ocean. We were caught in a severe storm and feared the ship would go to pieces. Much of the lading had to be thrown into the sea. I kept in good health during the voyage and had my hands full, working with the sick, many of whom died. The bodies of the dead were sewed in large gunny sacks and thrown overboard.

A few years later, Margaret married John Terry, a farmer ten years her senior. In describing their move from Ohio to Fulton County, Illinois, she said: "When we settled here, the best prairie land could be bought for a dollar or two an acre, but the people feared they would freeze to death."

Viola inherited a background rich in optimism, courage, and family solidarity. She passed those values on to her three children and named her daughter, Marguerite, after her Irish grandmother, Margaret Jenkins Terry.

Charles Rawalt, whose ancestors had been in Illinois for three generations, grew up a few miles from Prairie City in a family of prosperous farmers, deeply rooted in a Calvinist ethic that linked industry, patriotism, and religious zeal. Religious dissidents of German extraction, the first Rawalts came to America during the 1740s calling themselves Rehwalt or Rewald.

The first John Rawalt, born in 1775 in Pennsylvania, joined the Revolutionary Army near Boston and fought at the battles of Bunker Hill, White Plains, Trenton, Brandywine, and Yorktown. Charles's grandfather, Jonas Rawalt, moved westward to Illinois, became an entrepreneur–farmer, schoolteacher, lawyer and businessman and served in the Illinois legislature with Abraham Lincoln and Stephen A. Douglas.

In old age, Newton Walker, a fellow legislator, liked to tell how he set the young Lincoln up to a wrestling match with his agile friend, Jonas Rawalt. As Walker recalled it in 1899 in a Lewiston, Illinois, newspaper: Lincoln, an "unkempt, long-legged, rough-and-tumble country boy" taunted him. "Walker," he said, "I'll bet I can throw you down." Newton replied, "I'll acknowledge in advance, Mr. Lincoln, that you can throw me down, but I have a colleague from Fulton County, Major Rawalt, who will gladly wrestle with you." Early the next morning, a crowd gathered in front of the Illinois state house in Vandalia to see the contest:

> Rawalt was a splendid specimen of physical manhood, as stout as an ox and as quick as a panther. The two men had no sooner gripped each other than Lincoln's long legs went flying through the air and he was on his back with Rawalt on top of him. When Lincoln got his breath and had scrambled to his feet he said . . . "You're the best man I ever tackled, but you're the only man in the legislature I can't throw down."

In more important matters, Jonas Rawalt, his sons, and Abraham Lincoln stood together. At the earliest signs of war, Jonas (then fifty-seven years old) joined the Union forces, enlisted his three sons including Charles's father Enoch, and began putting together Company K of the Seventh Illinois Cavalry. Jonas and his sons became the first in a long line of Republican Rawalts devoted to the party of Lincoln, the Union, and individual freedom.

In 1864, Enoch wrote his wife Caroline from the Union camp near Poolesville, Maryland: "two days without bread . . . little meat." While Enoch was struggling to stay alive and keep his spirits up in the Army, Caroline managed to make payments on the land they were buying. According to family records, before his death in 1885, Enoch had increased his holdings to 630 acres "by strict attention to business and hard work."

When Charles left the Rawalt farm to marry Viola Flake in 1894, he carried with him a mandate to trust God, work hard, pay his dues — and prosper. Near the end of a long line of brothers and sisters, he knew he would have to make it on his own. Never close to his stern mother, he lacked his wife's strong sense of family connection. And, although his spartan nature softened with the years, he never lost the earnestness, the reticence, the moral rectitude of his heritage.

To Viola, Charles's intensity made him all the more romantic. Slow to speak and slow to smile, he was only an inch or so taller than the woman he married. His blue eyes, light skin, and black hair were in sharp contrast to her milder looks. At twenty, Viola was tall with soft brown hair, hazel eyes and an innocent, sympathetic face. Instead of making her bitter, her father's premature death and the hardships that followed made her all the more generous and understanding of other people's problems.

Two years after Marguerite's birth, Viola bore her second child, Louis. Still in his twenties, Charles had begun a lifelong habit of working two or three jobs at once, taking vacations only when his wife or daughter insisted, seldom resting during his long days.

Motherhood came easily to Viola. Hard times lay ahead, years of following the land, the Depression, Louis's war injuries. For now, she was happy, too full of hope and too busy with young children and the daily work of farm life to worry about the future.

As Marguerite grew older, her sympathy for the heavy demands and slender rewards of her mother's life increased. But the frequent refrain "and she never complained" implies a reprimand as well as praise. Perhaps she *should* have complained once in a while — and demanded more for herself. Somewhere in that family, Marguerite learned to make extraordinary claims for herself and other women.

Occasionally, Marguerite acknowledged the tougher side of Viola's love for her children as she did in this letter written to her nephew, Kenneth Rawalt, a few months before her mother's death in 1958.

> I will always thank her for having the unselfish courage to make me learn to do my share of work. . . . No pampering. She let her ducklings swim out where the hawks could see them and develop legs and wings to effect their own escape. It is the hard way for a mother, but it is a good way, I think.

Writing to "Kenney" again ten years later, she remembered Viola's reluctance to see her set out for Washington, "So far away where I knew no one," and her gratitude when her mother added "if you feel you must go, then have the courage to go . . . to follow your innermost judgment."

By nature less sanguine than his wife, Charles was not satisfied with the life they were living. Beginning in 1901, a year after their third and last child, Willis, was born, the Rawalts would wander for ten years, cover thousands of miles, and live in four states before settling in Texas. They traveled by train, by horse and buggy, by covered wagon. Charles and Viola were about to give the country's last frontier to their children for a playground.

The Rawalts' first attempt to improve their lot was not, however, a very adventurous one. In February 1898, they sold the mill and the property in Prairie City in order to buy a farm near Charles's mother. They lived there just long enough for Marguerite to start to school in McDonough County.

The white frame, two-room building that was to be the first of many "schoolhouses" for her, stood isolated in an open field, bounded on all sides by acres of farmland. A few trees shaded the neatly kept structure. The only playground equipment was a hand-pump that provided water and opportunities for horseplay among the children who crowded the spare classrooms for a few hours each day.

The Marguerite who started school there was a chubby, inquisitive little girl with light hair combed in bangs straight over her forehead. Only the solemn blue eyes suggested the meditative spirit growing alongside an abundance of childhood energy. School came easy for a child already adept at the word-games and riddles her mother loved.

Viola was proud of her daughter. She thought she was smarter than other children — more sure of herself. Leaving her daughter at school for the first time, and walking home in the dusty autumn sunlight, she hardly had time to wonder about Marguerite's future. She had two other children to care for, the youngest only a few months old.

Within a few years, she would know that Marguerite and Louis were brighter, more confident, more determined to go their own way than most children. Willis, too young to be included in their games and projects, grew up differently. He was quiet and dutiful, inclined to do whatever was expected of him. Driven by their own restlessness, Louis and Marguerite left home early. Willis married close to home and spent the rest of his life working the family farms at Robstown, Texas.

Viola and Charles lived the way farm families had always lived. While he plowed and planted, repaired equipment and sold the wheat he grew, she reared three children, did farm chores and cooked huge meals — sometimes for twenty harvest hands a day. She prepared and preserved almost everything they ate and helped Charles with the livestock and poultry. Except for her husband's heavy overalls, she made all their clothes and washed them in homemade soap. Although Viola worked hard, she was less intense than her husband; she looked for fun in what she did. Moving slowly but almost constantly, she managed to do all that was needed. Amid the ongoing labor, she told her children tales of Ireland, and taught them the songs she had learned as a child.

Early in 1900, Charles began hearing about good land to the southwest of them in Oklahoma Territory. People still talked about the "run" in 1889 when thousands of people lined up at the Oklahoma border to homestead rich Indian land just opened to white settlers.

As the century turned, the Rawalts shared with the country a fresh mood of expansionism and progress. The Spanish-American War wrested Cuba from Spanish rule and gave the people of America a new hero in Theodore Roosevelt. The United States had annexed the Philippines, Guam, Puerto Rico, and Hawaii. A spirit of reform and populism spread in the cities and across the rural heartland.

Like other American midlanders lured by dreams of a richer, freer life, Charles and Viola looked west. Even though the home-

steading days in Oklahoma were over, land was cheap and he believed he would find what he wanted there. Viola had her own reasons for wanting to leave Illinois. Never altogether comfortable
with the austere Rawalts, she liked the idea of going where they
could live to suit themselves.

Early in the summer of 1901, Charles bought 100 acres of flat,
wheat-growing land in central Oklahoma Territory, near the town
of Kingfisher. A few months later, traveling by train and accom-
panied by her twenty-four-year-old brother, Lewellyn Flake, Viola
set out with her three children to make the first leg of their ten-year
quest for "a place." Their travels began with a "fast train" to Kansas City, Kansas, in a coach car crowded with straight-backed
chairs and dimly lit by kerosene lamps.

After changing trains the next morning, the six-year-old Marguerite saw her first hills. But as soon as they dropped into Oklahoma, the landscape was flat again — and familiar. That night
they slept for the first time in the rambling farmhouse that would
be their new home.

Within a few days of their arrival, Lewellyn found the county
grade school and enrolled Marguerite. It would be just like her old
school, she thought, letting go of her uncle's hand. The school was
smaller than the one in Illinois. Everybody was in one room, with
one teacher, and many of the children were older and bigger than
she was. In the last few days, she had left the only home she could
remember, said good-bye to both her grandmothers and many relatives, taken her first train ride, eaten her first banana, and seen
her first mountains.

Among the white faces she saw a tall boy with black skin,
something she had never seen in Illinois. Frightened, she bolted
from her seat and escaped before the startled teacher could stop
her. Running the short distance home, she told her mother what
she had seen. Viola tried to explain — not everybody had white
skin.

Marguerite was just beginning to learn that all people were
not alike. She found it fascinating — and strange. But she made
friends easily, and soon she knew everybody in the small school-
room, including the lone black pupil called Harvey.

Her photographic memory put her at the top of her class in
arithmetic and spelling. When she won the regular Friday after-

noon spelling bees and ciphering matches, she was exhilarated. When she lost, she blamed herself.

From an Indian neighbor called Christian Star, Charles bought Piebald ponies that his children rode without saddle or bit. Some afternoons Marguerite returned home excited from hours of galloping through cattails that left red whelps on her bare legs. Other times she was wide-eyed and quiet, full of all she had seen — and her own dreams. Before she was old enough to ride, she had annoyed her father once by forging a secluded nook for herself in the middle of a lush alfalfa crop. In an emotionally reserved family, ill-at-ease with conflict, she learned to abide by the rules.

During long afternoons of play, she discovered the pleasure of solitude and developed a need for privacy that would become harder and harder to protect. The gregarious side of her nature would always be at odds with an abiding need for the nourishment gained from being alone, thinking her own thoughts, knowing her own desires — "working at home" as she called it so often in later years.

As soon as they arrived, Charles had begun working double and triple time, renting a second farm to tend, waking early, staying in the fields til dark. His efforts to pay for the land and make a profit absorbed all his time. Soon he was fascinated with the new farm machinery that promised a bigger profit and relief from relentless physical labor.

As soon as he could afford it, he bought a second-hand threshing rig and began running a threshing business at harvest time. Marguerite often rode beside her father, talking to the silent man as he worked, absorbing the dusty odor of the rich black soil. She waited all year for the exciting weeks in late summer when she would go with him to neighboring farms to watch men throwing bundled shocks of dry wheat into his steam-run threshing machine. Mesmerized, she watched the straw and chaff blowing out the separator's huge spout, looking to her like an elephant's trunk or the beak of a clumsy bird. As if by magic, the grain poured out underneath — into the waiting sacks.

She was fascinated by the slow, dance-like rhythm of many men and women working together for the harvest. The bundle wagoners, pitchers, grain haulers, a man to run the water wagon, boys and girls carrying water, women in the "cook shacks" preparing huge, heavy meals. The work ethic was in her bones; work was life, not something one chose to do or not to do.

She must have grieved when, in 1904, three years after their arrival in Oklahoma, her parents decided to give up the farm and move to town so Charles could take a job selling farm equipment for Rumley Tractor Company. Slowly farmers were trading horses for tractors and manpower for the first modern farm equipment — crude, lumbering machines that looked like dusky dinosaurs grazing the wide fields. Over the next five years, Charles worked for Rumley, Reeves, and J. I. Case, all young companies taking advantage of the wave of mechanization that would revolutionize the landscape of American agriculture before mid-century.

By 1903, there were 80,000 automobiles on the road and some-one had driven a Packard all the way from San Francisco to New York. Orville and Wilbur Wright had put a heavier-than-air machine in flight. Charles loved the new machines, loved reading about them, working with them. Soon, he thought, they would be doing the time-consuming, expensive labor that kept small farmers like himself from making it.

Marguerite finished the third grade in the one-room country schoolhouse where her uncle Lewellyn had left her almost three years ago. During the summer, they sold the farm, held a public auction, and got rid of everything they couldn't take to town. Farm equipment went, some of their furniture, and all the livestock except for their favorite buggy mare, Maud.

After a trip to Illinois, they returned to a rented house in the town of Kingfisher. Immediately things were different. Charles was on the road most of the time, calling on farmers, traveling by train all over Oklahoma, Kansas, and New Mexico. The Rawalts had neighbors close on both sides.

From new friends, they learned ball games to play out of doors. They invented new card games. They waited impatiently for the mail to bring bundles of newspaper comic strips sent by Viola's mother as well as the monthly *Youth's Home Companion*. Seventy years later Marguerite described those still-vivid memories to a niece:

> Our grandmother used to mail us copies of the comics from the Sunday paper which she saved up for a few weeks. When they arrived, and before we could open the package and enjoy the com-

ics, we had first to do all our chores, gather the eggs, feed the dogs and cats, wash our bare feet in the summer time, etc. before we could revel in the comics.

A barn large enough for Old Maud and some of Charles's tools occupied the broad lot behind the house. On a spring Sunday, a year or so after they moved in, Charles and Viola left their children on their own. Marguerite was playing in a friend's back yard and ignoring the noise other children were making in the street, until she heard them yelling "Fire!"

Running home, she found eight-year-old Louis trying to coax Maud out of the smoking barn, tears streaming down his face. They remembered: "You can't make a horse leave a burning barn." By now she was crying too, sure Louis and Maud were going to die. Hearing the horse-drawn firewagon still far in the distance, she grabbed a pitch fork and plunged it into the mare's backside. With that, Maud bolted into the yard, dragging the terrified Louis with her. In less than a year, Maud would be carrying them across the vast Texas panhandle toward the frontier town of Solano in the territory of New Mexico.

If Charles thought the selling job would enable him to save enough to buy another farm and some equipment, he was wrong. Recession set in. Farmers were pessimistic, afraid to spend money. A fervor of reform had taken hold in farm communities and in the cities. Many farmers sympathized with Populist Party ideas — farmers who worked the land and workers in the factories were entitled to share in the prosperity of the "Gilded Age." A few listened to Socialist Eugene V. Debs. But Charles, deeply moved by Theodore Roosevelt's patriotism and his belief in the rewards and perfectability of the free enterprise system, stayed with the Republicans.

In good times and bad, Marguerite absorbed the reform-oriented conservatism of the rural heartland. All Americans were entitled to the fruits of their own efforts. The American way was best, and it was everybody's responsibility to see that it stayed that way. Those who failed to do their part and shirked their responsibility to improve the world in which they lived, deserved little better than what they got. The Calvinism so deep in Charles Rawalt's own heritage pervaded the frontier: one got what one worked for — which was all anybody deserved.

Almost every day, Charles heard about opportunities farther to the west. By 1907, he had talked Viola into moving to New Mexico where, under the Homestead Act, they could "file a claim" on a quarter section (160 acres) of land. All they had to do was live on it for fourteen months, pay a few hundred dollars in fees, and the land was theirs.

A few days after Marguerite finished the sixth grade, Viola set out with her three children to travel some 300 miles across the Texas panhandle. Two mules hauled everything they owned in a covered wagon called a prairie schooner. Another mule and the long-suffering Maud pulled the family buggy. Tom Stucker and Lee Shaner, young men who had worked for Charles on the Kingfisher farm, joined the little caravan.

Going directly west from Kingfisher, they traveled a hot pathless route over ranches so vast that they were sometimes on the same property for days. Carrying little water, they charted their course by windmills that marked the watering holes where they spent the summer nights. As they approached the troughs of collected water, Marguerite, Louis, and Willis trotted ahead in the buggy scattering cattle, antelopes, and buffaloes.

At sundown, the men cared for the animals and pitched tents while Viola cooked supper — usually biscuits, cured meat, and beans — in a simple metal cookstove, fueled beneath with buffalo chips. Marguerite and Viola slept in the wagon, the men and boys in the tents — till daylight came and they could set out again.

After three weeks of moving slowly from water hole to water hole, they arrived in Solano and lived in tents until rustic, one-room houses were built. The town of Solano was nothing more than a handful of homesteaders surrounding a single wooden building. The ground floor of the building housed the post office and an all-purpose store. Upstairs was the single room in which Marguerite and her brothers attended school for a year. At twelve, Marguerite was one of Solano's oldest students. It is hard to know what — if anything — she was able to learn from one teacher managing a room packed with children of all ages.

As an investment, the venture would eventually pay off. But, for themselves, the Rawalts had neither the ability nor the inclination to try to cultivate the raw grasslands. Once the claim was proved up, as they called it, there was little reason for them to stay in the crude frontier town.

Since Charles's business was to be headquartered in Oklahoma City, they decided to go there, but not until they had earned the profits of another threshing season near Kingfisher. Leaving Marguerite with friends, the original caravan set out early in the summer, taking the same overland route back across the prairies. Charles met them in Kingfisher where he, Viola, Tom, and Lee put in several weeks with a threshing crew before making the return trip. On August 1, Tom Stucker wrote Marguerite a terse note: "We have one more week of threshing left."

Viola and Charles returned to Solano to find their daughter worried that she would miss the beginning of school in Oklahoma City. For her, education would come to mean the same thing land meant to Charles, a way to make it, something you could get by your own efforts that no one could take from you. She preached it in letters to young relatives throughout her life. Education was insurance, security, the only way to start with nothing and get somewhere.

Somewhere during the first twelve years of her life — perhaps at the Kingfisher town school, where she first heard classmates talk of going to college — she had learned the meaning of ambition and developed a desire to excel, to prove herself, to *be somebody*. Sometimes it seemed that her very existence depended on her ability to accomplish those things. For the rest of her life, she would suffer terrible anxiety whenever that urge — to learn, to grow, to make progress — was threatened or stifled.

Moved by his daughter's urgency, Charles arranged for her to live in the city with the family of his attorney friend, Claude Nowlin, until the rest of the family arrived. Together the two of them took the train from New Mexico territory to Oklahoma City, where Marguerite moved in with strangers and started school in another new place.

Her migrant life was teaching her to make friends quickly and accept lonely separations. She missed her playmates, Louis and Willis, and the gaiety that surrounded Viola and lifted the pall of fatigue that sometimes gripped both herself and her father. Still, the quiet, bookish Nowlins were kind. Reading Victorian poems and stories to each other every night after dinner, they introduced her to new worlds and new pleasures.

Despite halting progress and setbacks, the farm equipment industry grew steadily. Within weeks after their arrival in Oklahoma City, Charles was offered a better job in Wichita, Kansas, overseeing Rumley Tractor Company's manufacturing operation. Worn out with travel, he accepted.

In Wichita, Marguerite became active at church for the first time. Moved by familiar Protestant hymns and the rousing sermon of a traveling evangelist, she experienced a conversion that set her religious convictions in place for life. Her parents had already indoctrinated her with a code that combined integrity, fair-dealing, and the golden rule. A meditative strain enriched those simple standards for their daughter whose deepest beliefs would always be held close to her chest, carefully guarded riches beneath the surface of a gregarious facade.

Two events in her childhood left her believing that she and her family were protected and guided by the hand of Providence. One fall morning in 1906, Charles woke up late and missed the train that was to take him north on a selling trip. The buggy ride home was unpleasant for Viola and the Rawalt children as Charles railed against himself, the lost time, the money he would lose. They had hardly been home an hour when word came that the railroad trestle over the Cimarron River had collapsed taking the train Charles had missed down with it. Her father seldom changed his routine, and Marguerite wondered what had made him late that one time. She was sure the hand of God had spared her father.

A year or so later, Marguerite and her brothers stood in the second story window of the Solano school and watched a prairie fire sweep toward their house where Viola worked alone. They knew Charles was on the road and Tom Stucker and Lee Shaner had left early for work some miles away. Detained by the teacher for what seemed an eternity, they arrived home in panic and found Viola safe. For "no reason at all," Tom and Lee had returned early, seen the fire and — with the help of neighbors — built a back fire around the house creating a moat of scorched land to stop the flames. If they had not returned unexpectedly, Viola would surely have been trapped by the flames.

Three years after the move to Wichita, Charles was once again tempted into land speculation. Like many others, he was lured down to Texas on a land promotion junket sponsored by the Coleman–Fulton Pasture Company, which gave free trips to people interested in buying into the vast undeveloped range. Unable to resist the promise of a profit, he bought forty acres of coastal brushland at Gregory, Texas, across the Nueces Bay from Corpus Christi. In order to support his gamble, he began traveling again, this time for J. I. Case and Company, selling mechanical binders and tractors to Texas rice farmers.

The Mexican workers he hired would take a year to clear the tough, flat land, burning off the brush and forcing the stubborn mesquite roots to turn loose of the soil. By then, Charles would be nearing his goal. The profit from the sale of the Gregory property would enable him to buy the kind of farm he had wanted ever since he left Illinois.

Thinking back over their long-ago migration from Prairie City to Kingfisher, Viola packed her family for the 700-mile train trip south into another new state. Texas greeted them first with smoldering heat, and then a cold norther, a storm with biting north winds.

During his travels, Charles had heard about Bayview College, a small high school and junior college in Portland, Texas. Sending Marguerite there would mean dipping into the money he was saving toward a farm; still, he knew she would be unhappy and learn little in a settlement school where very few children attended the upper grades.

Bayview College was Professor T. M. Clark's second attempt to offer the young men and women of South Texas a liberal arts education. Clark was a classics scholar, an old-fashioned educator who valued discipline and scholarship above all else. Although the demand for such schooling was small, he had managed to keep his first school — Add Ran College at Thorp Spring, Texas — alive for twenty years. Bayview, situated on a bluff where the Gulf of Mexico and the Nueces Bay come together, lasted a little longer, until the hurricane of 1916 closed its doors for good.

Against all odds, their frontier wanderings had set the Rawalts down where Marguerite could get what she most needed. At Bayview she devoured a course of study that introduced her to classical and English literature and broadened her knowledge of mathematics and American history, which fascinated her.

For the first time, she faced a challenge in the classroom. To graduate from Bayview she had to complete four years of Latin.

Tossed across Oklahoma, New Mexico, and Kansas, she had almost missed Latin altogether. Now she had to make up for that, and she had to do it on her own.

If Marguerite's parents were baffled by her desires, her teachers were not. Clark had established his schools to inspire students like her, the talented children of a generation of pragmatic, unintellectual settlers. They should go to college. No excuses. They could work themselves through if necessary. Marguerite listened when he talked about how badly the country needed educators, teachers, doctors, nurses, lawyers. His was a "not by bread alone" message, and she was ready for it. She wanted to do things, to know things, to be one of those people who made the world better.

Louis was as bored and restless at the Gregory school as Marguerite would have been. A dreamy fourteen-year-old raised on the wide, dry prairies, he fell in love with the Texas coast as soon as he saw it. With his gregarious sister off at school in Portland, he spent many afternoons alone by the water, often bringing home shells, starfish, sand dollars, and driftwood, whatever washed up and caught his attention.

During the summer of 1912, the Rawalts moved to a small farm in Portland, a few miles from Bayview, so Louis and Marguerite could live at home and both attend school. Their long search for "a place" was coming to an end. As soon as it was cleared, Charles sold the Gregory land for a profit. He was selling equipment he believed in now: mechanical drills, binders, tractors, threshers. In Texas alone, rice farms were irrigating 300,000 acres, and some claimed an investor could make a forty-four percent profit on a 160-acre rice farm "and not put his hand to the plow." [1] Cattle and rice farmers were enjoying boom times and so were the Rawalts.

As soon as he could afford it, Charles bought an automobile and taught Marguerite to drive it. Soon she could be seen driving her friends around in a shiny black Lambert. Even when she wasn't running a machine like nothing any of them had seen before, people took notice. Tall and light-haired like her mother, and with her father's deep blue eyes, she carried herself in a way that demanded attention. Friends were apt to call her good-looking or handsome rather than beautiful. She was too big and her features too strong for their youthful ideal of beauty. Her magnetism lay not so much in her boyish good looks as in boundless energy and a powerful personality.

In later years, admirers would use the word *stylish*. Although the style would become more sophisticated and more feminine, the gusto would always show through. The combination attracted many people to her — and rubbed some the wrong way. She enjoyed the limelight too much, they would say.

For outings, Marguerite and her friends took the train across the causeway to Corpus Christi. Founded by a mixture of Mexican and American natives and European immigrants, the rural Western town would be a long time turning its hurricane-ridden shores into the glittering industrial harbor that Marguerite came home to in later years.

Wrung from both natives and sedate early settlers by a ruthless breed of cowboy-ranchers, the strip of land around the Nueces had survived 200 years of strife, and then been left almost devoid of civilization by Texas's struggle for independence from Mexico. When Zachary Taylor brought 3,000 soldiers to the Gulf to fight Mexico for the right to plant the American flag in Texas in 1845, he pitched camp during the summer on a coast now claimed by tourists. Newcomers flocked to the reborn city throwing up saloons, brothels, and an opera house to accommodate the soldiers — and exacerbate the everlasting clash between cowboy bravado and Bible Belt rectitude.

When Taylor marched his troops off to defend the borders at the Rio Grande, he left a ghost town soon to be sent reeling again by Civil War and reconstruction. In the years that followed, Corpus Christi made its compromises with Reconstruction, dealt with rampant frontier banditry, and survived a yellow fever epidemic that wiped out a third of the population. Amid the chaos, the great cattle drives began, moving huge droves east and south across the state to both black markets and legitimate ones. Men like "Captain" Richard King, founder of the legendary King Ranch, carved vast estates out of the free range and dominated the state with cattle and land money until oil wealth challenged their grip.

Coastal Texas merged the South's reverence for history and propriety with the West's exaltation of freedom, individualism, and "personality." The double tradition left an indelible mark on Marguerite — and some conflicts.

Despite her zest for the youthful social life of Portland and Corpus Christi, she was not interested in young men like Faye

Crites, good-natured and satisfied with the future their parents had made for them. Beneath the tomboy recklessness of the girl whose schoolmates called her "Mike," brooded a young woman with serious thoughts about her own future. Professor Clark encouraged the girls to become teachers. It wouldn't take long to get a teacher's certificate, she thought, and earn some money. She already knew she didn't want to dig a living out of the earth like her parents. For now, she didn't want to marry anybody.

Marguerite had begun a lifelong habit of keeping her deepest desires to herself. She wasn't sure where she was headed. She knew what she wanted but feared something unknown might stop her from getting it. Kids like Faye and his sisters didn't know what she was talking about. But sometimes Louis listened, and her parents had agreed to send her to The University of Texas in Austin the next year.

In years to come, the *Corpus Christi Caller* would claim Marguerite as a native and praise her activism. But in 1913, the tradition-minded newspaper had as little sympathy for women's rights — and the rights of blacks — as it had had in an 1884 editorial that admonished: "To permit the entrance of political contention to a home would be either useless or pernicious — useless if man and wife agree and pernicious if they differ." Man has a desire, the writer added, "To see woman forever the pure, refined, modest and gentle being that her sphere in life makes her." It would, however, be even more pernicious, the writer admitted, if the number of Negro voters grew large enough to put white women at a disadvantage in terms of property tax and ownership.

In 1912, while Marguerite was conquering Latin and making her first adult choices, Alice Paul, a fierce young Quaker trained in the British suffrage movement, was inciting 5,000 suffragettes to march at Woodrow Wilson's inauguration. No one Marguerite knew talked about women's rights. Susan B. Anthony was little more than a name to her. She had never heard of the firebrand Alice Paul.

While Paul and others focused single-mindedly on getting the vote for women, social welfare activists pushed for state laws that "restricted" or "protected" women working in industry. In 1908, in the *Muller* v. *Oregon* case, the Supreme Court ruled that laws limiting the hours a woman could work were constitutional and not contrary to the liberties guaranteed by the Fourteenth Amendment. In doing so, it placed women in a separate class saying that because "Healthy mothers are essential to vigorous offspring, the physical well-being of women becomes an object of public interest and care in order to preserve the strength of the race."

Marguerite's own ambitions were the narrow, personal ones of an eighteen-year-old. Although fascinated with being a grown-up in a grown-up world, she wasn't very interested in having children. She knew she did not want them any time soon, maybe never. She knew she did not want a life like her mother's.

Beneath the surface of a life filled with school work, parties, and courtships ran an anxious refrain: *Keep moving; don't let anybody get ahead of you.*

During the summer of 1914, after graduating valedictorian of her class at Bayview, Marguerite took the train to Austin with her father and found a boardinghouse where she could live with other university students. Two months later, her brothers heaved her heavy trunk out of their wagon and on to the train that would take her alone to an unknown life. Telling them good-bye, she knew she loved them, knew she would miss them and knew she had to go.

The first weeks in Austin were devoted to exploring the campus, admiring the powerful architecture of buildings like the Tower and Main where some of her classes met. It thrilled her to think she walked on paths made by decades of students like herself, generations of people who wanted to learn. Still, they were the loneliest weeks of her life. During all the earlier separations, she had been with families, friends or neighbors, and Bayview had been so close to home. Being on her own was not what she had expected. For the first time in her life, she had too much time to herself.

Sensing her homesickness, Charles scheduled trips to Austin whenever he could. Once they went to see Anna Pavlova perform; another time they saw Buffalo Bill Cody's Wild West Show.

Before long, she was part of a crowd again. When she wasn't studying or exploring, she went out with her new girlfriends or with a serious, good-looking law student named William Ware. He was smarter, wittier than the young men at home. He knew how to dress, and he took school seriously. She liked to hear him talk about practicing law in Houston, someday, perhaps, becoming a judge.

Maybe she would be a lawyer, too, she thought. She liked

reading and logic and she wanted to see justice done. But there were hardly any women lawyers in Texas. Some states had only recently begun to permit women to take the bar and practice law. Most people still agreed with the logic of the 1872 Supreme Court decision that refused Myra Bardwell, an Illinois woman, the right to practice law in her state:

> The natural and proper timidity and delicacy which belongs to the female sex evidently unfits it for many of the occupations of civil life. . . . The paramount destiny and mission of women are to fulfill the noble and benign office of wife and mother. This is the law of the Creator. And the rules of civil society must be adapted to the general constitution of things and cannot be based upon exceptional cases.

Any dreams the eighteen-year-old Marguerite had of becoming a lawyer were fleeting and barely conscious. She had other things on her mind. The whole country was in love with an erotic Latin-American dance called the tango — perhaps to take its mind off political discontent at home and fighting abroad. The fad outraged church and civil authorities alike. It was wanton, they said, and led to lewdness. One of Marguerite's housemates was teaching everyone to do it. Exaggerating a dip one afternoon, Marguerite caught her foot in the bottom of her new hobbled skirt and crashed to the floor. In the midst of final exams, she had sprained a knee so badly that she would be in the infirmary for days.

Suddenly, an unexpected letter from home put bitter disappointment in the place of schoolgirl pranks. With Louis still at Bayview, there wouldn't be enough money for her to go back to school in the fall. There was an over-supply of rice, and prices were falling. There were foreclosures on land and equipment.

Still distressed a few days later, not knowing what to do next, she walked out of her history exam with a dark, slender girl named Maggie (Mattie) Matthews. She found the girl's East Texas twang more irritating than usual.

Mattie was leaving school to take a teaching job near Waco, she said. The superintendent of schools, a woman named Lucy Moore, was interviewing people on campus that afternoon.

Close to forty, Lucy Moore carried her large, rawboned body in a way that demanded respect. She had no patience with either stupidity or sloth, and most people were afraid of her. But, for a few people, she was a wellspring of encouragement. Soon Marguerite found herself joking with the formidable woman old enough to be her mother; and, before she knew it, she had accepted a job teaching high school math in Lorena, Texas.

A few days later, a Hapsburg prince was assassinated in Sarajevo, Bosnia, hurling Europe — and ultimately the United States — toward war, Depression, and another war. Back in Portland for the summer, Marguerite was barely aware of world events that were shaping her life. She did sense she was leaving home for good this time and wanted to be with her family.

Lucy Moore handpicked her teachers and expected them to do good work. She liked to watch them grow up and go on to other things. She had seen too many of them — women like Mattie and Marguerite and classics scholar Amanda Bradley — make hasty marriages and waste their talents "following behind some farmer." Others grew old in places like Lorena, doing their jobs but never going "beyond their own back yards."

She appreciated Marguerite's ambition, her concern for students, her easy friendship with other teachers and her obsession with doing a job well. Soon she was giving her special duties and showing her how to become a better teacher. "Lower your voice, speak more slowly," she told her. "That's the way you hold attention." Marguerite hardly ever made a speech without recalling the advice — calm down, slow down, speak softly.

In 1950, after addressing an audience of 700 business and professional women, she wrote Moore, bedridden by then with a heart condition.

> It was such a sweet and satisfying letter you sent me in Austin. It lifted my spirits up, and supported my sagging confidence, as it came when I was facing into the making of a "speech" to that big group. [In another letter written that same year, she added:] Now if I could express myself as well, as intelligently, as entertainingly as you, I would not dread making these talks. I would have something to say. Yet here am I, without that high ability, rushing right in. . .

Moore, a born mentor, saw good judgment and intelligence balancing the enthusiasm that "rushed right in." Despite a twenty-year difference in their ages, the two became the closest of friends, and Moore told Marguerite something no one in Lorena knew except Amanda Bradley.

Encouraged by her longtime friend, Frank Hartgraves, himself a lawyer, Lucy Moore was planning to leave Lorena after one more school year and go to The University of Texas Law School. For the first time, Marguerite voiced her half-formed desire to become a lawyer herself.

Moore nicknamed Marguerite "Happy," and would never call her anything else. In the 1930s, when Amanda Bradley came to the Maryland coast to be Dean of Women at Washington College, the name spread. Friends from the past had a way of cropping up in Marguerite's life, calling her Happy — or Mike — if they went back far enough.

True to her plan, Moore headed for Austin during the summer of 1916, leaving Marguerite — not yet twenty-one — with the superintendent's job. Administration came easily to her, easier than teaching. She liked organizing classes, managing the teachers, the buildings, the budgets for two schools — the twelve-grade school for white children where she had taught and a one-room school for the few black children who lived near Lorena. "Managing" the black school meant talking to its one teacher a few times a year. "Separate but equal" public facilities had been the law of the land since 1896. Neither Marguerite nor Lucy Moore questioned it.

When Lucy Moore left, she and Marguerite already had plans for the next year. Marguerite would join Moore in Austin and pick up where she left off in school, work part-time and get into law school as soon as she could. There was good news from home. Charles had bought a 106-acre farm outside of Corpus Christi just west of Robstown, Texas, and had a good job as supervisor of the machine shops at the King Ranch.

The 2,000-square-mile ranch was a town in itself. The Kings and the Klebergs ran a vast empire that included not only cattle ranching but founding banks and colleges, building railroads, harbors and whole towns. Charles's job there gave him financial security for the first time in his life — and the opportunity to use all he had learned about the new machinery. He had gone to school the hard way and suddenly it was paying off. Every day he worked with the newest and best equipment that could be bought — automobiles as well as farm implements and big machines. He loved the feel of a good piece of equipment, the smell of it, the pleasure of putting every bolt in place.

Charles and Marguerite shared the joy of setting a task in motion, of working a crew. What she had seen him do so many times in the threshing field, she was doing for the first time in the independent school district of Lorena.

On April 6, 1917, just as Marguerite resigned her job as school superintendent to go to Austin, the United States declared war against Germany and Austria–Hungary. President Woodrow Wilson's rationale was convincing. As the divine agent of peace and justice, the United States had a responsibility to make the world "safe for democracy."

The country agreed and responded with frenzied patriotism. Louis finished Bayview one week and enlisted in the field artillery for the duration of the war the next. Clairmont Carroll, a friend and suitor of Marguerite's since her own days at Bayview, was less enthusiastic than most when he wrote, "I don't want any part of this fighting but I guess I will have to go."

As soon as school ended, Marguerite went to Austin to visit Lucy Moore and make arrangements for returning to the University in the fall. By September, all their plans had changed. When Moore was asked to direct the Hostess Houses for GIs in San Antonio, she interrupted her education one more time. Like many other women, she wanted to serve the country in any way she could.

By responding the way Lucy Moore did, women made a new place for themselves in American life. In the early days of the war, Harriot Stanton Blatch — a feminist in a way Lucy Moore never claimed to be — proclaimed, "American women have begun to go over the top. They are going up the scaling-ladder and out into All Man's Land." [2]

Women took up the slack in farm labor and filled factory jobs in droves, learning in record time to do jobs they had been thought incapable of doing. Efforts to get better working conditions for women in war industry ultimately led to the establishment of the Women's Bureau of the Labor Department.

By mid-1918, one-fifth of the country's 66,000 registered nurses had been assigned to military duty. Many civil service jobs were opened to women for the first time, and the expertise of women lawyers put them in prestige jobs and on boards where they had never been before.

Reconversion after the war would squeeze many of the new women workers out, but not all of them. The experience and know-how they gained, along with a new public image, were to be real and lasting.

But Marguerite was disappointed. In the light of war, her carefully made plans for going to law school seemed empty. Charles didn't think it was a good time for her to go back to college. Louis was going to war. All her friends were getting married. Karl Shipp, a man she had known in Lorena, wanted her to marry him. All of a sudden her "pal" Clairmont was serious — about her, about life, about war.

During the summer, before Louis left for Fort Logan in Denver, he and Marguerite settled back into the old intimacy of childhood. He was glad the war had come when it did; he had to get away. Neither of them liked the constant, deadening routine of farm life; they had their own plans and dreams.

Finally, Louis helped her make the decision to join Lucy Moore in San Antonio, rather than go to the University alone. He would have part of his soldier's pay allotted to her to help with expenses, half of his thirty dollar paycheck.

In September, Clairmont and Marguerite both headed for San Antonio — Clairmont for a few months of training at Travis Field before going to France to fight and Marguerite to attend business school to learn shorthand and typing. Marguerite shared an apartment with Lucy Moore and her younger sister, Kate, settling quickly into their routine, taking turns with housekeeping and cooking, driving the Ford that came with Lucy Moore's job.

By November, she knew enough about shorthand and typing to get a job as secretary to the manager of the St. Anthony Hotel overlooking San Antonio's downtown park. The work was monotonous, filling out forms, writing letters, dealing with complaints about hotel services in wartime.

Government-sponsored Hostess Houses like the ones Lucy Moore managed sprang up all over the country to provide soldiers with inexpensive entertainment and a convenient place to meet family and friends. For Moore, overseeing all the Hostess Houses in the area meant attending some kind of function almost every night.

Because she didn't like to drive — in fact never really learned how to drive — Marguerite often made her rounds with her.

For Thanksgiving dinner, 1917, the two of them set out for Kelly Field, where thousands of men were being trained by the Army. At the last minute Marguerite took off the blue suit she was wearing and changed into a gold satin dress Viola had helped her make. The scooped neck and short lace-trimmed sleeves exposed the smooth lines of her neck and arms. At twenty-two, the baby fat was gone, and an innate reserve tempered the ebullience. Her light hair was long and piled in curls around her face.

Master Sergeant Jack Tindale was a favorite at Kelly Field Hostess House. Blond and boyish, he took full advantage of his Scottish accent. He played the piano and sang the hits of his popular countryman, Harry Lauder. He moved about in the crowd when his act was done and seemed to know everybody.

Jack fascinated Marguerite from the start. The way he relaxed in a chair, paying the strictest attention to her. She was drawn to his sweetness, his vulnerability, his need to be cared for and admired.

He liked to have people around, but he was a wanderer, an entertainer, tied to nothing and no one. Parts of his past would always be a mystery. He was twenty-six years old, although he looked younger. He had gone to school in England at Eton College, he told her, then left home to escape the brutal discipline of his minister-father. He said he never wanted to see his parents again.

He had done a stint in the U.S. Marines before joining the Air Corps. He loved to play the piano and sing. It was a way to make people happy. "Everybody's not Happy," he would joke when he heard Lucy Moore's name for the girl he called Margaret or Margo. He would never play the piano for money, he said. His talent was the only thing that mattered, a gift from God, something he had to give back. Marguerite had never heard anybody talk like that before.

She was in love, not just with Jack's patrician good looks but with his mystery, his magic, his words. With all the force of her own personality, she wanted to make Jack happy, as happy as he made her. She wanted to provide the strength he lacked, to propel him toward the future she would have wanted for herself if she had been a man.

Torn with guilt, she finally wrote Clairmont who was in France in the infantry, defending his country. She herself didn't understand how she could have fallen so helplessly in love with Jack, she told him. Even though it had never been said in so many words, Clairmont had expected her to marry him — and she had thought she would. Now there was no one but Jack.

For a while, she stopped worrying about the future. The war went on, men came and went and died; women were working in offices and factories. People were moving around the country like never before. Louis was fighting in France.

On April 29, 1918, Marguerite and Jack were married by a Justice of the Peace at the San Antonio courthouse, attended only by two friends. Viola and Charles had met Jack once. Viola was charmed by his spontaneity and happy that her daughter was happy. But Charles was disappointed. Jack wasn't good enough for his daughter — too much of a dreamer.

Lucy Moore was hurt and disappointed. Marguerite never forgot the prophetic words she said partly in jest, "When two people think they can't live without one another, they get married and find out they can."

[2]

Finding a Place

While Jack and Marguerite honeymooned in their one-room apartment in San Antonio, the Great War in Europe came closer. Ten thousand American Marines were killed in France at Bouresche and Belleau Wood, and Louis wrote disturbing letters from "Somewhere in France."

In July 1918, Marguerite landed a job in the Quartermaster Corps Office in Fort Sam Houston and joined a generation of women going into the civil service for the first time. At work, she had the grim, exacting job of arranging railroad transportation for corpses going home to be buried. In late September, there was news of the largest battle ever fought, over 100,000 men killed between the Argonne Forest and the Meuse River in France. By the end of October, Germany had collapsed.

Within a week after the armistice was signed on November 11, the Rawalts were stunned by a notice that Louis was missing in action. On Christmas Eve, Marguerite received a letter from him, dated November 19. Wounded by shrapnel in the last battle of the war, he had recovered enough to start hiking across Europe.

> Well, Sis, . . . the main subject here is where do we stop. The war is over but hiking is not. We were right on their heels when they hollered time out. For the first few days we could not believe it was so.

Two months later, he described the long trek that took him from the Argonne front to the town of Kunft in Germany where he taught math in a German school for a few months before going to Paris to attend classes at the Sorbonne. Too exhausted and confused to study, he stayed in Paris a few more months before coming home. In April, he wrote bitterly to his mother:

> *Sunny France,* as poets desire to call it. But ask a soldier and you will hear # ! @ ★ France . . . Well, I celebrated my first year in France a week ago and in the year I saw and did enuff to make a man crazy.

Marguerite was worried about Louis, but she was also worried about Jack; he had been discharged into a marketplace flooded with returning GIs. He tried selling cars for a while, but what he loved was making people laugh, seeing his Margo smile. He wanted everything to stay the way it had been the night they met at Kelly Field. Choices came easy for Marguerite, but Jack was full of ambivalence.

For nine more years, Marguerite would support herself and her husband, learning the hard way what Lucy Moore had tried to tell her: *you can't give your dreams to somebody else.* Within a year, Moore would have her law degree and would be working at The University of Texas law library, teaching classes in the law school. It wasn't the same as practicing law, but it was better than most women with law degrees got.

Although, when the men returned, women lost some of the career momentum gained during the war, appreciation for their patriotism gave suffrage the nudge it needed. During the war years, several states, including Texas, were added to the list of those granting suffrage in state elections. On August 26, 1920, the national suffrage amendment became law.

All feminists and women's rights activists celebrated the passage of the "Susan B. Anthony Amendment," but with that the unity ended. Alice Paul's National Woman's Party took over the radical branch of the movement and began a long, uphill battle for total equality. Moderate suffrage workers established the National League of Women Voters to educate the new electorate.

The suffrage victory, combined with the raised consciousness of the war years, brought women into women's organizations in growing numbers. The National Association of Women Lawyers and the Medical Women's Association led the way as women became increasingly aware of the barriers raised against them in high-status professions. In 1919, an earnest young lawyer named Lena Madisen Phillips extended the work she had done with business and professional women during the war to found the National Federation of Business and Professional Women, destined to become the first large post-suffrage organization to advocate equal political, legal, and property rights for women.

Like most of her generation, Marguerite was ready to celebrate the end of the war that had interrupted her life. A new freedom was in the air, for everybody who was young, most of all for women. They had jobs, their men were coming back. Dresses were shorter, flimsier, easier to move about in. Bathing suits bared the knees. Women could dress and talk and do as they pleased. They smoked and drank bootleg whiskey just like their men. Everybody knew who Freud was and sex was no longer a forbidden subject. Nice girls were dancing cheek-to-cheek, painting their faces and bobbing their hair. Soon there would be radio, big bands, and the Charleston.

Marguerite's frontier roots left her freer of physical constraints than most of the women she would meet in later years. She was used to speaking up, moving about freely and going after what she wanted. Still, the bravado of the 1920s left its mark, intensifying the pleasure she took in trying the untried, heightening her desire to have the best and know all that could be known. But there was always a limit beyond which she would not go, a delicately maneuvered balance between pleasure and self-indulgence, responsibility and self-sacrifice. Certain things were not to be compromised: the work she had to do, her love for Jack and her family, the importance of a few friends.

For a while, she and Jack and a crowd of new friends joined the joymakers of their generation. Then there was reality again, the darkness beneath the glitter of the ballrooms, the speakeasies, the movie houses.

Not everybody was celebrating. The end of war brought an

ennui and meaninglessness to some, joblessness to many. The Bolshevik Revolution and the rise of Communism in Russia produced a "Red Scare" among Americans needing to replace the fascist enemy with the "Red Menace." Membership in the almost dormant Ku Klux Klan zoomed to over two million, fanning hatred and violence against everything "un-American" — blacks, Jews, Catholics, aliens — anybody who violated a narrow definition of "Christian" and "American."

By August 1921, the number of people unemployed and looking for work had risen to almost six million, and Jack Tindale was one of them. That same summer, without warning, a reduction-in-force abolished Marguerite's job along with hundreds of others. She did what she would always do in times like these, call on Viola for comfort and Lucy Moore for help.

Using Moore's political connections, she soon had a stenographer's job in Austin in the office of Texas's new governor, Pat M. Neff. She would be working under Espa Stanford, a statelylooking widow who supervised personnel and ran the governor's back office — as she had done before in his law firm in Waco. Marguerite was about to become a lifelong member of an extended Texas political "family" she didn't know existed.

As soon as Marguerite and Jack moved to Austin, Jack enrolled as a freshman at the University. Before long, he was entertaining at campus gatherings, organizing skits, volunteering for theatre productions. Although Marguerite thought he neglected his courses, she didn't say so. More and more, her own life was centered at work, where politics fascinated her and her knack for meeting people made her a favorite with the governor and his staff.

At fifty, Pat Neff had a reputation for two things: political independence and moral rectitude. A leader in the Southern Baptist Convention, he opposed the consumption of alcohol so adamantly that Marguerite refused to drink even in private for as long as she worked for him.

Over six feet tall, with strong features and a shock of black hair, he was an imposing combination of cowboy swagger and evangelical piety, twice elected governor despite powerful opposition from entrenched politicians with whom he refused to cooperate. In a collection of his speeches called *The Battles of Peace,* he wrote, "No one solicited me to run for Governor. I did not ask permission of anyone to get into the race. Just as a free-born American, and as a native son of Texas, without a conference with or advice from anyone, I announced my candidacy." Beneath a patina of sophistication and learning, he was like Charles Rawalt in many ways — solitary in nature, morally unbending, intense in his commitments. He loved only a few people.

No glad-hander and slow to make promises, Neff ran his campaigns on past performance and integrity. He was a solemn man, not given to quick laughter or casual relationships. Too much of an outsider to surround himself with political henchmen, he built a large and loyal office staff, retreating often into the spare, informal rooms where Marguerite worked. In the stark, oak-paneled domain of Espa Stanford — part mother hen and part organizational woman — he could be himself. There he played the patriarch often enough. But sometimes he relaxed and was more like a brother. When he asked for help, they gave it.

Neff was married to a conventional woman, completely dependent upon him in practical matters. His children Pat Jr., and Hallie Maude visited him in his office often and quickly singled Marguerite out. She was younger than the others, more fun. The senior Neff was attracted to her, too. He liked the casual, confident way she moved and dressed; there was something natural and comforting about her.

He didn't like to call her by her first name, yet the formal Mrs. Tindale seemed awkward. When she and Jack were divorced and she took back her family name, he began calling her "Rawalt" in jest and never again called her anything else. For her, he would always be Governor Neff.

The relationship grew steadily over the next thirty years. In 1942, when Pat Neff was president of Baylor University and Marguerite a prominent lawyer, he wrote: "You and I have been comrades in arms under so many different conditions, places, and environments that out of these rapidly receding years any thought of you is stimulating and helpful."

Neff's first campaign had been a remarkable one-man show, built on the simple principle that you shake as many hands as you can. Alone, he canvassed the huge state for months, speaking five or six times a day, going into thirty-seven counties that had never before seen a candidate for governor.

He was planning the same kind of shoot-from-the-hip approach to his 1922 reelection campaign until Marguerite began working with him, imposing order on an impossible schedule. She started by sorting the vast piles of letters he had saved, cataloging his supporters by county, profession, attitudes, any useful bit of information. She collected the information in a black notebook binder, listing the names of Neff's supporters county by county.

For Marguerite, organization was second nature. For the introverted, idealistic Neff, it looked like genius. The young woman who so appealed to him had depths of initiative and intelligence beyond what he had expected. He would call on it again and again and never be disappointed. But when she told him that she wanted to be a lawyer, he turned paternalistic.

Who would hire a woman lawyer? She'd starve to death. Anyway, a woman shouldn't have to deal with hardened criminals. Adamantly opposed to probation for convicted criminals, he had seen Marguerite moved to tears by letters from prisoners and their families. She wasn't tough enough, he insisted. He didn't like to think how embarrassed she would be trying a rape case in front of a jury. Neff would always applaud Marguerite's accomplishments and honor her interest in women's rights, but he would never rid himself of the notion that she belonged on a pedestal.

Despite his ingrained protectiveness, Pat Neff had a respect for the abilities and accomplishments of women and made clear his intention to recognize them. He made Espa Stanford the first woman to serve as private secretary to a Texas governor, appointed many women to state boards, and named three women attorneys to the Texas Supreme Court for the disposition of a specific case.

Margie Neal was one of several women political regulars in the governor's office. A graceful, sturdy woman in her forties when Marguerite met her, Neal's warmth and Deep-South gentility made her an unlikely choice to be the first woman in the Texas Senate. Everything was personal with Margie Neal. She was easy to be with, a little like Viola.

Active in the suffrage campaign that enabled women to vote in Texas primary elections two years before the national amendment passed, Margie Neal was the first woman Marguerite ever heard complain in mixed company about unfairness toward women.

Harry Crozier was a journalist and another frequenter of the back office. He became Marguerite's lifelong mentor, friend, admirer. And sometimes suitor. Estranged from his wife but devoted to their one child, a son, Crozier roamed the state, writing news stories, political stories, business stories. He had connections everywhere and hung his hat wherever his stories took him.

In Austin, Marguerite met the colorful Texas politico "Colonel" Sarah (Sank) King. She heard about Sarah Tilghman, an aggressive woman her own age who was graduating from law school and coming to Dallas to practice law with George Hughes, the young Texan she had married.

Though intrigued by her new political friends, Marguerite stayed in close touch with her family. When Louis returned from France in the fall of 1919, he was mixed up and restless. He couldn't concentrate well enough to go to school, and he disliked farm life as much as ever. At home with his parents for a few weeks, he was restless and disagreeable. He couldn't think clearly or make decisions. Marguerite wanted him to go to college. All he wanted was to forget. Forget the smell of fear and death. He couldn't talk about it, and he couldn't forget.

By the time school started in September 1922, Marguerite had talked him into coming to Austin to live with her and Jack and enroll in the University. Always uncomfortable with a debt, she wanted to pay him back for the money and encouragement he had given her during those uncertain first months in San Antonio.

But the war had done something to Louis. He didn't pay attention, and his combat memories had turned into nightmares that kept them all awake. When she asked him to tell her about it, he always said the same thing. "Forget it, Mike."

In December, Louis came to her office to say he was leaving school and leaving Austin. "I can't," he said, "do something I can't do. And you can't do it for me." A month later, he enlisted in the Navy and served for three years before being discharged with a kidney ailment.

He could have been talking about Jack as well as himself when he said "you can't do it for me." As determined in her ambitions for her husband as she had once been for herself, Marguerite ignored Jack's flagging interest and insisted he stay in school through the fall of 1924, when Governor Neff's second term ended. Finally, she admitted he was not doing well enough to continue and agreed to go with him across the state to El Paso.

Full of hopes and promises, Jack had acquired the Real Silk Hosiery franchise for the Southwest. He would be managing dozens of door-to-door salesmen selling stockings and lingerie. Business was good again. People liked him; he knew he could do this. He was going to support them now, he said. He didn't like her going to work every day, coming home tired, staying long hours, working with men. They took advantage of his Margo.

She wanted to believe him. She knew he tried, and she still liked to hear him talk like that. But he got so upset, so depressed. How could it all be his fault, he kept asking.

Before they moved in November, Marguerite took a three-week vacation with Charles and Viola, back to Illinois for the first time since that long ago summer after they sold the Kingfisher farm. On the train ride home, she admitted she was worried about Jack, about her life with him. Using words she knew her parents would understand, she said, "I wonder if he is ever going to amount to anything, or am I always going to be the head of this family? I can never turn anything over to him and think 'My husband will take care of that.' I am beginning to feel more like his mother than his wife."

They got to El Paso in time to celebrate Christmas, just the two of them, in their rooms at the Laughlin, a small residential hotel occupied by friendly people who already knew one another. Many of them came there believing the dry, mountainous air cured asthma and tuberculosis. For a while Marguerite and Jack took advantage of the ideal climate and the tourist location, driving into New Mexico to the parks and crossing the border at Juarez for the night life.

With no other prospects for employment, Marguerite began helping Jack in the Real Silk Hosiery office, keeping the books, scheduling sales trips, filling orders. From the beginning, she was afraid to leave the business to him — afraid there wouldn't be enough money.

Worried about Marguerite, Harry Crozier paid the Tindales a visit in the spring. It didn't look good to him. He wanted her to come back to Austin where she had friends and could get a good job. When she refused that, he insisted she take some writing assignments he got for her. Under Crozier's guidance, she wrote an article on the varieties of cacti for *The Cattleman* magazine. Although she stayed in El Paso with Jack and turned down other writing assignments, Crozier's concern sealed the friendship.

In addition to running Jack's office, Marguerite was working for a new friend, Norman Henry, a forty-year-old bachelor, an entrepreneur and a loner. He liked the work he did, traveling the Southwest and Mexico managing sales for businesses that were moving or closing down. Seeing Marguerite working harder and harder while Jack grew more and more bitter, he wanted to help but didn't know how.

Within six months, Jack was desperate with the sense of his own failure. In the spring of 1925, he left for Denver following a lead on a job Norman Henry told him about. From there, he wrote Marguerite. "I have done the one thing I vowed I would never do. On Easter Sunday, I took money for playing six times in a motion picture theatre. I feel utterly degraded."

They hung on for a few more months in El Paso before all three of them — Jack, Marguerite, and Norman — went back to San Antonio where Marguerite got a job as clerk-typist for Ormsby Chevrolet Company. She was enough her father's daughter to be fascinated by the sleek new automobiles that came in. Everybody, including L. D. Ormsby, seemed to be making money in 1926 and 1927. Soon her knack for organization and delegation gained her a promotion to bookkeeper and then office and credit manager.

Suddenly her dream of becoming a lawyer was back in full force. It annoyed her that Ormsby's lawyer could come into their office and get a high fee for work he delegated to her. As soon as she could afford it, she enrolled in San Antonio Junior College for courses at night.

Pat Neff came to San Antonio occasionally. She had new friends, she told him. She was making good money and saving toward law school. When he said she would make less as a lawyer than she was making at Ormsby's, they both laughed. They had had this conversation before. As for Neff, he was headed for Washington to fill an unexpired term on the U.S. Board of Mediation, a prestigious, presidentially appointed board to mediate labor disputes in the railroad industry.

Jack heard rumors of opportunities in Chicago and went there for a few weeks, finally writing Marguerite for money to come home. Exhausted and no longer in love with the boyish dreamer she had met at Kelly Field, she agreed with him this time when he said "I do everything wrong. I am just dragging you down."

On August 1, 1927, after a tragic nine years of marriage, Marguerite and Jack were divorced. The passage of time had widened the breach between them, exacerbating Marguerite's determination to make it, both for herself and for the man she loved, and dulling the spontaneity and joy that had attracted them to one another in the first place. Seemingly against his will, Jack had been drained of the confidence and drive he had brought to their courtship.

Marguerite was saved, at least in part, by her unerring ability to focus — sometimes too narrowly — on whatever task seemed most urgent. During most of the years with Jack, the task was sheer economic survival. Drained by years of emotional and financial struggle, she told her mother: "Jack never did anything mean to me. Love just turned to pity. That is no way to be married." Following her own instincts and her father's advice, the woman who had called herself Margaret Tindale for so long became Marguerite Rawalt again.

The Rawalts had reason to grieve for two of their children. A few months earlier, doctors at the Naval Hospital in Chelsea, Massachusetts, had operated on Louis, removed a kidney, and diagnosed persistent malaria. Instead of going home to die as they said he would, he married Violet (Vi) Bell, the sister of another hospitalized soldier, and went back to Texas to make a life for himself by the water.

Early in 1928, Marguerite was surprised by a telegram from Pat Neff.

RAWALT, HERE'S YOUR CHANCE. COME TO WASHINGTON AS MY SECRETARY, ATTEND FIRST-RATE LAW SCHOOL AT NIGHT.

In the first flush of excitement, she called her friend Tess Allen and then her parents. Tess thought it sounded like too much trouble. Weren't they having a good time with their fighter-pilot friends Captains Moon and Quinn? Viola and Charles seemed stunned. She was just getting over the bad times with Jack. She was making money, having fun. Why didn't she relax and enjoy herself? Washington was a long way off. She didn't know anybody there.

The postwar boom had been good to both Ormsby Chevrolet Company and to L. D. Ormsby, an ex-racecar driver and shrewd investor who made money in oil and land speculation as well as in car sales. When Ormsby offered Marguerite a raise to stay, she refused; when he suggested part ownership in the business, she hesitated. He had never had anybody he trusted to leave in charge before, he said. Still, she vacillated.

Money was getting tight in the big cities, he warned. The city
of Chicago was out of money, he heard, paying its teachers in
scrips. In Washington, she would probably find herself out of work
with no money to pay for law school. Finally, in frustration, he
scrawled a single sentence on an office note pad, *If you go to Washington you're a D. Fool.* Although not so bluntly, Charles and Viola
agreed.

Marguerite had seldom acknowledged it during her marriage,
but frustrated ambition had festered. She had always wanted to accomplish things on her own, to be somebody. She had wanted a college education, then the money ran out. When she was ready to go
to law school, the war came. She had married Jack and wanted success for both of them but had been unable to get it. If she let this
chance go by, there would be no one to blame but herself. She was
thirty-two years old and thought this chance might be the last.

Finally, she wrote Lucy Moore and got the approval she was
looking for. "Go, Happy. This is what you wanted."

By the end of June, she was on her way to Washington, taking
time to visit with her parents and stop with Lucy Moore in Austin.
In Moore's wooded Medina Lake cottage, they talked the nights
away and revived their old plans for Marguerite. She would go to
Georgetown University, they decided, since it was the highest-
ranking law school in Washington, and it offered courses at night.

After only a few days at her new job in the new city, all Marguerite's hopes were dashed. She was talking over her plans with
Anne Bauerlein, her first friend in the office, when a young man, a
lawyer named Hugh, asked what she was talking about. When she
told him, he smiled and called to a colleague, "She says she is going
to my school, Georgetown, because it's the best law school in
town." They began to guffaw.

Marguerite was already worried that some of her junior college credits wouldn't be accepted: "I've got good grades from The
University of Texas," she argued; "I know I can get in." After
more smirks and nudges, Hugh told her that Georgetown University Law School did not accept women — no matter what kind of
grades they had.

She had never heard of a school that refused women. At first she thought they were joking. She felt like she had been hit in the stomach with a sack of grain. The blood ran to her hands and feet, and she thought she would faint. Why had she left everything to come here?

Her heart pounding, she called the law school at Georgetown. A woman answered the phone. Yes, it was true, no women students. George Washington University had a law program at night. She should call there.

In years to come, she would say, *The fight doesn't begin until you get opposition.* For now, she wasn't looking for words, she was moving on stored-up adrenalin — and rage. By the time school started in the fall, she had gotten herself provisionally admitted to the law program at George Washington and enrolled for a semester of required undergraduate courses. But not without a fight. First there had been the disappointment about Georgetown and the terrible fear that she had left Texas for nothing. Then her Bayview credits were refused.

Before it was over, she had challenged the registrar's ruling to a complaints committee and then gone above that to GWU's new president, Cloyd Heck Marvin. She was indignant, she told him. If those credits were good enough for The University of Texas, they ought to be good enough for George Washington University. "You people out here in the East think no learning takes place west of the Mississippi." Amused, he reminded her that he came to Washington from the University of Arizona. Finally, the credits were accepted.

Suddenly years of pent-up momentum propelled her in all directions at once. She was working, going to school, making friends. She learned to play golf. She joined the Texas State Society and added many Texans to her growing network of friends. With a little coaxing, L. D. Ormsby forgave her betrayal and arranged for her to buy a Chevrolet at cost. She took the train to Detroit one weekend in September and drove back to Washington alone in her light green coupe.

With the automobile, she could drive to all the places she had read about — Gettysburg, Valley Forge, Harper's Ferry, Mount Vernon. The more she learned, the more she wanted to know. When her San Antonio friend, Tess Allen, moved to New York, she added Manhattan to her list. She was exhilarated by the night life, the rampant Stock Exchange, types and races of people she had never seen before.

Marguerite was creating a style and a pattern for the rest of her life. From that time on, she would lead a fiercely disciplined life — at a breakneck pace. By packing immense amounts of work and play into short periods of time, she created the illusion of doing two or three things at once. Her real secret lay in her ability to concentrate totally on whatever she decided to do.

Busy as she was, she dreaded the upcoming holidays, the first she had ever spent away from old friends and family. As Christmas approached, she heard other people saying they couldn't go home either. With Christmas Eve on a Monday, they faced a long, desolate weekend. Soon Marguerite had plans for five or six single friends to "come together to make their own happiness." Forty years later she described it to a niece:

> The first Christmas after I came to Washington in July, I could hardly bear the thought. We didn't have money and couldn't afford in those days to go home for Christmas. But I had made a few friends thru men and women in the office. And among them and others, there were about six persons just like me — alone, single, and could not go home. I was living in an efficiency one-room apartment, but I had an electric toaster and broiler. So — I invited them in for Christmas Eve. We all went to a famous Catholic Church here for midnight mass and then came back for whatever I could fix on that grill. And the same on Christmas day — we got together. And all enjoyed it. But it always takes one person to act as the catalyst — come to think of it, I think that is just about what I have been all my life — one who stirs others into action, myself along with them.

Marguerite's first year in Washington was marred by a near-tragedy much graver than spending Christmas holidays alone. Accustomed to dry cleaning her clothes out of doors with high-test gasoline, she came home one night after classes and tried to clean some blouses in the bathroom, closing the door behind her. Overcome by the fumes, she fainted, lying unconscious for hours in a pool of gasoline in the tightly sealed room. Early in the morning, she became conscious long enough to get to the bedroom and call Louise Wright, a nurse who lived some blocks away. With layers of skin burned off her back, she was deep in shock by the time Louise arrived.

She awoke to find herself in a strange hospital being cared for by people she hardly knew. Two were Dr. Earnest, whose father taught criminal law at GWU, and Louise Wright, with whom she established a bond that would endure over many years and changing circumstances. Samuel Winslow, chairman of the Board of Mediation, took care of things at work and notified Pat Neff, who called her parents.

Herbert Hoover's election to the presidency in November had been good news for Pat Neff and his staff since it had been Hoover — then secretary of commerce — who had recommended that President Coolidge appoint Neff to the Board of Mediation in the first place. As expected, Coolidge reappointed Neff late in the year with Hoover's approval.

Suddenly there was trouble. The Klan-backed incumbent, Senator Earle Mayfield, had been defeated by Tom Connally with the help of Pat Neff and his friends. Bitter and bent on revenge, Mayfield invoked senatorial privilege to blackball the presidential appointee from his state. For three months, Neff's staff worked around the clock locating people who might influence the disgruntled senator, trying to find some way to break Mayfield's resolve.

Marguerite and Neff worked in tandem as they had done in his second campaign for governor, writing letters, calling people they knew, trying even the longest shots. Before giving up, Marguerite went in person to speak to Mayfield. Apparently, for Senator Mayfield, revenge was enough. Congress adjourned in March with no action on the confirmation, and Pat Neff returned to Waco to practice law.

From the beginning of 1929, Marguerite's anxiety over Pat Neff's departure and the possible loss of her own job was intensified by word of economic troubles surfacing across the country. Wall Street was like a gigantic slot machine with everyone hitting — or about to hit — the jackpot. But banks and businesses were overextended; in the midst of boom times, workers were losing their jobs. Charles Rawalt said even the King Ranch had to economize.

When her job was made secure again by the appointment of another former Texas governor, O. B. Colquitt, to the Board of

Mediation, Marguerite turned her attention toward law school. The handful of women in her class were immediately beset with invitations from the two leading legal sororities for women, Phi Delta Delta and Kappa Beta Pi. Representing the sororities, Washington's most distinguished women lawyers congregated in Stockton Hall's large, bare "ladies lounge" with tea, sandwiches, and encouragement for the new students.

In the sixty years since 1869 when the first woman was permitted to practice law in the United States, women lawyers had climbed a steep, uphill path in the profession. During the decade after World War I, they had grown increasingly conscious of themselves as a small, competent group, with skills and knowledge rare among women. Through the sororities and the National Association of Women Lawyers, the know-how and rising consciousness passed from one generation of women to the next.

Marguerite was particularly impressed with a sophisticated, gray-haired Washington lawyer named Elizabeth Cox, whose husband was also a lawyer. She got her degree from GWU after her children were grown. Now she had a successful private practice of her own in probate law. It looked like a good life. Good work. Money to travel. Good-looking clothes. All the things Marguerite never had.

Membership in the Nu Chapter of Kappa Beta Pi began Marguerite Rawalt's career as a leader in professional and women's organizations. It was her first taste of an avocation that would become a way of life for her. The rough and tumble of organization life came naturally to her. She liked to be in charge. She didn't mind competition. And she could stand to lose. The uninhibited camaraderie of the women reminded her of those carefree days in Lorena.

Later, Marguerite would be critical of Kappa for its lack of activism for women's rights. But during those early years in law school, she simply appreciated what women like Elizabeth Cox were giving her — moral support, friendship, and recognition. They were a group of admired women from whom one could learn much.

Early in September 1929, the stock market reached its glittering peak — and began to fall. On October 23, the panic began, and on October 24, "Black Thursday," the market collapsed.

In 1926, Charles had traded the farm west of Robstown for 240 acres of cultivated cotton land across town. In order to make the swap, he had borrowed $27,000 from the Martindale Mortgage Company in San Antonio. With Willis farming the land on shares, the Rawalts needed both Charles's salary and good profits from cotton to support the two families and make the mortgage payments. Between 1927 and 1930, cotton prices dropped from twenty cents to nine cents a pound and Charles lost his job at the King Ranch.

Charles and Viola moved in with Willis and his new wife, Anna. For a while, Louis and Vi were there as well. Desperate, Viola bought a little hamburger and lunch stand in town and sold short order meals. Later, Louis and Vi camped on Padre Island and fished for a living.

As the only member of the family with an income, Marguerite became a pivot and a still point in their troubles — and eventually the absentee head of the family. With the farm close to foreclosure in the spring of 1930, she borrowed $200 to help pay the interest on the farm loan and sent home smaller amounts when she could — to pay insurance, interest, fees, whatever their most pressing need happened to be. As hardships took their toll in family tensions, increasingly it was her combination of logic, fairness and tact that kept them all working together.

By December 11, 1930, some 1,300 banks had failed, including the Bank of the U.S., a major private New York bank with some sixty branches and 400,000 depositors. Convinced the Depression-ridden Republicans would be swept out of office in the 1932 elections and that her democratic credentials would stand her in good stead, Marguerite insisted on taking the bar exam a year before she finished her courses. Government lawyers were politically appointed; and, although it wasn't easy, it was not impossible for a woman with connections to get one of the coveted spots.

She took the exam in June 1932, and passed it. In October, she was admitted to the Bar of the Court of Appeals and the Supreme Court for the District of Columbia. A month later she was appointed to George Washington University's first Law Review.

But her successes were overshadowed almost daily by heart-rending letters from her family in Texas. In their attempts to protect one another, they turned to her. Charles didn't want the rest of them to know how bad things were; for the first time in his life, he felt he couldn't protect his family.

They needed the money Marguerite sent and they hated to take it. Abandoning the remnants of his Republican sentiments, Charles joined the hoards of farmers and despairing workers who hoped to be saved by Franklin Delano Roosevelt.

In the city, Marguerite saw poverty and black despair deepening all around her. Before Christmas, thousands of hunger marchers petitioning for work were turned away from the White House. While she studied for the bar exam in a frenzy of anxious concentration, the first of thousands of veterans came to town to claim advances on their soldiers' bonuses. For two months they poured in from all directions, bringing their families and camping out in parks, dumps, and abandoned buildings. Many of them built shanties and settled outside Washington on the banks of the Anacostia River.

On June 29, in one of the bitterest moments of a bitter time, United States troops marched on "Anacostia Flats," driving the veterans out and burning down their makeshift houses. The 17,000 settlers were only a fraction of the army of the unemployed whose numbers would reach thirteen million by the end of the year. By then wages would have dropped sixty percent since 1929, and cotton would be selling for a nickel a pound.

Now president of Baylor University in Waco, Texas, Pat Neff wrote Marguerite about the Depression in Texas:

> Any kind of place to work now, on any kind of a salary, is a good place. People down here in Texas have no choice any longer about work. . . . All salaries of all kinds have been greatly reduced. Public school teachers' salaries have been reduced, and some teachers have not been paid for months and some for a year, even their reduced salaries. Baylor, like practically all other institutions, is hard-pressed, and at present is paying teachers in scrips.

Suddenly Marguerite was hearing from Jack again. He had remarried. Something was wrong with his back. The trouble started, he said, when he was in the Air Corps in San Antonio. He wanted her to help him get veteran's medical benefits. For several years they corresponded, and she watched his handwriting deteriorate and his paranoia increase. She did what she could to help him get the medical attention he needed, and grieved over his occasional, pathetic letters: "There is only one Marguerite and during the years that we have not seen each other, my prayers have been for your success and it looks as tho they have been answered. . . . I only think of you when I need help evidently. . . I am just now beginning to appreciate what you did for me. . . . You are the only one who was ever in my heart."

In less than a month after Marguerite was admitted to the D.C. Bar in October 1932, she and the rest of the country were celebrating the landslide election of Franklin Roosevelt. A nation about to collapse into revolution had to have action. More than that, it had to have hope. Here was a man who offered both.

All the Texans Marguerite knew were exuberant with new hope. John Nance Garner, the vice-president elect, was a Texan. Sarah King, honorary state National Guard colonel and chairman of the state's prison board, would be representing Governor Miriam A. (Ma) Ferguson at the inauguration. Marguerite had known the elegant, white-haired Mrs. King, whom everyone called "Sank," since her days in the governor's office.

Loaded with suitcases and bags carrying her uniforms, evening clothes, and fur coats, she refused accommodations at the fashionable Willard Hotel, insisting on staying instead in her younger friend's two-room apartment at the Chastleton. Knowing Marguerite was trying to get a government law job, she set out to introduce her to everybody who might help.

Sarah King arrived a few days in advance of the Saturday March 4 inauguration. In Texas, the Rawalts were living off what they could grow or shoot or catch with a fishing pole. Marguerite was campaigning for two jobs and knew she might end up with none. But there were parties every night; and, for a while, no one talked about money.

March 4, 1933, dawned gray and overcast. Nearly 100,000 spectators surrounded the Capitol. In anticipation of trouble, Army machine guns guarded the east lawn. Marguerite sat with the Texas delegation in front of the platform, close enough to see John Garner borrow a scarf and wrap it around his neck in the bitter wind. Franklin Roosevelt, wearing neither coat nor hat began,

> This is a day of national consecration. . . . the only thing we
> have to fear is fear itself— nameless, unreasoning, unjustified ter-

ror which paralyzed needed efforts to convert retreat into advance.

Later on Saturday afternoon, movie idol Rudy Vallee visited the Texas delegation. Snuggled inside Sarah King's mink coat, Marguerite posed for photographs with Rudy Vallee and the rest of the delegation. A month later, she described it all to Lucy Moore.

> Cinderella right — that was me. I forgot all about being tired, or having nerves. I had no sleep and no rest for a week, yet everyone said I looked so much better! Excitement! You understand.

King took Marguerite to Congressman Richard Kleberg's office to talk about the law job she wanted at the Bureau of Internal Revenue. She was a good Texan, a good Democrat, and she was going to be a good lawyer. She had passed the bar exam a year before graduation; she was on the Law Review. Her grades were topnotch. She had just been elected to the honorary Order of the Coif. She had chosen Internal Revenue because tax law was growing. It was a field with a future. She liked to work with figures, and she understood money. It was what she wanted to do. Both Kleberg and his brash twenty-four-year-old assistant, Lyndon B. Johnson, promised to help.

On the day after the inauguration, the president's four-day bank holiday put an end to the run on the banks by depositors and began the famous "One Hundred Days" of New Deal reforms. Some reforms promised relief to farmers like the Rawalts.

At five o'clock on Saturday afternoon, April 1, Marguerite joined a handful of other guests for tea in Eleanor Roosevelt's private quarters at the White House. The invitation had come through Margie Neal, who was doing everything possible to help Marguerite get a job usually reserved for men. A few days later, she wrote Lucy Moore about it.

> Was I proud? It is always customary for the President's wife to receive guests on the second floor, in the Blue, or Red, or Gold Rooms. But we were promptly invited to Mrs. Roosevelt's private living room on the third floor, which is the family living quarters. There we had tea and talked. Mrs. Roosevelt is more interested in accomplishment than in clothes; no inane talk and actions in her make-up. Mrs. Dall [Anna Roosevelt] and the little granddaugh-

ter were present. . . . Just plain folks, I call it. I was very proud of
such a wife in the White House.

On June 8, the morning after her graduation from law school,
Marguerite wrote a long letter to "Precious Mom."

> Last night was the big night as you know. I should have
> given a whole lot if you could have been there. . . . When my
> name was called, I stepped in front of Dr. Marvin for my di-
> ploma, he held it a moment, to cause me to stop, and said to me:
> "I think you have a lot of success stored up in this."

> Getting elected to the Order of the Coif was the big honor. I
> was the only girl in the June class who made it. The men were all
> so fine to congratulate me and seemed glad that I was included
> too.

> I am anxious to know what Pop has learned about the farm
> loan. I think of that constantly and all the time. . . . I was relieved
> beyond word that you had had rain. Thank goodness for that. . .

She was temporarily secure in her job at the Board of Mediation. But hardships had both strengthened her ambition and deepened her desire for security. She was unwilling to remain — like so
many lawyers — in the ranks of overly qualified female secretaries.

She thought a woman who worked hard would have a better
chance of success in the bureaucracy than in private practice. Pat
Neff agreed but said the prejudice against women was greater than
she seemed to think. To get the government job she wanted she
would have to be recommended as high up as they could get, the
president if possible. He would arrange for her to see the vice-president.

Marguerite met with Mr. and Mrs. Garner. Harry Crozier,
Lucy Moore, Margie Neal, and Sarah King called on everyone they
knew. By June 1933, she had the personal backing of Senators Morris Sheppard and Tom Connally along with letters of recommendation from Neff and O. B. Colquitt; Jed Adams, Texas Democratic National Committeeman; Roy Miller, director of the Texas
Democratic National Committee; Margie Neal, Sarah King, and
L. D. Ormsby, all prominent Texas Democrats.

Finally, during the fall, in order to secure the appointment,
Senator Connally arranged to go with her to meet the newly appointed chief counsel, E. Barrett Prettyman. Leaving the building

on the arm of the prepossessing senator, Marguerite laughed, "You would think I had gone after a Cabinet post."

Early in October, she had a call from the senator's office — she could count on the appointment. The vague message came at a time when she was too anxious about the situation on the farm to be excited. The letters from home were breaking her heart. With every letter, she was sure the farm had been lost.

In May, President Roosevelt had signed the Agricultural Adjustment Act (AAA) which promised farmers parity prices for certain products and subsidies for land taken out of production. There was also hope of low-interest federal mortgages to relieve farmers of the high charges of companies like Martindale. But relief was slow in coming and the Rawalts were losing hope. Now Martindale refused to give them a release on the previous year's crop mortgage, which they hadn't paid — and couldn't pay. Every letter sounded more hopeless than the one before.

There were other problems. Charles was having "heart spells." He was tired. He couldn't provide for his family. They lived from day to day.

Marguerite's was the only income her family had. At a time when a quarter of the work force was unemployed and the average worker made less than $1,000 a year, she was making $3,000. A beginning lawyer's salary with the government was just $2,000. A third less. She kept going over it in her mind. The money, Mom and Pop, the missed opportunity, all the years of schooling.

That night she wrote Pat Neff, Lucy Moore, and her parents: What did they advise her to do? Neff responded immediately, "Take the job with Internal Revenue. You've earned it." Lucy Moore said the same thing.

Confused and unable to make up her mind, Marguerite wrote Neff again.

> I am the only one drawing a salary in all my family of six adults, and not even the money for plowing up cotton has come to hand, though there are a dozen places where it must go to pay off old obligations. "The plight of the farmer" is no mere platitude — it is an actual fact, as I am sure you too know. And every one of these six adults would welcome a job that would bring in a salary. You see I just HAVE to carry on, hence my consternation at a reduction of $88.33 per month. These are hard luck tales that one doesn't like to talk about nor have to admit, but those are facts

which all the philosophic reasoning or Aristotelian logic in the world do not cure.

During the weeks before she was officially notified of her appointment, Marguerite vacillated. Finally, word came from her parents: "Take the lawyer's job. We'll get by." She didn't see how they could get by, but she let them make the decision and loved them for their faith in the future — and their trust in her.

In December, she began work in the Office of the Chief Counsel, Bureau of Internal Revenue. Now, as Pat Neff had once promised, all she had to do was "work and be happy."

[3]

Moving Up

Marguerite had been forewarned that being a lawyer in an office full of men was not going to be easy. Pat Neff had tried to tell her. Aline Stillwell, a Women's Bar Association friend who had been a lawyer at Internal Revenue for a long time, warned her. "Watch out," she said, "the first thing they are going to do is offer you some clerical or administrative job rather than the docket of cases they would give a new man. Don't take it. Tell them you want your cases." As soon as she was sworn in — one woman out of thirty new appointments — it happened.

She was greeted by the office administrator, Mr. Clifford Beckham. "I have the very place for you, Miss Rawalt. Our docket clerk has just retired. This is a very important spot, keeping up with the dockets of cases here and the assignments to the attorneys, and the issues involved in the various cases, keeping a close record of all cases that come into this section. . ."

No, she insisted; she had been hired as an attorney and if he didn't have any work for an attorney she would go to the chief counsel and see about getting herself transferred to where she was needed. Immediately she had her twenty-five or thirty cases like the others, and for four years, she worked on "compromise cases," collecting unpaid taxes and negotiating with taxpayers.

She didn't want to believe that — despite her own intelligence and hard work — she was going to be treated unfairly because she was a woman. She had to learn the lessons over and over again. Gradually, she accepted it. She would have to fight and fight again to get her due.

In 1933, the Bureau of Internal Revenue liked to call itself the second largest law office in the country, second only to the Justice Department. Marguerite was invigorated by the work. She liked organizing information, concentrating under pressure, using logic and common sense to untangle knotty legal problems.

Still, the pressure to compete with men who thought they were superior to her never lifted and neither did the pall of anxiety over her nearly destitute family. A letter written to Jack Tindale a few months after she joined the civil service reveals the strain.

> My work is heavy and I am rushed. I have not had any rest or vacation for three years because I could not afford it. I feel it needs extra effort to make good for women have to be not just as good, but almost better than the men, to hold the same kind of position. . . . I might offer sympathy but that is not what you need. You will be out and going again if you just have determination and courage.

As soon as she was settled in the law job she had wanted for so long, Marguerite began carving out the avocation that would become a demanding additional career. Automatically, she joined professional organizations.

She joined the D. C. Women's Bar Association as soon as she passed the bar exam. There she heard Laura Berrien and Burnita Shelton Matthews talk about the Equal Rights Amendment. She saw Alice Paul, Mabel Vernon, and a handful of other suffragists valiantly holding together the National Woman's Party. A few years later she joined the National Association of Women Lawyers (NAWL), a forward-looking group deeply influenced by the feminist philosophy of the Woman's Party. In 1935, she added the Federal Bar Association, an almost all-male national organization of government lawyers. She joined the D.C. Bar Association when women were admitted in 1941.

At the start, her organizational work grew out of her professional interests. But many of the organizations she joined were women's groups, and soon she knew the country's leading women lawyers. Burnita Matthews, a suffragist who had come to Washington to get the law degree she couldn't get in her native Mississippi, had helped Alice Paul write the uncompromising version of the Equal Rights Amendment that had been introduced in Congress in 1923, and every year since then.

Social welfare reformers wanted to see women protected by special conditions in the marketplace. Because the Woman's Party insisted on total equality with men rather than protection or special treatment, the amendment read simply:

> Men and women shall have Equal Rights throughout the United States and every place subject to its jurisdiction.

By the 1930s, Matthews and a few others had become a link between the Woman's Party and the women's organizations that Marguerite joined. In 1935, led by Matthews, NAWL became one of the first professional women's organizations to endorse the Equal Rights Amendment. Later, Matthews would become the first woman named to a Federal District Court.

Through Kappa Beta Pi, Marguerite established a lasting friendship with Judge Florence Allen, appointed by President Roosevelt to the U.S. Court of Appeals. Those first years in the law flooded her with new influences, new interests, new aspirations. Undoubtedly, they gave birth to her first conscious interest in women's rights and organizational work — and probably inspired her desire to become a judge herself.

Feminist sentiments lingered into the 1930s. Women influenced by the suffrage movement urged a new generation to get involved in politics and the professions and continued to press them into altruistic causes — social work, campaigns against war, crime, alcoholism, prostitution, all the ills of society.

In 1937, Eleanor Roosevelt, the country's first activist First Lady, began inviting women executives in government to White House garden parties. Marguerite attended the first one. According to the Sunday, May, 16, *Washington Post*, the lawn in front of the south portico swarmed with "every prominent woman and wife in town." Mrs. John Nance Garner co-hostessed the event. Mary Anderson, chief of the Women's Bureau, was there, standing in for

Frances Perkins, secretary of labor and the country's first woman cabinet member. Some women lawyers already saw the pro-labor Women's Bureau as unfriendly to the cause of women's equality because of its endorsement of the protective labor laws.

Marguerite had new friends now. The women she knew in her legal sorority and the bar associations, Anne Bauerlein and Colonel Murphy from the Board of Mediation office, Louise Wright, and her mother Hattie Crawford.

During the early 1930s, a new and flamboyant suitor named Louis Bennett came to town for a week or so every few months — long enough to take her to the best restaurants in Baltimore and Washington and to the horse races at Bowie, Maryland, which she loved almost as much as he did. Louis was a gambler, following the horses up and down the East Coast. He only appeared when he was flush, buying extravagant gifts for her, making her laugh. Nothing was too good for her, he said. When she tried to stop short of eating everything he ordered for her, he teased her, "Come on Marguerite, get fat, Marguerite. Get fat and be somebody."

There was nothing serious about the relationship between the two of them, she thought. She enjoyed his worldly good humor and was too busy to miss him when he left.

One Sunday, in the spring of 1935, Marguerite and two friends from her office drove along the Potomac to Hains Point to play golf. They needed a fourth and Harry Secord was looking for a game.

She had heard of Harry Secord from Louise Wright and her mother. Years before, when he was in the Army Air Corps, he and his wife had rented an apartment in the Crawford home in Junction City, Kansas. Now he lived in Washington. His wife had died recently. Despite her mother's urging, Louise hesitated to introduce their two friends. At fifty-one, Harry was too much older than Marguerite, Louise thought, and not exciting or intellectual enough for her ambitious friend.

That afternoon, he made up their foursome for golf, and Marguerite agreed with Louise. Harry wasn't very exciting. He was quiet — shy almost — and slender, not much bigger than she was. She couldn't tell exactly what he did. He was slow to speak, with a military bearing and a steady gaze. He had a nice smile that started with his eyes and moved slowly down his face, only occasionally turning to laughter. She was good at the old game — the clever banter between aggressive, sophisticated men and women. Harry Secord seemed oblivious to all that, and she found it disconcerting.

Weeks passed before Marguerite saw Harry again and months before she took him seriously. He was nice to be with, but she felt, he didn't know how to dance, didn't enjoy crowds. He spent most of his spare time alone or with one or two friends. He was learning to cook and liked to give small, congenial parties. Sometimes he included her friends among his guests.

Eleven years older than she was, he had left high school in Jackson, Michigan, to join the army in 1901. Spending years in the Philippines when he was little more than a boy, he had accumulated enough active-duty time to retire as a captain in 1933. A year later, at the request of Army Air Corps General Henry H. (Hap) Arnold, he had gone back to work as civilian superintendent of Bolling Air Field.

Harry's life had been different from Marguerite's. He wasn't intellectual but he knew things she didn't know and had a wisdom and maturity that she had known only in her father and Pat Neff. Harry didn't need much outside himself. He liked the work he did at Bolling, but he had earned his retirement, he said. He didn't plan to spend the rest of his life working for money he didn't need. She was the only thing he wanted that he didn't have. But, at forty, Marguerite's career was just beginning. The joys of retirement were unfathomable to her.

While Marguerite insisted she had better things to do than get married, Harry courted her deliberately, confidently. They went to the nightclubs she was used to and spent leisurely evenings with Louise and Hattie. They took long weekend drives to the Patuxent River home of Colonel Murphy, Marguerite's old friend from the Board of Mediation.

By the fall of 1935, she was interested enough in Harry to describe her birthday as a "wonderful night with Harry that he later wrote 'I will never forget' " and to note in her diary his departure for a vacation alone at Miami Beach. Still, she wasn't ready to give up her freedom again.

Christmas letters from Harry Crozier and Pat Neff brought back memories. During the winter she was busy with work, club functions, and the graduate law courses she was taking. Harry, she felt, would want a full-time wife.

Harry loved good automobiles and always had a new one. Every night during the summer, he parked on Twentieth Street in front of the plain brick building where she had gone to school for nearly six years. At seven o'clock it was still light and hot, but the humidity would be lifting. Some nights after class she walked out of the stuffy classroom and found an icy martini waiting on the dashboard. Often they drove into the countryside to relax and cool off before going back to town for dinner.

Marguerite was settled in her job. Master's degree courses came easily. Harry was around all the time. Finally, the Depression was loosening its iron grip on the farmers in South Texas. In January 1934, the Federal Farm Mortgage Corporation was set up to help farmers refinance their mortgages; and, by fall, the Rawalts had the low-interest federal loan that would enable them to keep their land. Willis and Charles were working the farm and with the help of AAA subsidies managing pretty well again.

When his oldest brother died in the spring of 1935, Charles inherited $7,500 cash from his mother's estate, enough to enable him to build four small houses in Corpus Christi, one for him and Viola to live in and three to rent. Louis and Vi were operating a bait and tackle shop on Padre Island. Living and working near the water, collecting Indian relics, guiding tourists and beachcombers around the barren island, Louis was happier than he had been since the war.

Charles never fully recovered from the blows that fell so heavily and unexpectedly during the Depression. In 1936, he was sixty-six years old and completely exhausted. In the spring of that year, he bought a new Ford, the only thing he wanted, and agreed to take a long trip with his wife and daughter.

Marguerite got her master's degree that June and set out for Texas early in July. The vacation marked the end of one period of her life and the beginning of another.

By then Marguerite had agreed to marry Harry. Gradually, she had come to appreciate the depths beneath the quiet surface. With him, she relaxed in a way she had never done before. She had looked after herself a long time. She wanted someone, not to take care of her so much as to share with her the responsibility for both their lives. He was, she said, someone she could "lean on" when she needed to. They were strong in different ways.

In retrospect, it seemed that what she had with Harry was

what she had wanted with Jack, but she had ended up taking care of him. Pat Neff and Harry Crozier cared for her. They would always be there. Louis Bennett, for all his protestations, had a wife somewhere. She was ready for more than that. She loved the limelight and attention from men, but the hardships of the Depression years and her time in Washington away from her family had dulled the glitter of independence and freedom — for Marguerite and a whole generation of women no longer enchanted by the 1920s wave of liberation. Styles for women were more formal, more ladylike. Dresses were longer and bobbed hair was growing out. A woman could be glamorous again and reticent about her private life.

On her way to Texas, Marguerite stopped in Dallas where she met Pat Neff for the Fourth of July holiday. The city was alive with the carnival atmosphere of the Texas Centennial. They saw a few people they knew, had their silhouettes made at the fair, and she told him about Harry.

After a week in Austin with Lucy Moore, Marguerite joined her parents and set out with them on a long westward journey that recalled the magical landscapes of her childhood. There were the plains of Illinois, Oklahoma, New Mexico, her first glimpse of the Mississippi River, the Cimarron, the Gulf of Mexico, the Texas range as flat as the sky above it as far as you could see.

The 8,000-mile marathon she had planned drew a rough semicircle on her map, across the South to the West Coast and back through the Northwest where they stopped for a series of visits with Rawalt and Flake relatives in Illinois. Before it was over they had toured Carlsbad Caverns, the Grand Canyon, the Petrified Forest, the Painted Desert. They drove across the Mohave Desert and through the Redwood Forest, tromped through Lincoln, Yellowstone, Bitterroot and Sequoia National Parks. If Charles and Viola were exhausted some nights, they kept it to themselves.

Harry telegraphed every day and wrote, "I wake up blue and lonesome."

In Illinois, they saw old friends and met in-laws they had never heard of. They were country people, farmers, some more prosperous than others, all descendants of the same sturdy line of immigrants. Among them, Marguerite's city ways fell away. Charles and Viola were as at home as if they had never left Prairie City.

On September 3, Harry joined them in Galesburg, Illinois, for a huge gathering of Flake relatives. Charles and Viola met him and introduced him as their future son-in-law.

Marguerite was going to marry Harry, but she didn't know when. She was going to Chicago in October with a full docket of court cases. She had waited almost three years for the opportunity, and she had to be ready. She was enrolled in Catholic University's doctoral program in law. She had just been elected president of her Kappa Beta Pi chapter.

Her friends' questions echoed her own doubts. Wouldn't Harry want her to stop traveling, to stop working, to give up her work in organizations? Was there really time for the demands of a husband in a life like hers?

A practical consideration threatened her job and bothered her more than all the rest. In 1932, Congress had passed the National Economy Act in a Depression attempt to reduce government spending. Section 213 of the law prohibited two members of the same family from working for the government. The regulation, which covered military as well as civilian employees, had been controversial from the beginning. Women called Section 213 discriminatory, insisting that it was aimed at women. Civil servants thought it undermined the merit system which called for the hiring and firing of government employees on performance alone.

Marguerite knew a few people in the Treasury Department who had been fired under Section 213. All of them were women. Later studies showed her suspicions to be well-founded: three-fourths of those separated had been women. Between 1932 and 1937, when the law was repealed, the federal government dismissed 1,600 married women from government service. To make matters worse for Marguerite, who was making a name for herself as Marguerite Rawalt, a 1933 ruling required government employees to take their husbands' names and report that change to their department or face disciplinary action.

Unable to decide what was best, she and Harry prolonged their courtship. On the cold and brutally windy Saturday after Thanksgiving, Marguerite and Harry boarded a special Baltimore and Ohio train headed for the Army–Navy football game in Philadelphia. They arrived an hour before the game on the same train with Eleanor Roosevelt and her friend Lorena Hickok. Joining the second largest crowd ever to watch a football game, they ate a picnic lunch in Municipal Stadium and saw Navy beat Army 7–0.

Marguerite fought the wind with a borrowed aviator's jacket and pilot's boots. Everyone was dressed up, bundled up. Many of the men were in uniform. Harry looked wonderful in his custom-made suit and Borsalino felt hat.

For Marguerite, the holidays were darkened by word that Jack had died of tuberculosis of the spine at a hospital in San Antonio. The newspapers described him as a native of Edinborough, Scotland, "war veteran, radio announcer, entertainer." For a while, all the old feelings came back, her infatuation with the boyish entertainer, the exhilaration and then frustration and impatience. Finally, all the feeling dissolving into pity and disappointment.

On a Christmas trip to Cuba, Marguerite made up her mind. She would marry Harry and keep it a secret for as long as she had to. They drove through Florida for four days before embarking on rough seas to the Cuban capital. Harry had never had time for sightseeing before. He was learning from her. He was learning to dance. With him, she could say and do what she pleased. And she could count on him. She felt the weight of years of responsibility falling away. Harry wasn't like Jack. She could be married a different way now.

In February, she moved into a roomy apartment on New Hampshire Avenue. It was close to town, convenient to her job and big enough for the two of them. For discretion's sake, Harry kept an apartment in the Chastleton.

A few days later, she left for Dallas with her second big docket of compromise cases. For two weeks, she and four other government lawyers worked on delinquent taxpayer cases. As a woman lawyer and a Texan, she attracted attention. On Saturday February 20, 1937, she made the front page of the *Dallas Morning News* in a story captioned "Women Entering on Careers Find Selves Welcomed as Men, Washington Attorney Asserts." Despite the handicaps, she was moving up. If a woman worked hard enough, she could have whatever she wanted. "Just like a man," she told the Dallas reporter. "Any field in which women can qualify themselves is open to them. . . . It is all a matter of merit. If a woman has the ability she can go anywhere and the men in that same field will welcome her."

Sent to New York a few months later, she was featured in the

Washington Times-Herald and the *New York Sun.* Alma Sioux Scarberry, author of a woman's page story in the *Times-Herald,* wrote with tongue in cheek: "This is a most unusual task for a woman and it is believed the lady attorney from Prairie City, Illinois, is the only one ever sent out by Uncle Sam on this difficult Job." There is a hint of disbelief as she records Marguerite's description of fair treatment in the courtroom.

> 'Any field in which a woman can qualify is open to her,' the lawyer said, seriously. 'I don't know how long men have been acting fairly toward the woman in business, but I know never in my day have I met any opposition because I wore skirts at the bar.'

On Saturday, May 1, Marguerite and Harry were married at the Presbyterian church in Snow Hill, Maryland, a quaint 300-year-old village on the banks of the Pocomoke River. May Day and the air was still cool, the damp countryside just waking up with the pale foliage of spring. They knew the Maryland coast from visits with Colonel Murphy, Tom and Irene Scott, and Amanda Bradley, Marguerite's friend from Lorena who lived at Chestertown. But today they were alone. They had agreed — if you wanted to keep a secret you didn't tell anybody at all. The church was empty except for a handful of youngsters waiting with rice and flowers to throw as they left.

"Work and be happy," Pat Neff had told her in 1933, when she graduated from law school and went to work as a lawyer. She could do that now. She had found the man she loved.

For three years, they lived on New Hampshire Avenue together but kept separate addresses and told no one in Washington they were married. Only Charles and Viola and Lucy Moore knew for sure. Although Congress repealed the dreaded "Section 213" shortly after their marriage, women remained vulnerable to government economies. And Marguerite was still a political appointee only partially protected by civil service regulations. Not until Roosevelt was elected to a third term in 1940, did she feel secure enough to reveal her marriage in Washington.

The three-year interlude became a long honeymoon and a secret love affair, and it gave Marguerite time to prove to herself that this time marriage would not halt her career. For a while, her two lives were completely separate. Even after the marriage became known, she guarded her private life jealously, sharing Harry only with close friends. In public, she was still the independent woman, quick to take charge. Only those closest to them knew her as Harry's "Dulce."

They had three peaceful years to learn to live together. Harry taught Marguerite to enjoy leisure in a new way. They shared elaborate weekend breakfasts, getting up late, reading the papers, not dressing until afternoon. They cooked meals together and sometimes invited friends to join them. Their closest friends may have known they were married but never asked.

Together they became inveterate sightseers. During those first years, they traveled at a breakneck rate, as if they were afraid the time would get away and one of them would have missed sharing something with the other.

They spent their first vacation as a married couple in Texas. Viola and Charles already knew Harry. If Willis and Louis had reservations about him, they were soon erased by the ease with which he won over his niece and nephew. Harry enjoyed children in a way Marguerite never would. In a flash of jealousy she thought, they like him better than they do me. And then, he should have children. In love with Harry, she wondered if she should try to have a child before it was too late. But she had never really wanted children and they had so much already.

Every trip to Texas included sightseeing in Arkansas, Tennessee, Kentucky, West Virginia. Sometimes they took new routes, going through Louisiana, Mississippi, Georgia, touring everything in Virginia that either one of them had missed. During the first four years of their marriage, they made three trips to Texas, took a long journey through rural New England, absorbed the romance of Charleston during azalea season, and made several trips to Michigan to be with Harry's family.

Charles died during their Christmas holidays in 1937, just a few months after their marriage. Following their trip to the West in 1936, he had been weakened by a series of heart attacks. Knowing how ill he was, Marguerite took her Christmas leave early and arrived in time to spend Thanksgiving Day with him at the Fred Roberts Memorial Hospital in Corpus Christi. On December 2, when she arrived at the hospital to relieve the night nurse, he was conscious enough to joke with her and reminisce about their trip. He trusted Harry, he said; he was leaving her in good hands. A few minutes later he was dead of heart failure.

In a tribute written years later, Marguerite praised her father's honesty and his singular devotion to his family and his craft. "He was a restless pioneer and a disciple of land-owning. Land was wealth, land was life-giving and sustaining. . . . As an intense worker his entire physical and mental drive was focused on doing the job and doing it right. Father refused to learn the meaning of 'vacation.' " In a few years, Marguerite would be working with the same single-minded intensity, but thanks to Harry *she* had learned the meaning of vacation. For as long as he lived, she would be able to escape with him from even the most pressing demands.

In October 1938, Chief Counsel John P. Wenchel told Marguerite: "I've passed over you several times and I won't do it again. I'm sending you to the Appeals Division to do court work. They don't want you, but I'm sending you anyway." The transfer, which she had wanted for a long time, came with a promotion and the opportunity to appear before the Tax Appeals Board (now the Tax Court of the United States).

Her enthusiasm was dampened when she found herself isolated in a small office with a hostile director and two male lawyers, left to struggle with a difficult fraud case alone. Working weekends and holidays she dug out for herself information that could easily have been provided for her. Eventually, one of the other lawyers offered to help, admitting they had given her a raw deal because they thought having a woman in the division lowered their own status.

Although most of her appeals work was done in Washington, in April 1939, she went on special assignment to the chief counsel's New York City office. Three days after she arrived, the World's Fair opened in Flushing Meadow.

For six weeks, she spent her days working with others to clear out a backlog of tax cases. Nights and weekends were devoted to the Fair. "The World of Tomorrow" they called it. A thousand acres of things she had never seen before. Machines from the past and the future, a 100-year-old daguerreotype, television sets, nylon stockings, a robot that talked and smoked cigarettes, automobiles of the future. Harry came for the weekends, and they joined the crowds experimenting with foreign foods, gawking at parachuters jumping from a 250-foot tower.

Influenced by other women lawyers, Marguerite had begun to follow the political activities of the National Association of Women Lawyers and the National Federation of Business and Professional Women, an organization to which she did not yet belong. During the 1930s both groups made firm commitments to the Equal Rights Amendment and began calling attention to economic and legal discrimination against women.

Women, especially married women, were universally discriminated against in terms of pay. Most states limited a woman's right to serve on a jury. Many states denied married women the right to own or manage even inherited property. Marguerite was beginning to see how those things affected her.

Soon she was going to lectures given by the National Woman's Party. She was particularly impressed by suffragists like Mabel Vernon, Dr. Agnes E. Wells, and Alma Lutz. All three of them were scholarly women and compelling speakers.

Mabel Vernon, who regularly addressed small crowds that gathered in her suite at the Hay Adams Hotel, made a strong impression on Marguerite when she spoke about "the rightness of things." Her message was always the same — *women did not have the same opportunities men had. It was wrong. Something had to be done.*

When the Kappas honored Judge Sarah T. Hughes of the Fourteenth Judicial Circuit of Texas at a reception in January 1937, Marguerite began a long working relationship with someone she had wanted to know since her days in the governor's office in Austin.

Also through the Kappas, she came to know Judge Florence Allen, who had been appointed judge of the United States Circuit Court of Appeals by Franklin Roosevelt in 1934. Allen reminded Marguerite of Lucy Moore. Both were confident, opinionated, witty. Allen was stout like Moore and wore her hair as short as a man's. Always singling Marguerite out, pushing her forward, she became another of Marguerite's motherly-sisterly encouragers.

Unexpectedly, in April 1939, Marguerite heard from Pat Neff for the first time since the summer of 1936, when she had told him about Harry. Since 1932, he had been president of Baylor University. Georgetown University was celebrating its Sesquicentennial. He wanted her to attend the festivities in his place.

The irony wasn't lost on either one of them. Georgetown's refusal to admit women to its law school ten years before had been one of the great disappointments of her life. She would be celebrating the founding of a school that still rejected even the best qualified women.

Women lawyers drew together instinctively. But Marguerite had a knack for working with the men as well. When she was elected third vice-president of the Federal Bar Association in 1939, she broke all the records and put herself in line to become president of a powerful national organization of government lawyers. Since joining in 1935, she had done her share of leg work in the Washington chapter and national headquarters, recruiting new members, working on committees, arranging weekly luncheons and huge annual receptions. Few women belonged to FBA and none had ever aspired to be president.

Her closest friends in the organization were women: Ellyne Strickland, a lawyer with her at Internal Revenue; Lucy Howorth, member of the Board of Veterans' Appeals; Mary Connelly, assistant solicitor at the Veteran's Department; Annabel Matthews, first woman on the Tax Court; and Mary Agnes Brown, who would become a colonel in the WACs. In order to get Marguerite elected third vice-president and put her in line for the presidency, the women in FBA had formed a secret network. Individually, they set out to learn which men would support her. When she had to go to New York for the six weeks prior to the election, the network carried on. They didn't want anyone to wonder "what are those women up to?" It wouldn't have worked.

On May 2, Marguerite was still in New York when a telegram came from the women of her HAPPY COMMITTEE announcing her victory, 200 to 180, over Labor Department solicitor, South Trimble. Harry was there with her to celebrate two things at once, her election and their second anniversary. That same day, the *Washington Times Herald* announced, "Woman Wins Vital Federal Bar Post."

After a short Thanksgiving visit to Corpus Christi in 1940, Marguerite and Harry announced their marriage. By Christmas day, they had moved into a spacious apartment in the Somerset House on Sixteenth Street. In a living room without furniture, they opened presents around a silver Christmas tree. Although their best friends might have suspected it, friends at work, like Irene Scott, could hardly have been more surprised.

She had known Irene since they sat down beside one another in the same graduate law class at Catholic University. She was immediately attracted to the Alabama lawyer whose down-home wit and practicality matched her own. Their professional interests coincided as well, and Irene soon joined Marguerite at Internal Revenue and later became a judge on the Tax Court. As Marguerite became more involved in organizational life, the Scotts' vacation house on the Chesapeake became a retreat for her and a place for Harry to be with friends when she was traveling.[1]

By the middle of January, Marguerite had made another trip to Texas, in order to legally change her name from Secord back to Rawalt. When she divorced Jack, she had promised her father she would be a Rawalt for the rest of her life. "Rawalt is a good name," he had said, "don't change it again." Furthermore, she was proud of the reputation she was earning in her own name and saw no reason to change it. The more she understood the nature of the restraints placed on women in the professions, the more determined she became to get around them.

By the time they announced their marriage, Marguerite and Harry had settled into a routine. Her days included a demanding load of tax cases plus meetings, luncheons, receptions and lectures. The weekends were full for both of them with trips to the bay and visitors from out of town. Occasionally Harry would attend a banquet or lecture with her, but gradually she established the habit of attending such affairs alone or with other women.

At home, she kept work and organization problems to herself. And, for many years, she kept their Sundays free to use as they pleased, cherished days shared only with their closest friends. On a Sunday in September 1939, she jotted in her diary, *Harry working. Home all day. Beautiful Indian Summer. Hattie and Louise for dinner, hash and rum apples.*

Shortly after Marguerite and Harry announced their marriage, Viola surprised her children with her plans to marry a sometimes home-builder named C. M. Bardwell. He wasn't Charles; but he took her dancing and made her laugh. Her first marriage had been built on work. This was something different. Marguerite could understand the attraction, but she didn't like it. Her father had worked hard for what he had left his wife and children. None of them wanted to see any part of his estate go to a man they hardly knew.

At Marguerite's suggestion, Viola deeded all her property to her children to be administered in a trust. Then she married Mr. Bardwell. The marriage, which was happy for a short time, would end in divorce in 1948.

The bond between Marguerite and her mother grew stronger over the years that were increasingly trying for Viola, and demanding for herself. At last, she was in a position to try to repay Viola for what she would always see as the sacrifice of her life to husband and children. A few days before Mother's Day, 1941, Marguerite wrote her.

> I shall be thinking of you many times on that day, May 11th and I shall be wishing, oh, so hard, that I could knock at your door, or hear your footsteps in the hallway outside mine. Both Harry and I shall speak of you — we often do. We remember that between the two of us, you are the only living parent — though you seem less like a parent and more like sister particularly to Harry. Mother, I do so want to do things for you, to be able to make your daily living more pleasant.
>
> Most of all, I'd be happy to send you the railroad fare for a visit to Washington. In absence of that, we are sending something you have expressed a wish for — silverware. I hope you will like it — it's Rogers 1847.

While Marguerite and Harry enjoyed their long honeymoon, the nation geared up for another war. Like the rest of the country, they watched the rise of military dictatorships in Europe, and the rearmament of Germany, with alarm. Women in the United States were particularly disturbed by the loss of civil rights and the subjugation of women under fascism. As early as 1935, Molly Dewson, head of the Women's Division of the Democratic National Committee, could write bluntly to Eleanor Roosevelt, "The women's organizations have the jitters on the attack on women made by Hitler and others. They feel the trend is toward prohibiting women from functioning in any other capacity than as wives, mothers, and homemakers. Of course, I myself think we handled dynamite when we passed 213 of the National Economy Act." [2]

For four years the United States clung desperately to neutrality while friends in Europe defended themselves against unremitting encroachment by Germany, Italy, and Japan. With the invasion of Poland by Germany in September 1939, France and

England formally declared war on Germany, making it clear that the second great world war of the century had begun.

The speed of events astonished most Americans. In April, Hitler marched through Denmark and invaded Norway. Then Belgium, the Netherlands, and Luxembourg. On June 14, Paris fell. Britain seemed sure to be next. Still, the United States remained technically neutral, although supplying military arms and supplies to the Allies. When the Japanese bombed Pearl Harbor on December 7, 1941, the country went to war on two fronts.

With the approach of war, there were jobs for everybody, promotions and responsibilities for women where there had been none, opportunities to make more money and get better training. Remembering the progress made by women during World War I, the Washington community of women lawyers began admonishing its members to take advantage of the changes.

Two months before Pearl Harbor, Marguerite wrote Pat Neff of wartime changes already beginning.

> Washington is certainly a hub of the country just now. . . Rents and food prices are going up. And, although everywhere the eye looks there are new apartment houses, new homes, though Washington has spread for miles, still there is the cry that there is inadequate housing for all the new workers who are coming to engage in defense activities. As for our tax work, it will double and triple within two years.
>
> Air Corps activities are at a peak, and Harry finds his presence at Bolling demanded many Sundays, and regular hours are unknown for the men actually servicing the planes. The ferry service which takes our official passengers overseas is also being handled out of Bolling Field.

Once again, the mood of the country changed overnight. All talk of neutrality was gone. Harry and Marguerite's red-white-and-blue Christmas card carried two American flags, a silver liberty bell, and the message,

> Bringing you Holiday Greetings
> and Best Wishes for the New Year
> In the Real American Way.

On Christmas Eve, she wrote in her diary, *Bad news from the Philippines, Japs are gaining, landing — it is hard to enjoy so much at Xmas.*

For men and women alike, the word opportunity was replaced

by responsibility. Everybody had a job to do. Marguerite was flooded with the memories and worries of the last war.

Harry, now fifty-eight years old but always a soldier, immediately began trying to resign his job at Bolling Field in order to return to active duty. By early January, he had passed the required physical examination and requested a commission.

Home with a variety of minor complaints — colds, headaches, laryngitis, dizziness — Marguerite missed more work because of illness during January and February than she ever had before. On March 10, Harry turned down a promotion at Bolling; and, in less than a month he had been commissioned as major and assigned to Keesler Field, Mississippi.

On Sunday, April 26, two days after Harry left, Marguerite wrote, *Alone at Home,* in her diary, and hurled herself into a week-long frenzy of social activity, spending as much time as she could with her friend, Annie Perry Neal, a lawyer and a relative of Margie Neal.

When Congress established the Women's Naval Reserve (the WAVES) a few months later, Marguerite tried to join. The wives of servicemen were not eligible, she learned. Anyway, a forty-seven-year-old woman was too old for the service. Why, she wondered was forty-seven too old for a woman and fifty-eight not too old for a man? She didn't want to stay in Washington without Harry, and she wanted to do her part.

Soon an increased work load, heavy involvement in organizations, and weekend trips to Mississippi to see Harry were filling all her time. Unexpectedly in March, she was nominated for the presidency of both the D. C. Women's Bar Association and the NAWL. When election to the vice-presidency of FBA put her in line for the presidency of that organization as well, she removed her name from the D. C. Women's Bar slate. If she were elected president of NAWL and FBA, there would be a three-month period when she would be president of two national bar associations at once; nevertheless, she allowed her name to remain on the NAWL ticket.

The leading women lawyers in the country belonged to NAWL, yet neither NAWL nor any other women's bar association was represented in the American Bar Association's (ABA) House of Delegates, the profession's major policy-making body.

George Maurice Morris, a prominent Washington tax lawyer

whom Marguerite knew and admired, was the incoming president of ABA. If she could get elected president of NAWL, she thought she could — with Morris's help — get the organization into the House of Delegates.

At the NAWL convention in August, Marguerite learned lessons about politics that she would never forget. Months earlier she had been asked by current president Gertrude Harris to take the nomination. Harris was from Atlanta, Georgia, and so was the other presidential prospect, a woman named Daphne Robert, the association's recording secretary and a lawyer for the Coca-Cola company. Since it didn't seem a good idea to have two consecutive presidents from the same city, Marguerite came to the convention unopposed and, she presumed, with the support of both Harris and Robert.

A few hours after arriving at Chicago's Book-Cadillac Hotel for the convention, she learned that a group from Chicago planned to nominate Daphne Robert from the floor. Robert had agreed to run.

Feeling confused and betrayed by the turn of events, her first instinct was to withdraw. Raised in a family where anger was seldom expressed, she had learned to retreat from conflict and get what she wanted by reason, compromise, and persistence. When those things didn't work or her opponents played unfairly, she would always react with shock, anxiety and the temptation to yield her position, thinking to herself, if they want it that badly they can have it. Later, she learned to react more quickly and to fight when she was angry, but it would always take courage. Over and over in times of crisis, she repeated a pattern of retreating and struggling with the temptation to withdraw before committing herself to battle. Increasingly the metaphors of battle dominated the language she used to describe her work in women's rights, but the big battles would never be engaged without ambivalence and suffering.

The next day at breakfast, she told her friend Anna Hogan of her decision to withdraw from the race for president. Hogan, a fiery, disheveled woman with long experience in New Jersey politics, was horrified: "No, what they are doing isn't right. You stay in there. I know politics. This is just politics. You don't have a fight on your hands until somebody opposes you. You're a fighter aren't you?" Heartened by Hogan's confidence in her and her practicality, Marguerite decided to stay on the ballot. Hogan would conduct a write-in campaign for Marguerite for vice-president. If Marguerite lost the presidency, she was sure to win the second spot and be in line for next year.

Her supporters worked for two days, determined to see her elected to one of the two offices. She was learning her first lessons about politics and leadership.

> One makes enemies;
> The opponents don't always play fair;
> One has to fight to win.

Hogan's words became a slogan in many later struggles: "It's not a fight till you get opposition."

The next day — thanks to their write-in campaign — Marguerite was elected both president and vice-president of the organization. Daphne Robert came in second in both races. Gertrude Harris, in the chair, didn't know what to do. Marguerite, who would soon be an expert on parliamentary procedure, relied on common sense and chose the presidency. Robert would be vice-president.

Prepared to have to persuade him, Marguerite was surprised at George Morris's response when she approached him about getting NAWL into the House of Delegates. "I'm all for it," he said. "If you can meet the qualifications, I'll back you. You must have 1,000 members and twenty-five percent of them have to be in good standing as individual members of ABA — I'll back you."

The presidency of NAWL made Marguerite one of the most notable women lawyers in the country. The three Washington newspapers ran lead articles. Clippings and letters of congratulation poured in. Anxious to claim her as a native or at least a resident, several Texas papers featured the story.

The Sunday *Washington Star* printed a long piece based on an interview she had given Jessie Fant Evans. The story ended with a quote: "This woman lawyer admits to being 'a fairly good cook, a poor golfer, an indifferent bridge player and an ardent collector of English bone china and eggshell porcelain.' "

In September, Harry left Keesler Field to become technical inspector and later executive officer of a new Army Air Force Technical Training School near Gulfport. A month later, Marguerite made the first of many train rides to Gulfport. Harry met her in Slidell, Louisiana, and drove her to his quarters at the Edgewater Gulf Hotel for a long birthday weekend. Her diary records it.

> *My Harry! A moonlight drive at midnight. . . . My birthday —*
> *flowers and cards from Harry — fruit too. . . . Dinner, cocktails at Biloxi*
> *Hotel. . . . All day at Hotel, a morning walk thru the pines, sunbath and*
> *plunge. Dinner at 6. A precious day with Harry.*

She returned determined to get NAWL into the House of Delegates. If it was going to be done during her term, the qualifications would have to be met before the House of Delegates convened on March 29, 1943.

She had two jobs to do: increase the size of the membership and the percentage in ABA. With the help of Washington lawyer Charlotte Million, she divided the country into regions, got mailing lists from all the state bar associations and began writing women lawyers inviting them to join NAWL. At the same time, they wrote letters to all members of NAWL who did not belong to ABA.

Some said they couldn't afford the ABA dues. A few were put off by rumors that Marguerite only wanted to get NAWL into ABA so she could be the first woman delegate. Others suggested, erroneously, that ABA would not accept NAWL because, thanks to Marguerite's sweeping membership campaign, they had admitted three black women, making NAWL the first national bar association to remove all barriers against minorities.

In 1942, racial segregation was just beginning to be challenged. The first crack in the rationale of inequality probably sprang from the New Deal and the need to provide relief to historically poor blacks as well as Depression-poor whites. Although the president did little to address the issue, Eleanor Roosevelt's symbolic refusal to abide by the customs of segregation attracted attention. And, although "separate but equal" remained the law of the land, the war years laid the foundation for serious protest among black people and their white sympathizers. Old prejudices were just beginning to give way.

Although steeped in a tradition of white supremacy with its abhorrence of the social and sexual mixing of the races, Marguerite's egalitarian sympathies would always bring her to the defense of the "qualified woman." As members of state bar associations, the black women who wanted to join NAWL were by definition qualified.

Finally, however, it wasn't the racial question so much as the sheer weight of the work to be done that threatened NAWL's effort to get into the House of Delegates. Beginning in mid-October, Marguerite and Charlotte Million worked nights and weekends at Marguerite's dining room table — writing letters, making calculations, contacting the fence sitters.

Louise Wright pitched in. Beer in hand, she entertained them with her jokes, stuffed envelopes and licked stamps. Sometimes her mother, Hattie Crawford, came too and beamed her encouragement. "What would Harry think of all this Marguerite?" she would ask. "You couldn't do this if he were here." Her reply was always the same, "If he were here, I wouldn't want to."

Like many women living alone during the war, Marguerite occupied herself with outside interests. But, unlike most others, she made an abiding commitment during those years to women's rights and organizational work. For the next twenty years, there would be moments of conflict between her career, her activism, and her marriage. Gradually, her career became less important than her work for women. When she had to choose, she put Harry above everything else — without regret. She needed Harry to temper the force of her own drive. When he wasn't there, she pushed too hard, tried to do more than was possible for one person to do.

She and her NAWL team, which now included a network of state vice-presidents, worked frantically through the first week in March. Finally, with less than two weeks to go, both Marguerite and ABA were satisfied. Officially, NAWL had 1,033 members, thirty-one percent of them in good standing with the American Bar Association.

On Monday, March 29, the American Bar Association admitted the National Association of Women Lawyers as an affiliated organization, and Marguerite was heralded as the first woman seated in the House of Delegates, the first woman ever elected to the legal profession's governing body.

Laura Miller Derry, a NAWL member from Louisville, Kentucky, watched her walk down the aisle of the Edgewater Beach Convention Hall and described it later for the *Women Lawyers' Journal*.

As they advanced with dignity and solemnity to the platform, I felt I was witnessing the completion of a great accomplishment, brought about by the foresight of many of our able visionary members. . . . Delegate after delegate congratulated our representative and spoke highly of our organization.

For the time being, Marguerite was satisfied; it was, she thought, the most important thing she had ever done.

Exhilarated by her NAWL triumph, she set out to complete her climb to the presidency of the Federal Bar Association. Although she had struggled for three years to stay in line for the job, she had opposition. There was grumbling about a woman being president. Some said she shouldn't be permitted to hold the presidency of two national bar associations at once. Her opponent, David S. Davison, claimed there was no precedent for the first vice-president becoming president.

Marguerite wrote Harry describing the criticism. She was thinking about withdrawing, she said. She didn't like the criticism, the anger. It wasn't worth it. Again she had to decide whether to fight for something she wanted or let somebody take it away from her. Harry wired his opinion as soon as he got her letter.

DO NOT BE A QUITTER/FOLLOW THRU WITH FEDERAL BAR.

A letter he wrote the same day put the situation in perspective.

You go ahead and run for the Federal Bar. . . I would like to see
you elected. Roy Vallance has run that organization long enough.
He is afraid of you. If you should happen to be defeated, what of
it? But I don't believe you will.

Swallowing a deep aversion to hostility and confrontation, she made up her mind to win — and set her election committee of women to work once more. Early in April, Sarah Hughes visited for several days, offering advice and calling lawyers who might help. As soon as Hughes left, Margie Neal moved into Marguerite's apartment and took over the campaign, saying over and over: "When you run for something, you have to ASK people to vote for you. Ask them; they like it." For three weeks Marguerite asked for votes in every way she could think of — and managed to defeat Davison by 100 votes.

Too tired to celebrate with friends, she spent a few days catching up on legal work before leaving for ten days in Mississippi with Harry. On the long train ride back to Washington, she planned her year as FBA's president. She had speakers to line up for the weekly luncheons. She wanted to increase membership and establish more local chapters and strengthen the few they had. As soon as she got to town, she scheduled an organizational meeting and put her vice-president, Federal Trade Commission lawyer Wilbur Baughman, in charge of local chapters.

Nineteen forty-three was a year of firsts for Marguerite. Shortly after her election to the presidency of FBA, she was invited to address the annual meeting of the Texas Bar Association in Houston — the first woman ever to do so.

Immediately, she wrote Pat Neff, Lucy Moore, and Amanda Bradley. To Neff, she said, "I am scared to death. . . . Will you give me any suggestions you have?" Give a short speech and don't read it, he suggested, adding that "during these uncertain and disturbing days when our nation is drifting so far from its original moorings," she might want to talk about some "fundamental principle of government."

Letters to Lucy Moore and Amanda Bradley carried the same message: she was "petrified," and wanted them to tell her what to talk about. Although the scholarly Amanda provided some images and quotations for her speech, Marguerite followed her own instincts and wrote a speech about the two things she knew best: what it meant to be a woman lawyer and how increased government regulations were changing the practice of law.

She began with a brief history of NAWL, founded in 1899 because women were not permitted in existing bar associations. In order to praise women in the law and forgive men for the omissions of their forebears, she elaborated on an allusion to Thackeray's *Vanity Fair* suggested by Amanda Bradley.

> . . . the barristers who drew up the first such by-laws can scarcely be censured for lacking prophetic vision of the advent of women in the legal profession. Who, in the age when Becky Sharp and Amelia were representative feminine types, could reasonably have predicted that any women would turn away from the crinoline and laces and court affectations of a *Vanity Fair* to become proficient in Blackstone. . . Who then would have predicted that in 1943, in the United States alone, there would be not less than thirty-five women lawyers serving on the bench?

But, with the first blush fading on wartime opportunities for women, she refused to ignore the problems of discrimination. She told the *Houston Press,*

> If women make a good showing now when they are faced with a plurality of opportunities, they will be chopping down many barriers that might otherwise fence them in again after the war.

Her message to the women of the Texas Bar was less heartening.

> . . . getting a degree from a university doesn't put women on an equal footing with men. . . . There is no pattern the individual woman can follow in trying to achieve equality with men in her chosen profession.

It was the second part of her speech, "How Our Tax Laws Grow," that would most interest the media and her audience — and cause unexpected trouble for her later on.

Most lawyers didn't know it, she told them, but the growth of federal laws and regulations had created a "promising professional gold mine." She challenged them to take advantage of the new opportunities in administrative law, and compared the plight of the legal profession to that of Alice in *Wonderland,* who had to run to stay where she was and run twice as fast to get somewhere else.

Euphoric with success and relief, she wrote in her diary,

> *My speech Friday was successful, I think. Many compliments from men who introduced themselves. Women lawyers beamed and all expressed pleasure.*

She described the event to Pat Neff. "The hall was crowded. . . . Many were curious to see whether a woman lawyer could talk, or how."

Marguerite was triumphant. She had gone home to Texas as a celebrity and leaped another hurdle for women. Now, thanks to Pat Neff, she was to receive an honorary doctorate from Baylor University. Her presidency in NAWL had established her as a leader among women, someone who could move forward and move other women with her. She was headed for the presidency of FBA as well. In a few months, Harry would retire from the military and be home to stay. When she was offered a promotion to go to Chicago to do trial work, she turned it down. She had everything she wanted.

After Christmas, the euphoria began to fade. It was good to have Harry home; but Marguerite was worried about Viola, who had returned to Texas and a troubled marriage. Everyone was talking about an international organization to establish world peace; yet, it looked as if the war in Europe would never end. Coffee, meats, and dairy products were rationed; so were shoes and automobile tires. Nightly "dim-outs" and "black-outs" made the reality of a ravaged Europe impossible to forget.

Marguerite's presidency of FBA started off with the usual gusto. She invited some of the most important people in Washington to speak at their weekly luncheons and many accepted: Eleanor Roosevelt; Chief Justice Harlan Fiske Stone and top federal judges; Secretary of Interior, Harold Ickes; Admiral Thomas L. Gatch, judge Advocate general of the navy; and an array of ambassadors, senators, judges, and prominent lawyers.

She established several new local chapters across the country but was disappointed when the big drive she had planned to set up a nationwide network of chapters fizzled. Her first vice-president, Wilbur Baughman, had agreed to head up the drive — and let her down. She resented him for it and didn't think he should be allowed to walk into the presidency he hadn't earned.

Assistant U.S. Attorney General Tom Clark was a Texan and a friend of hers. From his position in the Justice Department, he could easily spearhead the drive to establish new chapters. In early spring, Marguerite met with Clark and urged him to run against Baughman for the presidency. She would back him, she said. Clark, who was on his way to becoming attorney general, agreed. He would do it, and they would put her on his slate as FBA's delegate to ABA.

Marguerite's solitary decision left her isolated and vulnerable. Immediately, she was attacked from all sides. Rumors and interpretations of what she had done were rampant: she had handpicked Clark (a friend, a Texan) without consulting anybody — and built in a spot for herself. Just a year before, she had insisted that the vice-president deserved the presidency, that to refuse it to her could only be attributed to prejudice against women. Now they said she was trying to create a political machine, using the organization to perpetuate her own influence.

In April, the papers began to follow the controversy. W. O. Chatterton, a Justice Department lawyer and candidate for first vice-president on Baughman's slate, resigned from the executive council and told the *Washington Times-Herald* that Marguerite was using the organization "for her own personal aggrandizement."

In a statement reported in the *Washington Star* she insisted, "The lawyers of the Federal Bar Association are capable of evaluating charges of this nature. So far as I know this is a stimulating but clean contest between members for office in the FBA."

A few days later, the *Times-Herald* called the controversy, "the first wide-open split in the ranks" in the organization's history and reported the rumor that Marguerite's attempts at self-aggrandizement extended to seeking an appointment to a federal bench in Texas. Still confident in herself and flattered by the rumor, she refused to deny it, "A federal judgeship is an ambition worthy of any attempt and if presidency of the Federal Bar Association leads to that end, it would be an honor indeed to serve."

Meanwhile another FBA problem continued to plague her administration. Since early in 1942, a handful of Justice Department lawyers had been trying to get black lawyers admitted to FBA. From the beginning of her administration, Marguerite was pressured by both sides. The executive committee opposed the change on the grounds that FBA was a social as well as a professional organization. In fact, NAWL remained the only national bar association to admit minorities.

Despite the recent desegregation of NAWL, Marguerite sympathized with those who were reluctant to see the races mingling socially. Furthermore, she was convinced that, should the issue come up, the admission of blacks would be voted down by her executive council. Then she would be blamed by one side for allowing the issue to come up and by the other for the organization's failure to accept blacks.

Early in the year, a black assistant attorney general named Lewis Mehlinger had been nominated for membership with the support of Attorney General Francis Biddle. When FBA's civil rights committee insisted that Mehlinger be admitted, Marguerite stalled, finally (under increasing pressure and troubled by reports that Biddle intended to resign from FBA unless the highly-qualified Mehlinger was admitted), she scheduled a meeting between the civil rights committee and the executive council — too late in the year for any action to be taken.

Her carefully worded statement to the executive council acknowledged the importance of both the moral issue and the division in the council and recommended: that local chapters establish their own criteria for membership, that by-laws be changed to separate national and local functions, and that the issue of admitting black lawyers be taken to the Washington membership and decided by the whole body rather than by the executive council and the membership committee.

Early the next year, Tom Clark made the decision to admit black attorneys through the executive council despite her continued complaints about the procedure. She expressed herself impatiently to friends: "I have become less interested in whether we admit colored attorneys than in seeing that the action is determined in the democratic manner by the membership. I cannot subscribe to the 'do it first and let them holler afterward' sort of approach."

Early in April, in the midst of the worst of the accusations against her in FBA, Marguerite was suddenly attacked from another quarter. In his widely syndicated column, "Fair Enough," the reactionary Westbrook Pegler, archenemy of the New Deal and anyone he associated with Franklin and Eleanor Roosevelt, unearthed her speech to the Texas Bar. Pegler's vitriolic attacks on Eleanor Roosevelt had become legendary. She was, he railed, "a wily old conspirator" who deserved "far less respect than any conventional woman."

Apparently, Marguerite Rawalt, whom he called "the lady counselor" deserved no better. He called her Texas speech

> . . . the most cynical confessions of the brutal rapacity of the professional New Deal bureaucrat to be found in all the sordid record of this parasitic horde. . . . a plain exhortation to her fellow lawyers to take full advantage of the unfortunate citizen's uncertainty and his dependence on legal counsel for the interpretation of the law in countless, perilous daily relations with his government.

FBA was a regular "bund of New Deal lawyers," he added, ending with an abusive attack on New Deal "spooks."

On Friday, April 7, she came to work and found a telegram from the *Corpus Christi Caller-Times* waiting for her. The editors planned to print the Pegler column the next day. She could have as much space as she liked to reply. Astounded by Pegler's interpretation of what she had said, she wrote a short explanation but never mailed it.

By Monday, she was a national figure. Newspapers nationwide were running the column. Two Washington papers carried it, and everyone she knew seemed to have read it. Friends from out of town wrote to console her. Reporters wanted her comments. The men at Internal Revenue were concerned. She didn't know what to say.

Within the day, George Morris telephoned insisting that she let him reply for her since he had heard the speech. "Don't you say anything," he added. "Pegler is bound to have the last word and use anything you say against you." Morris defended her speech in a conciliatory letter sent to a number of major newspapers and in an editorial written for the professional journal, *American Law and Lawyers*.

Harry's advice was succinct. "The man's a fool, Marguerite. Forget it." Still she worried that something she had done in innocence was causing so much trouble. As she saw it, the speech had been good sound advice to fellow lawyers. If she had made a mistake, she didn't know what it was.

In a letter to Meyer Casman, president of FBA's Philadelphia chapter, she made a connection between her problems in FBA and the Pegler incident, hinting that her enemies in the organization had sent the speech to Pegler.

> They [Baughman and Chatterton] are carrying on an underhanded campaign by phone, etc. which I should like to answer with the same tactics, but refrain in favor of the dignified silence. I am not sure I should alone be silent, but because of the others on the ticket, I do not want to launch into replies. The most potent reason for my silence, is that newspaper publicity certainly does not raise the prestige of the Federal Bar Association. . . . I am convinced that the Pegler publicity was animated from the same source.
>
> These boys are making undercover attempts to influence votes respecting the admission of Negro members. . . . I suppose that is politics, Meyer, . . . We can only hope it all blows over and that strong leadership for next year is put in charge.

On May 1, the *Washington Times-Herald* announced the results of the FBA elections: "Rawalt Slate Wins as Federal Bar Names

Clark." Everyone on her slate won — except herself. They were sending someone else to ABA.

As a woman in FBA, she was an outsider, put into office by a clandestine circle of women. Thinking she could play power politics on an equal footing with the men, she had overstepped her bounds.

During her first month as president of NAWL, she had written to Grace Harte, a prominent Chicago lawyer many years her senior.

> May I address you as Grace? In that respect, I like to copy
> the men folk, who, in addressing each other in that way, generate
> an atmosphere of friendly concern which begets the reality or at
> least helps to that end.

In FBA, she had tried to "copy the men folk." Modeling herself after George Morris, she had learned how to conduct a meeting and orchestrate crowds of people. FBA had been a good place to practice, but she had never been as surefooted there as she had been with the women lawyers.

Forty years later, Marguerite remains the only woman ever elected president of FBA. The luncheons had been grand affairs; no one would forget them. Despite war times, she had increased FBA membership by thirty-three percent and set up the first new chapters in years. It had been thrilling to introduce speakers like Chief Justice Stone and Eleanor Roosevelt.

Marguerite enjoyed the gala receptions, the excitement and stimulation of so many people, friends, acquaintances, new and old faces. Everybody knew her. But even as she enjoyed the breathless life of a Washington career woman and celebrity, she was being drawn in another direction.

[4]

Going Forward

On June 6, 1944, D-day, General Dwight D. Eisenhower, supreme commander of the Allied Forces in Europe, landed his troops in Normandy and began the long-expected invasion of Europe.

That night, Eleanor Roosevelt mailed invitations to 200 of the country's leading women asking them to meet in the East Wing of the White House on June 14, to consider "How Women May Share in Post-War Policy-Making." Women had made progress during the war, but no one could say how they would fare once the war ended.

Invited to the conference as past president of NAWL, Marguerite had high hopes that a "concrete plan" for women would be presented. What she didn't know was that she was about to make a commitment that would govern the rest of her life. From then on, the energy and concentration that had gone into making her one of the best-known women lawyers in the country would be devoted to changing the world for women.

The meeting began at 10:00 A.M. with Eleanor Roosevelt calling for the participation of women in all phases of American life. Secretary of Labor Frances Perkins argued against special consideration for women, who, she said, ought to get positions of authority for the same reason men did — and no others. In the afternoon Helen Rogers (Mrs. Ogden) Reid, vice-president of the *New York Herald Tribune*, called it "a major tragedy" that women had not been drafted like men during the war. Women had been subordinate too long, in part, she said, because of their own passivity.

Helen Reid and Frances Perkins talked about women in a way that appealed to Marguerite and many of the younger women. Participation meant doing one's share. Women were entitled to both equal rights and equal responsibility with men.

At the afternoon session, Marguerite was flattered by the attention of Marjorie Webster, a flamboyant woman wearing a dark, expensive-looking suit and a spectacular hat. A prominent Washington educator and civic leader, Webster grew up wanting to be an actress. In mid-life, she was tall and stylish, every dramatic gesture demanding attention.

Meeting that day in the East Room for the first time, Marguerite and Majorie Webster established one of those rare friendships based on instant rapport. Webster had her own college for young women in fashionable Northwest Washington. Like Marguerite, she had ambitions for herself and other women.

Webster, who came to the conference as the president of Washington's Business and Professional Women's Club, wanted to know why Marguerite hadn't joined the large, prestigious organization. Flattered and charmed by her new friend, Marguerite filled out her application on the spot.

With that gesture, she unknowingly committed herself to a struggle which would absorb the second half of her life and bring her more disappointment and more satisfaction than anything she had ever done.

Despite a surface bravado, it would always be hard for her to ask for things for herself. Her own ambitions were sometimes a burden. Ten years of battling the odds at Internal Revenue, the exhilaration of the NAWL presidency and her address to the Texas Bar, then the Pegler attack and the trouble in the Federal Bar. Working for herself alone had left her bruised and uncertain. She wanted to belong and she wanted her accomplishments acknowledged. As she had put it to herself so long ago, she wanted to be somebody.

Marguerite learned not from meditation but from action. Viscerally, she was beginning to realize that those simple desires were barred to most women — sometimes even to her.

She was baffled when friends asked what "drove" her. She didn't reflect on it. She just tried to do what needed doing and to get other people to help her. She sometimes forgot the White House Conference had been a turning point. Something had just "taken hold" of her. She didn't think of it as a choice exactly. In the 1970s she would quote Elizabeth Boyer, a meditative activist who liked to paraphrase Martin Luther: "Here I stand. I can do no other."

The changes came fast but not suddenly. By the end of the year, she had joined every national organization that worked for women's rights and endorsed the Equal Rights Amendment. To the Business and Professional Women's Clubs she added the General Federation of Women's Clubs and Zonta International, a service club of progressive business women. At about the same time, she began paying dues to the National Woman's Party, still dominated by suffragist Alice Paul's single-minded commitment to ERA.

Above all else and sometimes despite the evidence, Marguerite had come to believe that groups and individuals could, by banning together, accomplish almost anything. Like many women influenced by the women's club movement, she clung to that belief with unflagging — almost romantic — loyalty.

As a member of a generation twice hurled into global war, she was convinced that the only hope of lasting peace lay in some kind of cooperative international organization. In November 1944, she wrote Pat Neff:

> . . . Do you suppose every generation in history has regarded itself as living in the most interesting era of the world? It seems to me that we of this present one are witnessing an enormous transition. I do not say "progress" though I hope the sum total of it all will in retrospect be a forward and not a backward movement.

Nations organizing for world peace and women working together for equal rights were closely linked in her mind. Over the next few years her speeches often combined the two messages. The postwar woman had two major responsibilities: the fostering of world peace and the pursuit of equality.

Still, throughout the 1940s, her admonitions carried an apology. Hers were not, she said, the words of a militant feminist:

> . . . Men are not to be censured for continuing to run and to control an organization which is theirs by long practice — don't blame them. If women had been in control of the political parties in this country for 165 years, we too would have placed the interests of women first — passed laws and governed for the benefit of women.

For a while Marguerite's new enthusiasm for women's rights seemed to be taking her in all directions at once. In addition to her commitment to ERA, she was increasingly involved with other campaigns for women's legal rights. As her convictions grew stronger and merged with her own ambitions, she became more aware of the problems and conflicts of leadership. Women didn't seem to be as forgiving as men. They never forgot your mistakes.

Late in 1945, she wrote Lula Bachman, then president of NAWL, about the possibility of forming an international bar association for women. The letter shows an increasingly realistic view of leadership, a growing concern for all women, and a stubborn insistence (often against the tide) that women's organizations use systematic, prescribed procedures to make decisions and establish policy:

> . . . we women lawyers. . . owe it to the women in some of the South American countries to lend a helping hand. . . . The shackles of seclusion for womanhood, the protective idea, are still accepted in many places. Not all of them outside the United States. You and I, as Presidents of the one national organization of women [lawyers] here, have an increased responsibility and accountability for our action.
>
> . . . let's get the facts, the actual facts. . . . And then present them to others, and let the collective judgment be soundly arrived at.
>
> Criticism seems to be part of taking the lead, and of having ideas, as you have. On the other hand, I have seen the "mugwump" type of leader who says yes to all, fail to make any progress and fail to end up with the good will of all. So. . . just a choice of pathway for us, I guess.

Over the next ten years, her "leadership pathway" would take her to the top in the National Federation of Business and Professional Women's Clubs. There she would make lasting friendships and learn the lessons that would prepare her for the essential role she played in the reborn women's movement of the 1960s and 1970s.

With over 800 members, the Washington BPW club was one of the federation's most visible and influential groups. Prominent politicians, business leaders, entertainers — men and women alike — welcomed an invitation to its large, posh affairs. As Marjorie Webster's good friend, Marguerite was flooded with new opportunities. Her first year in BPW introduced her to hundreds of people she had not known before.

In the spring of 1945, less than a year after joining BPW, she was unanimously elected president of the D.C. club. *Washington Times-Herald* columnist Vylla Poe Wilson praised the organization's choice in extravagant terms:

> The Business and Professional Women's Club. . . with an astonishing quota of top-flight women leaders in many lines of feminine endeavor. . . is rejoicing over its new president, Miss Marguerite Rawalt, a dynamic woman lawyer, known beyond the District borders.
>
> It is small wonder that the club members brag about her when they meet. This brilliant follower of Blackstone, magnetic and winning instant attention and admiration for her legal acumen, knows the art of correct dressing as well.
>
> Her friends marvel at her costumes, extremely well cut with individual touches, which, while on the conservative side of modern costuming, are the acme of good taste and just rightness.
>
> Charm is contributed to this new leader of Washington business and professional women by a gentle, gracious personality and a low, sweet voice whose resonance carries to the far corner of any room without effort, and the fact that she has an abiding interest in her fellow human beings.

In addition to BPW activities, Marguerite was finishing the course work toward a doctoral degree in the law. Early in 1944, she had set out to write a dissertation on the history of women in the law only to discover that there was no collected information on the subject. A year later, she described her efforts to Pat Neff:

> I have been delving into papers yellowed with age and laboring through the pages of legal periodicals which were without index, and putting together piece by piece the mosaic of the 75-year record of women in the law profession. . . I am fired with the

ambition to some day complete and publish such a record. No bound volume treating of women lawyers had been published since 1891.

She wanted the degree because she thought it would give her an edge at work — and a title the men couldn't challenge — but a dissertation like the one she planned would take years and more time than she could spare from work. She gave up the idea reluctantly, finally choosing leadership in organizations over the desired "top degree."

The honorary doctorate from Baylor eased the disappointment. Across the date, May 28, 1945, she wrote on her calendar, "Baylor Centennial. I am to become a 'Dr.' " Pat Neff and all the world, she felt, would be recognizing her as a woman of accomplishment.

On that morning in Waco, in a ceremony that was solemn and hot, Pat Neff conferred sixteen honorary degrees — to scholars and college presidents, Baptist dignitaries, three millionaire philanthropists. When he came to her name he paused and paid her the highest of compliments, "Marguerite Rawalt — receiving financial aid from no one, but relying alone on your own brain and brawn, climbing the ladder round by round. . . ."

Nineteen-forty-five brought change for the country as well as for Marguerite. On January 20, she stood in the cold to hear President Roosevelt make his last inaugural address. Three months later, the country was stunned by the death of a president credited with saving the country from revolution and the world from fascism. Many shared the sentiments of the *New York Times* writer who said, "Men will thank God on their knees a hundred years from now that Franklin Roosevelt was in the White House when a powerful and ruthless barbarism threatened to overrun the civilization of the Western World."

Marguerite stood with the mob that mourned in the streets the next day and prayed for Harry S. Truman, the great president's little-known and ill-prepared successor. Within days, the new president announced victory in Europe. On July 16, after months of secret research, the first atomic bomb was exploded in the New Mexico desert. In less than a month, the apocalyptic new weapon fell on Hiroshima, Japan, annihilating the city and killing 100,000 people. On August 9, a second bomb was dropped on Nagasaki, bringing the war in the Pacific to an end.

Criticism swirled around the president for his decision to drop the mystery weapon on a country already on the brink of surrender. But America was tired of the war and Japan seemed determined to fight to the death. People like Marguerite and Pat Neff backed the president. He was a man of the people — a man willing to make a hard choice and stand behind it.

When Marguerite's installation as president of Washington's BPW club fell on Eisenhower Day, June 18, she joined the throngs and walked to the luncheon celebration at the Statler Hotel, wearing the green silk dress she had bought for the occasion and a white orchid from Harry.

Later in the summer, she learned that Tom Clark was to be the next U.S. attorney general. When Leonora Graham, a friend in New Orleans, wrote suggesting that she speak to Clark about a judgeship, she demurred: "I don't know where I would stand if I asked for anything. Haven't tried it."

By November, circumstances had thrust her into the fray — as she explained in a letter to Lucy Moore.

> I'll never reach that rocking chair! The Womens Bar Association of D.C. last Saturday recommended my appointment to the Municipal Court of Appeals for the District of Columbia. This is a Presidential appointment, which is made on the recommendation of the Attorney General. It is first necessary to get the recommendation of Attorney General Tom Clark. The appointment is political.

Despite the endorsement of NAWL, help from friends in Texas, and a letter-writing campaign aimed at both Clark and President Truman, the appointment went to Judge Brice Claggett, who was being moved up from the Municipal Court.

Marguerite's supporters immediately shifted their ambitions to the lower court spot made available by Claggett's promotion. In June, she was disappointed again when the job went to Justice Department lawyer, Nadine Gallagher.

Ignoring the advice of friends, Marguerite never went to Clark in person, never asked outright for his support. Naively adhering to her own standards of justice and fair play, she refused to believe in the need for political pressure. Tom Clark knew her, knew her qualifications, and knew she wanted the job. She thought he would do the right thing. Standing on principle, she forgot one of Margie Neal's rules of politics: ASK for what you want, people like to be asked.

Trying to console her, Harry said it was a blessing she didn't get the job; he was sure she would tire of the petty issues that came before the city courts. But she wanted to be a judge, she said, wanted to join the ranks of the women she admired most: Florence Allen, Annabel Matthews, Marion Harron, Sarah Hughes.

Soon she was back at work in BPW, organizing seminars on postwar employment problems and the role of women's organizations in peacetime. At her invitation, Margaret Hickey, BPW's national president and chair of the Women's Advisory Committee of the War Manpower Commission, told a huge crowd of Washington men and women that sixteen million women were going to need jobs after the war.

Marguerite was impressed by the women who took time from demanding careers to run the Federation of Business and Professional Women. Its national board included president Margaret Hickey as well as the famous writer and lecturer, Margaret Culkin Banning and Ellen Woodward, a member of the Social Security Board. Dr. Frances Scott and Dr. Minnie Maffett were both medical doctors, one from Massachusetts and the other from Texas. Maffett was a past BPW president and Scott, a professor at Smith College, was sure to be president soon. "These women are real stalwarts," Marguerite thought, feeling almost shy in their presence.

Though change seemed slow in coming, Marguerite and others like her were beginning to see a different future for women. Writing in her *Washington Post* column on February 13, 1946, Malvina Lindsay spoofed male preconceptions and predicted a new day. Clubwomen were educating themselves on the issues, she said. They weren't the kind of politicians men were used to:

> . . . they haven't been in politics long enough to know that a thing has to be done a certain way because it always has been done that way. They're likely to want change. You know how women are — always wanting to move the furniture, or clamoring for a new rug or for college education for the children. . . . Do something, anything, quickly to get their minds off Congress.

Two weeks later, Lindsay wrote more seriously about the "dual system" of social and organizational life:

> . . . It is possible that American men, recognizing the energy, ambition and organizing talents of their women, have sensed that their own groups, if opened to them, might become as overfeminized as have the church and the home. Perhaps subconsciously they are in a last ditch retreat from "mother knows best."

For Marguerite, the next few years were a steady climb toward the national presidency of BPW. As national legal advisor and a sought-after banquet speaker, she attended state conventions across the country and practiced the essentials of politics as she had learned them from Pat Neff and Margie Neal: meet as many people as you can, don't forget them and don't let them forget you.

As her year as president of the D.C. club came to an end, she made plans for a short, nostalgic trip to Texas, stopping first in Waco, where on March 6, 1947, Baylor was to award President Truman the same degree she had received.

She arrived at the Hotel Roosevelt on Wednesday, in time for a banquet for her old friend's guests. Neff loved such occasions. The next day's *Dallas Morning News* called him and Senator Tom Connally dignified representatives of "a gracious Southern era near-vanished." Following the ceremony and a speech by the president, Marguerite lunched in Burleson Hall with Neff, Tom Clark, President Truman, and other guests of the University.

But neither the honors nor the achievements in organizations made up to Marguerite for the fact that less competent men passed her by at work and got the promotions and raises she deserved. She didn't like to pester men into giving her what she had already earned. In staff meetings when she said women were not getting promotions, she got the same old saws, "But Marguerite, you know the men here have families to support." Sometimes, her colleagues said she devoted too much time to organizational work. Other times, they accused her of working *too hard*. She was married; they said she didn't need the job.

In the spring of 1947, income taxes were due; the telephones had been ringing constantly for weeks. They were all getting edgy. At noon, Marguerite learned that a young lawyer in Brief Review had just received a promotion. He had been promoted twice since her last raise. By three o'clock she was furious. She grabbed her coat and walked across the street to see Attorney General Robert Jackson at the Justice Department. Rumor had it that Jackson was going on the Supreme Court. She had worked for him when he was chief counsel at Internal Revenue and knew him well in FBA.

She told him what was happening. She was being taken advantage of; she was deeply offended. She wanted to leave Internal Revenue and come to work for him at a grade raise in the Justice Department. All she had to do was fill out the forms, he said.

Back at her office, her anger cooling, she thought about Macon B. Leming, the assistant chief counsel with whom she worked. He was a competent man. She respected him. She didn't like the idea of walking out on him. Later that afternoon, she told him how long it had been since she had a promotion. He refused to believe her until he checked with personnel. Chagrined, he found out she was right and ordered a grade raise immediately. He didn't know how it had happened, just an oversight. She should have said something sooner.

Finally, she decided to stay. She enjoyed the work, she liked Leming, settling into a new job would take time away from other things that were important to her. She had made her point, but she would always be annoyed that it had to be done.

On April 30, 1947, Harry retired from his job at Bolling Field. He had done his duty and served his country; now there were things he wanted for himself— to be with his friends, to go to Michigan to see his family whenever he liked, to travel for pleasure with Marguerite. Most of all he wanted to spend time in Texas, fishing and combing the beaches with Louis. No, he told Marguerite, he did not want her to retire and he didn't need a hobby. Looking after her, he said, would be his hobby and his job.

With his retirement, Harry and Marguerite began a pattern of separation and reunion that would make them both happy for the next fifteen years. On Friday, May 16, after putting Marguerite on an airplane going to Tampa, Florida, Harry headed for Corpus Christi in his Oldsmobile. For the next two months, he lived in a motel at the beach, sleeping late, visiting with Viola, making the rounds on Padre Island with Louis, getting better acquainted with Marguerite's nieces and nephews. His life was his own.

Following his own instincts and defying the odds, Louis had made a good life for himself. He and Vi and their two children,

Louise and Charlie, fished and camped and worked on Padre Island buffeted by the tides and winds that supported them. In an article about Louis as the archaeologist of Padre Island written for the January 1948, *Saturday Evening Post,* Lewis Nordyke described the harsh shore that had proved the salvation of the war-damaged veteran and his family:

> Padre Island, which lies off the Gulf coast of Texas almost within sight of bright lights and traffic jams, is one of the most untamable spots in this country. What the storms don't blow away, the sifting sands cover up. Man has been bucking the island for some 400 years. But today it is uninhabited, and its chief attractions are things which have been lost at sea, and which have somehow turned up on Padre. . . . With possibly a few exceptions, Padre is the world's richest territory for beachcombers. . . . Every person who has stayed long on Padre has been virtually blown off, ultimately. It is no place to be in a bad storm.

Working at a variety of jobs in town, Louis always returned to the island and eventually found a way to make his living there — fishing, selling and renting equipment, guiding oil company geologists, tourists and sailors, combing the beaches for relics and plunder. As Padre's unofficial archaeologist and historian, he put together a rare collection of artifacts culled from the island's debris or washed in by the waves — the teeth and bones of ancient animals, a carved Mayan statue, 400-year-old Spanish coins, Indian arrowheads and spearpoints. By 1947, when Harry began making his long pilgrimages to Corpus Christi, Louis knew the island and its lore by heart — the myths, the wildlife, the constantly changing shoreline, the harsh, unrelenting winds.

With Harry in Texas, Marguerite worked harder than ever on BPW affairs. Between May and July, she traveled to Florida, Ohio, and Indiana. At home she worked with ERA lobbyist Geneva McQuarters and began pressuring ABA to appoint women to its prestigious committees. She herself chaired the ABA's Committee on Facilities of the Law Library of Congress, a rare and prestigious appointment for a woman.

During May, there were personal demands as well. Louise Wright's aging and always frail mother, Hattie Crawford, was so ill that someone had to be with her constantly. For two weeks, Louise and Marguerite shared the duties with a hired nurse. On June 4,

Marguerite called Harry to tell him that Mrs. Crawford, who had introduced them, was dead. For twenty years, Marguerite had shared weekend afternoons and nights with Louise and Hattie — sewing, cooking, getting ready for whatever the week would bring.

Hattie Crawford died on Wednesday. Marguerite kept to her rigorous schedule through Friday then cancelled all obligations for the weekend. On Saturday, she wrote in her diary, *Very tired — wanted to be alone.* By Sunday afternoon, she was recovering. *At home all day, clouds and showers. Sewing.*

Her next round of travels began with a five-day BPW board meeting in French Lick, Indiana. From there, she took the train to Austin, Texas, to spend a night with Lucy Moore, who was retiring and moving to the little town of Stephenville, near Fort Worth. Moore was ill with a heart condition for which her doctors prescribed only "rest and more rest."

A few days later, Marguerite headed for Corpus Christi and then Padre Island for several days of camping and fishing with Harry, Louis, Vi, and their children. The size forty-six blue trousers she bought at Sears-Roebuck for the occasion became a permanent joke among her nieces and nephews. Several months later, she described the outing in a long letter to Lucy Moore:

> Louise (13-year-old) discovered she could have a good laugh by holding them aloft in the back of the truck, letting the breeze fill each leg like two huge wind-directed tubes at the airport. . . . They were so immense that it invoked a seige of giggles in which I too had to join. Mom contributed a 10-year-old black milan hat, which I tied down with Louise's girl scout bandana. Harry contributed shirts. I owned shoes. . . . Vi had gotten Harry's attention and called him to "take a picture of Mike pulling in her first fish." But when he aimed his camera at me, as I ungracefully arose, hat over one eye, I dared him to take it in tones that wrote finis to that.

After being ribbed about her citified ineptitude for five days, Marguerite redeemed herself at the last minute by catching a four-pound redfish — the sweetest meat in the Gulf of Mexico. Her brothers wanted her to come back to Texas.

Leaving with mixed emotions, she returned to more conflict and another challenge. The Tax Section of the American Bar Association was opposing the reappointment of Marion Harron to the

U.S. Tax Court. Yet all agreed that one place on the court should go to a woman. Marguerite was being considered.

As always, she hesitated before plunging into the contest. She didn't want to lose and she didn't like to condone criticism of a competent woman already on the court. But India Edwards, the director of the Women's Division of the Democratic National Committee and the Truman administration's most outspoken advocate for women, encouraged her. The DNC might, she suggested, recommend both Marguerite and Marion Harron for the sixteen-member court.

A long letter written to Pat Neff on New Year's Eve shows how much the Tax Court judgeship appealed to her.

> . . . Good friends, with good judgment, tell me that I should not fail to give this a real try. . . This would be the ideal place of service for me. . . a most wonderful and satisfactory culmination of the years I have spent in getting the law education, and in working to establish a good reputation in tax law. The appointment is for 12 years, so I am just the age for it to coincide for the remainder of my working years, and old enough, I would hope, to be ripened in judgment and experience.

In March, she learned that ABA was recommending sixteen tax lawyers for consideration, including two women lawyers from the Justice Department. Her name had not been mentioned. In the first flush of uncertainty and disappointment, she wrote Sarah Hughes,

> . . . [Cecil] Kilpatrick assured me that my name was a cinch to be on the list. . . . Two other members of the [ABA tax] Council told my immediate office chief that my name was certain to be included. Kil is ill; in the hospital, so I cannot ask him just what took place, but I am at a complete loss as to why this is. Two things have been suggested: first, there is no one from the Bureau [of Internal Revenue] on the list. . . Another suggestion was made to me, as a collateral remark, to the effect that the "Department of Justice" took a hand. That is hard to interpret, very.

> But just at this state, I am in a state of quandary, and disbelief that almost undermines one's self-confidence. From the lawyer slant, it is facts I want. . . You can keep an ear to the ground from there.

The facts were harder to come by than she had expected. A nationally prominent tax lawyer and a friend of Sarah Hughes, Cecil Kilpatrick, had thrown all his weight behind Marguerite's nomination. Taken ill suddenly, he had missed the crucial ABA tax council meeting. Some of the men resented her club work, he said afterwards. Some didn't think a former IRS lawyer could be unbiased in tax cases. A few recalled her uncertainty on racial matters in FBA. Some said she was too aggressive.

A few months later, President Truman made the whole issue moot by reappointing all four incumbents, including Marion Harron. By the end of May, Marguerite had accepted the disappointment well enough to support a women's campaign to assure that the Senate confirm Harron, who was still being opposed by influential tax lawyers. Sarah Hughes said, "It's a shame that a woman so unpopular had to be appointed in the first place. It makes it that much harder for the next woman." If Marguerite agreed, she never said so.

She was as close to taking defeat in stride as she would ever be. Her success in BPW made up for some of the disappointments. The same letter that told Hughes of the reappointment of Harron, described her plans for the national convention in Fort Worth and revealed her growing enthusiasm for her work in BPW: "I get a thrill out of attending the state conventions. Last week, I was over the coals [during ERA controversy] at Pennsylvania state meeting. . . 650 in attendance at the dinner. I was bedecked and be-dined."

Internal conflict over ERA surfaced again in Fort Worth, where Southern delegates led an unsuccessful attempt to curtail the federation's endorsement of the ever-controversial amendment. But, amid the convention's "wild west" atmosphere, there was plenty of "bedecking and bedining" to temper the political troubles.

Sarah and Marguerite were impressed with some of the younger women, especially Virginia Allan from Michigan. Allan had seemed shy at first. She had never known women as boisterous and outgoing as Sarah and Marguerite, riding horses at the rodeo, showing off, attracting attention, staying up all night — but always getting the work done.[1]

Driving back across Texas to Corpus Christi, Marguerite and Harry took a hot, two-hour detour to Stephenville to see Lucy Moore. Her big frame was frail now, her wispy hair thinner than ever. She missed her friends in Austin. Inactivity depressed her. Earlier in the summer Marguerite had been moved by a letter lamenting her forced retirement, ". . . so far, I've stood it like a man (Even they do cry a little sometimes, you know.). . . Lord, I'd love to see you!"

They talked about Texas politics and books. Moore had seen the article about Louis and Padre Island in the *Saturday Evening Post*. Marguerite told her Viola was getting divorced.

In November 1949, she wrote Moore an unusual letter, a sketchy, rambling attempt to tell her friend what the work in BPW meant to her. Always more given to action than to introspection, the letter makes a rare attempt to analyze her own behavior and speak candidly of her ambitions.

> Travels? . . . One weekend in Dover, Delaware, one in Richmond, Virginia, and one in Southern Pines. . . attending statewide meetings of officers of clubs in the state federations of B&PW. I enjoy it thoroly [*sic*]. There are really fine and earnest and sincere women in the organization. Perhaps I enjoy feminine gatherings too much. . . . I take a leader part.
>
> My name is to be proposed to the nominating committee in San Francisco next July for a national office, i. e. for one of the national vice presidencies. Sarah Hughes, now 1st VP, will be nominee for President. . . . Trouble is that there will be other potential nominees from other states, in goodly numbers. . . . One thing: I am interested and would like to hold national office. But I don't NEED it, and the disappointment would be temporary.

She had other things to tell Lucy Moore as well. In September, she had been made chief of the Brief Review Section in the Appeals Division at Internal Revenue. She was the first woman to be put in a supervisory position in "the second largest law office in the world."

Near the end of four closely-typed pages, she returned to the subject most on her mind, her ambitions in BPW.

> I may or may not get nominated. And of course can't foresee who my opponent may be. In my favor is the membership promotion work done for two years which has made many in the Federation acquainted with my name and my work.

Once she was at ease in a situation, Marguerite loved the limelight. Amid the resolutions, the parliamentary procedures, the constant strife between factions, they gave gifts and applauded one another. The excitement of the crowd, the exhilaration, the flood of relief when tensions relaxed, those things thrilled her and gave her energy for the hard work that came with it. She found women she admired at the top in NAWL and BPW. They were "the stalwarts," strong in their convictions, committed.

Suddenly, in the midst of it all, she would be flooded with an unaccustomed peace, a joy she couldn't name. Like a well-bred animal, she was doing the work she was made for.

In BPW, the only large women's group in the country that could possibly call itself "activist," Marguerite and a handful of others were dreaming of a stronger BPW that would lead women to equality under the law. Over and over, she would tell them,

> . . . We have to have the facts; we can't just keep going around throwing up our hands and saying 'It isn't fair. . . it isn't right. . . we're second class citizens. . .' If the men in Congress know what we are talking about, they don't care. If we give them the facts, they might have to do something.

First, she thought, they should study the laws nationally and state by state and collect statistics on unequal pay and discrimination. They had to *know* how state laws would be affected by ERA. Without the facts, they would remain powerless.

In the meantime, BPW continued to keep itself in the public eye and to do the things it had always done well. In January 1949, the D.C. club sponsored a luncheon at the Statler Hotel to welcome Margaret Chase Smith to Washington. Smith, a national office-holder in BPW, had just been elected senator from Maine. Both Senator Smith's assessment of BPW and her feminism coincided with Marguerite's. At the luncheon, Smith commented:

> My work in the BPW taught me the very touchstones of political success. . . . I know of no organization that has as much to offer business and professional women. . . No organization that can provide better training in cooperation, tact and efficiency. . . . no better way of increasing one's chances of success.
>
> I was elected in spite of the fact that I am a woman. And that in itself was a victory for all women, for it smashed the unwritten tradition that the Senate is no place for a woman. The point that so many miss is that women do not blindly support some candidates just because they are women; we are not headed for the

Amazonian world — rather that no one should be barred from public office just because she is a woman.

Slowly, very slowly, concern among women was rising, new stirrings ran deeper than the traditional, futile support of uniform jury service, equal pay, and the Equal Rights Amendment. India Edwards at the DNC spoke openly of discrimination. Her frankness startled some — but not all — women when she said: "If the Party backs a woman, you can be pretty sure they do it because they think it is a lost cause but they know they have to have *some* candidate." [2]

Marguerite herself was less hesitant now, more confident of her own stand on issues, less likely to defer to others or hide behind procedures and majority opinion. Her speeches of the late 1940s and early 1950s attacked problems that were unique to women — and seldom mentioned. Women were living longer and many needed to return to the work force at middle age and after; they would have to be trained and retrained; since most working women were mothers, something would have to be done about child care. Women, who bore the children and reared them, had a special responsibility to speak out against atomic war. From now on, world security would require world unity.

In addition to the philosophy and the questioning, she packed her talks with realistic advice to women on getting along in a male-dominated work world. They had to do their share of the work — and then some. They were not to engage in office squabbles or gossip or discuss personnel matters at work.

She liked to end her speeches by quoting John Mason Brown:

> . . . The pitiful people are those who in their living elect to be spectators rather than participants; the tragic ones are those sightseers who turn their backs deliberately on the procession. The only true happiness comes from squandering ourselves for a purpose.

For Marguerite, years of experience and struggle were coming together.

As she and others like her grew more ambitious for women, the country was feeling the first tremors of the cultural earthquake that would shake the 1960s. A radical movement for equality, still smoldering in the black churches of the South, would soon sweep up the

East Coast. Women would see black activism get results where their methodical plodding had failed.

With the explosion of the Soviet Union's first atomic bomb during the summer of 1949, the possibility of an annihilating world war became real. A year later, the United States was battling Communist Chinese troops in Korea.

People were practicing air-raids and building bomb shelters; they were afraid of nuclear war, afraid the power of communism would destroy the country from within if not from without.

Marguerite and Sarah Hughes helped set up an Assembly of Women's Organizations for National Security to act as a clearinghouse for information and encourage the participation of women in national defense. Harry scoffed, saying the next war would destroy everything, including their plans and organizations. Like most people, Sarah Hughes and Marguerite acted as if a nuclear war would differ very little from the two wars they had known.

In March 1947, spurred by the country's mounting fear of communism, Harry Truman had created a Loyalty Program requiring security checks on all government employees and applicants for federal jobs. In October of the same year, the House Un-American Activities Committee launched a series of sensational hearings aimed at uncovering Communist influence in the movie industry.

But it took until 1950 for the incipient panic over "the Communist influence" to rise to the surface full-blown. On February 7, in a hardly noticed speech in Wheeling, West Virginia, Joseph McCarthy, a renegade first-term Republican senator from Wisconsin, made the first of many accusations, insisting that the State Department harbored Communists. As chair of a Senate subcommittee, he conducted over 150 investigations of supposed Communists and Communist activities in the United States. While he rode his hobby to its destruction, and his own, a tide of character assassinations and blacklistings swept through universities and business and professional organizations.

Early on, Marguerite feared the idea of a "Communist dictatorship" and supported public attempts to expose communist and socialist influences in the government. Her patriotism, her abiding belief in democracy and free enterprise ran deep. She distrusted the idea of community ownership and feared the loss of political power and personal freedom.

In a version of a speech given frequently during the early 1950s, she told her BPW audiences, "The aim of Communism is conquest, power conquest, power lodged in the hands of a few and maintained by treachery and conspiracy. Power once attained, the masses and their needs are soon forgotten. Communist effort is devoted to conflict rather than any attempt to improve human well-being."

In 1951, she reported her reaction to the "All American Conference to Combat Communism," held on March 9 and 10, in Philadelphia. The conference "consisted of presentations of the communist menace by outstanding leaders from church groups of all denominations, from press, and from Federal Government Departments. . . . It is my conviction that we [BPW] should continue our support of this necessary and worthy cause. It is unquestionably sanctioned by Federal government, and by church and lay leaders."

A year later, she responded to a BPW colleague who asked for tips on speaking out against communism by recommending articles by J. Edgar Hoover, director of the FBI; reports from the Committee on Un-American Activities; and pamphlets from the American Legion, the National Catholic Welfare Conference, and the National Association of Manufacturers. She concluded with a familiar line of advice — don't do or say anything until you've got the facts.

Ultimately, her innate distrust of excess and the danger she saw to individual freedom and privacy turned her against the drastic methods of McCarthy and the House Committee on Un-American Activities. She hadn't forgotten her dismay at Westbrook Pegler's misinterpretation of her own opinions and motives. Some of Senator McCarthy's fans wanted Eleanor Roosevelt investigated and Pegler said,

> The time has come to snatch this wily old conspirator before Joe McCarthy's committee and chew her out. . . Joe McCarthy or Bill Jenner could tear her to tatters if either of them should ever drag her to the stand. She deserves far less respect than any conventional woman.

When the enemies of communism began maligning the leaders of democracy whom Marguerite most admired, they went too far. Again she agreed with Margaret Chase Smith: the Republican Party should disdain to ride to victory on the coattail of a man like Joseph McCarthy.

On Sunday afternoon, January 20, 1952, Marguerite was on her way to a reception in town when she learned that Pat Neff was dead. There was no mistaking what she heard through the static of a distant radio station, . . . *former Governor of Texas dead of heart failure at his home in Waco.* A year before, Margie Neal had seen him and written: "He didn't stand out above the crowd as he always had done. His hair was white and his body seemed to be shrunken up. I wanted to cry he seemed so broken. . . . The years take their toll on the youth, vigor, and personal charm of the best — and worst — of us, don't they?"

The next day, Marguerite sent a telegram to the Neff family.

FROM THE DEPTHS OF DEEP PERSONAL SORROW
MY PROFOUND SYMPATHY. . .
THE COUNTRY HAS LOST A GREAT SOUL.

Within months Lucy Moore was gone too. Suddenly, in her sleep, like Pat Neff. They had believed in her, taught her how to live, to find the things worth living for. They had taught her to do her part — in work and friendship and love. Know who your friends are, they had said, and don't worry about your enemies.

Always in the past, Marguerite had built her political efforts on the advice of Lucy Moore and Pat Neff. Now when two new vacancies appeared on the Tax Court, she turned to Margie Neal and Sarah Hughes. With two Texans already on the Court, she knew her chances were slim, but she wanted to try for it anyway. She had the support of Senator Tom Connally. Both Neal and Hughes were close to Senator Lyndon Johnson. Again she had the encouragement of India Edwards.

Still a voice to be reckoned with in Texas politics, Neal sent Johnson a long personal letter praising Marguerite and reprimanding the administration for its failure to recognize Texas women.

> It will not be amiss, I trust, for me to say that as far as I am informed *Texas women* — (and I am not one who has ever felt that *sex* should have a part in the selection of public officials) — have not had the recognition by the present National Administration that they are entitled to and which political considerations have warranted.

In April, Marguerite wrote optimistically to Neal saying that India Edwards had spoken to both President Truman and the secretary of the treasury. Edwards thought she had a good chance but warned of the unpredictability of political appointments. She had heard that Vice-President Alben Barkley was "suddenly" advocating someone for the position. At Neal's insistence, Marguerite had finally gone in person to see Tom Clark, now a justice on the Supreme Court. He promised to mention her to the president or the secretary. She could, he added, refer anybody to him for his high opinion of her.

Nevertheless, on April 18, two men were appointed to the Tax Court, one of them from Kentucky, the vice-president's state. A letter to Margie Neal barely conceals the depths of Marguerite's disappointment.

> I am not going to grieve about the appointment I didn't get, but as you have known for years, it is the one spot to work in which seems to me the most to be desired. It is the one for which I am trained. . . . Anyway, it is worth much to me to have you tell me that I don't have to be a judge for you to appreciate me.

The same letter tells of her promotion to assistant chief of Internal Revenue's Appeals Division, third in command of a staff of 230 lawyers, another unprecedented position for a woman. As she explained to Neal, ". . . some years ago, it would have been unthought of that I would ever be made an assistant head of the Division. I am very glad; and it will pave the way for other women to do likewise in the office if they care to work at it."

Although the disappointment of losing the appointment subsided, Marguerite became more and more convinced that, had she been a man, she would have had one of the spots. Never one to show bitterness or grieve for long over something she couldn't change, she was soon immersed in a drive to become national president of BPW and strengthen the Federation's position as a leader for women's rights.

By now, her attitude toward leadership was firm. She had found most women to be too timid to express themselves. They had to be led by the few who were not afraid. Elected officers like Sarah Hughes and herself had the authority and the responsibility to see that the paid staff was efficient and productive. In 1952, she wrote Hughes encouraging her to take a strong position with an ineffective staff member and added, "The Federation is important to me, and the views of the fine women over this country. . . . Not only the

Federation, but your leadership of it, and YOU are important to me too."

Carrying added pounds with ease, Marguerite was a commanding presence. Every gesture came naturally now. Beside her, Sarah Hughes was diminutive. Both women were leaders; but Hughes, absorbed in her own political ambitions, thought of herself more as an example than an organizer of women. Marguerite seemed to want to embrace the whole race and carry all women along with her. She was ahead of the pack, maybe too far ahead.

On Friday, May 4, 1951, Marguerite arrived in Oklahoma City for the Oklahoma state BPW convention. As National's second vice-president, she was treated like an expert, a celebrity. She had done it a million times. She would address the banquet on Saturday night with a plea that women get involved in fighting communism and "aggressively defending Constitutional democracy." She didn't give "ladies' club speeches," she said. She liked to leave them with something to think about and something to do.

For years BPW had worked for uniform jury service in all the states, and Oklahoma still did not permit women to serve on juries. A bill was stuck in the Senate Judiciary Committee. Once again, the state convention was about to pass a resolution in favor of the bill. The state Legislature was meeting a few blocks away. Why, asked Marguerite, didn't they recess and lobby in force, all 500 of them? It would become a theme song with her. *Stop "resoluting" and do something.*

That afternoon, they flooded the halls of the legislature and packed the galleries; and by the first of the week, a bill thought to have been hopelessly stuck in committee had passed both Houses. Oklahoma's governor finally signed it, but not without reservation: "I'll sign it, but I've been on juries — they don't know what they're asking for."

In 1952, BPW was determined to get a woman nominated for vice-president of the United States. Margaret Chase Smith, who had agreed to let her name be presented at the Republican convention, backed out when she learned that Richard Nixon had already been chosen. Sarah Hughes allowed herself to be nominated from the floor of the Democratic Convention as a symbolic gesture, then withdrew saying: "I am not so naive as to believe that this year we will have a woman as vice-president of the United States, but we do have to get into the arena and fight."

These were brief, exhilarating moments, but progress for women was slow. They slogged endlessly over the same issues, constantly retracing their steps. At every national convention, the resolutions sounded good, and every year sounded like the year before. Every year, the National Woman's Party saw to it that ERA was introduced in Congress; and every year, NWP and BPW waged a losing battle to get it passed. And usually Senator Carl Hayden introduced an amendment which would prevent ERA from impairing "any rights, benefits, or exemptions now or hereinafter conferred by law upon persons of the female sex." Since the "Hayden Rider" exempted protective labor laws from coverage under ERA, it was totally unacceptable to ERA advocates. There the stalemate stood year after year.

Compared to the narrowly focused National Woman's Party, BPW was big and unwieldy. Events during the summer of 1953 confirmed Alice Paul's doubts about the political viability of an organization as far-flung and young as BPW. Following the group's decision to do everything possible to get ERA through Congress before the session ended in January, BPW lobbyist, Marjorie Temple, and Isabelle J. Jones, a capable political organizer in Pennsylvania and chair of BPW's legislation committee, organized a letter-writing campaign designed to force the Senate to bring the amendment to the floor for a vote.

Immediately, BPW and the Woman's Party were at cross purposes. Alice Paul knew ERA didn't have a chance in the Senate without the Hayden Rider attached. Under those circumstances, they should all be working together to see that ERA did *not* come up for consideration.

By Wednesday, July 15, even Marjorie Temple could see the danger. If ERA came up in the Senate, it was going to pass — with the rider attached. If the same thing happened in the House of Representatives, a parody of the Equal Rights Amendment would go to the states for ratification. Assured by Majority Leader William F. Knowland that he had no room on the calendar for the bill, Temple relaxed and passed the message on to the Woman's Party.

Early the next day, a quorum having been dispensed with, and only a handful of senators present, ERA was presented for debate without warning. Even its primary sponsor, Senator John M. Butler from Maryland, was caught off guard. By afternoon, the amendment — plus the Hayden Rider — had passed the Senate, 73 to 11.

Everyone was blaming everyone else. Senator Knowland insisted an opening had appeared unexpectedly, that was all. Senator Margaret Chase Smith thought the sudden action on ERA had been planned, perhaps with the cooperation of the Women's Bureau. Alice Paul would remain convinced that Marjorie Temple had sold out to the Women's Bureau and the labor union people who favored the "nullifying rider." [3]

Uninvited, the 1953 debacle catapulted Marguerite to a new level of awareness and activism for ERA. In the absence of president Helen Irwin and executive director Laura Lorraine, who were in Europe at BPW's international convention, she was bombarded with calls and telegrams from the Woman's Party and from lawyers and BPW members all over the country.

In a letter sent to her fellow officers on July 20, she reached the only conclusion she could have reached: "Opponents of ERA could not have chosen a more cunning time and manner" of attack. Now "maximum effort" would have to be made "to prevent the House acting, and acting in the same manner as the Senate." The letter ends with a familiar admonition: "We have a responsibility, and you and I can discharge it only if we all know what is to be known."

Writing more openly a few weeks later, she told Massachusetts lawyer Susanne Shallna: "It turned up . . . that we do not keep our officers apprised; that our Federation has need of executive coordination and management. Finally, after 'sweating' with it for two weeks, we have a respite by reason of adjournment of Congress."

She was even more forthright in a note to second vice-president Hazel Palmer: "I too, get very discouraged, as year after year, I spend my weekends over a typewriter, and trying to meet emergencies. . . ."

As soon as that crisis was over, BPW leaders had other decisions to make. Should they continue their push for ERA now? And if so, how? If they were going ahead with it, they would have to develop a better system, coordinate the local clubs, and educate the membership — as well as Congress — on the difference between ERA with and without tempering riders.

In October, the executive committee met in New York and agreed to spend $10,000 for publicity to launch a new kind of ERA campaign. Swallowing their pride, they hired a male lobbyist with the kind of experience they had not been able to find in a woman.

Executive director Geneva McQuarters was sent to the New York office to coordinate the effort. Isabella Jones hired professionals to design a bold red, yellow, and blue brochure which proclaimed: 174,064,000 WOMEN VERSUS A "BOTTLENECK." Inside, redfaced donkeys and elephants read Republican and Democratic platform pledges endorsing ERA. The brochure gave the exact wording of the amendment and called for passage without the nullifying rider. By November, BPW members all over the country had brochures and instructions to contact their congressmen and senators while they were home for the winter holidays.

Yet finally, despite their pride in the campaign called "Operation Buttonhole," BPW activists had to agree with Alice Paul. They were a long way from getting ERA through Congress without the Hayden Rider.

As BPW's first vice-president, Marguerite was making plans for a presidency that would leave its mark. The ranks of educated working women was growing; many women supported themselves and their families. Yet, they almost never got equal pay with men. There was more to the woman's cause than ERA, and she wanted the women in BPW to take the lead. To start with, they should move the main office from New York to Washington and make BPW a headquarters for legislation concerning women.

At IRS, Marguerite had watched the growth of foundations. She knew that with a tax-exempt foundation, BPW could raise money to fund research and gather data on sex discrimination. As simply a network of clubs, they would never be able to attract donations for the work that had to be done.

Funds collected in 1929 for the purpose of buying a headquarters building in Washington had been unused for almost twenty-five years. By 1952, the Lena Madesin Phillips Building Fund, named after BPW's founder, had grown to $50,000. In five years, the fund's bonds would mature at $63,000. Marguerite saw the fund as the basis for a building fund drive that would make possible the purchase of a permanent headquarters in Washington.

Gradually, Marguerite took a few women into her confidence: Hazel Anderson, a lawyer from Kansas and BPW's legal advisor; Libby Sachar, a New Jersey lawyer whom Marguerite had long admired for her cool intelligence and commitment to women's rights;

Grace Daniels, an employee of the State of Pennsylvania whose common sense and good nature often saved the day for her literal-minded cohorts; and, of course, Judge Sarah T. Hughes.

Immediately there were difficulties. BPW's current president, Helen Irwin, resisted her ambitious vice-president's plans for moving the headquarters and — despite Marguerite's protests — signed a five-year lease on new offices in New York. Then hoping to get Lena Madesin Phillips to modify her long-held view that a headquarters should be built in Washington, and nowhere else, Irwin called a special luncheon meeting for the executive committee and Phillips.

At seventy-one, Lena Madesin Phillips was a serene and stately woman with short white hair and strong features. She had known what she wanted ever since 1915, when — after a year of exhaustion and self-examination — she left behind her life as a failed musician to become a lawyer and activist for women.

Now, as always, she stood her ground. When Irwin questioned her, implying there wasn't enough money for a move and suggesting the fund be used for operating expenses, Phillips replied,

> The fund cannot be used anywhere but in Washington. . . . I would not pay too much attention to the amount of money you have. What we have was spontaneously given. . . . the additional money will be forthcoming just as the original fund was forthcoming.

Marguerite was outraged and embarrassed. The nerve of it — pressuring such a woman! For years Phillips had dreamed of BPW's having a suitable headquarters in Washington. Her example gave Marguerite courage, and now the dream was hers as well.

While Helen Irwin's headquarters committee prepared to present its findings at the national convention in June, Marguerite lined up supporters both for her candidacy and for the headquarters move. To be pro-Rawalt for president was to be pro-headquarters.

On Thursday, June 24, Marguerite arrived in St. Louis with her election forces in line. Years of traveling to local clubs and state conventions were going to pay off. When she said she was confident they could raise the money and move the headquarters, they believed her.

During a stormy all-day meeting on Sunday, the board of directors heard reports from members of a divided headquarters committee. Finally, they agreed on two things: purchasing suitable headquarters in Washington would require an additional $325,000; and it was up to the convention body itself to choose the location of a permanent national headquarters.

All week, Marguerite campaigned, wearing the white suit and bird-of-paradise corsage that were her trademarks. On Wednesday morning, the convention body "took action" when it voted to 1) move the headquarters to Washington, 2) raise the money to buy a headquarters building, 3) empower the executive committee to enter into contracts and appoint the necessary committees. Amid the applause, Lena Madesin Phillips wished them well and Dorothy Titchener, a board member from New York, brought down a flutter of one-dollar bills with her "Bucks for Bricks" slogan. Before the day was over, they had an $8,000-start on their goal.

When rumors that Helen Irwin was going to run for a second term proved false, Marguerite was elected national president without opposition. She wasn't going to have a do-nothing administration, she said.

By the time she got back to Washington a week later, she had firmly in mind a plan for raising the headquarters money and re-ordering the staff. Immediately she hired a new executive director, Genevieve Rogers Riley. Clara Longstreth, a lawyer and former D.C. Club president, was added to the staff in Washington in the newly created position of assistant executive director. As soon as she could be replaced, lobbyist Marjorie Temple would go, too.

A few weeks later, Marguerite traveled alone to the board meeting of the International Federation in Venice. Leaving from New York on Friday, September 17, she had time to spend one night alone in Paris. For two days she walked the streets and museums of the famous city and enjoyed perfectly served meals in her hotel. At the Louvre she stood entranced before the "Nike of Samothrace," a woman pushing forward.

On her return, Frances Lide from the *Washington Star* insisted on interviewing her at home with Harry. Reluctantly, she agreed to let the persuasive reporter come to their apartment and talk to them both. On November 7, the *Sunday Star* featured a Marguerite unfamiliar to most of her admirers. There were two large pictures in the newspaper, one of her and Harry seated together on the

French Provincial sofa in their traditional living room. No, Harry admitted, he was not a joiner, but he admired Marguerite for all she was able to do, holding down a demanding job and running a national organization of 165,000 members.

A second photograph showed her in the kitchen, going through filing cabinets that stood beside her stove. Harry told the reporter, "Marguerite puts the eggs on to boil, sets the timer, and then works on something until the alarm goes off."

Frances Lide presented a deceptively tranquil picture of Marguerite's life. An average week day began at 5:30 A.M. with work at home and often ended only when Harry called the BPW office and ordered her to let the staff go home. She could work all night if she wanted to, but she mustn't expect Clara Longstreth and office manager, Isla Benedick, to do the same thing. She worked most weekends and holidays, as she told her friend, Sara Creech, in a holiday note: "My 'family' is doing fine. Thanksgiving Day the two of us had a roast chicken and chestnut dressing all by ourselves at 6:30 P.M. after I had completed a day's work here in the BPW office. It was a good day all around."

Marguerite had returned from Venice obsessed with raising the headquarters money and increasing membership — but she refused to employ professional fundraisers. She thought about having a Miss Membership Contest modeled on the Miss America Contest, making up a gold-scroll for people who gave $500 or more to the headquarters fund, running a national advertising campaign, "selling" membership in BPW. She considered hiring professional consultants to recruit new members.

To Margaret Wilkinson, who chaired the membership committee, she wrote: "I have no hesitancy about advertising and selling my product. I do not think it will detract from our dignity to get out a poster on membership."

Within a few months, she had turned BPW's staid monthly magazine *Independent Woman,* usually dominated by career advice, into a vehicle for promoting her goals. Beginning in September, the inside front cover displayed a "Scroll of Achievement" listing the names of individuals and clubs contributing over $100 and adding state organizations as they made their quotas. For months, every issue featured the building fund drive. There were architectural renderings of "dream headquarters," photographs of imposing buildings available in prime Washington locations, accounts of how the clubs were meeting their quotas, pep talks by prominent past presidents.

Marguerite told them over and over, "Buy a home for the Federation. It's our Number One Project. Aim High." In April, she and Isla Benedick created *Betty Beep*, a cartoon figure mounting the stairs every month, step by step, to the $325,000 they needed. Two months later, inspired by the sweepstakes theme of the national board meeting coming up in Louisville, Kentucky, they added a two-page horse race chart of state organizations galloping toward the finish line month by month. In August, *Independent Woman* carried an account of the board meeting's mock Kentucky Derby and Headquarters Sweepstakes Award.

> Colonel Marguerite Rawalt, as Chairman of the Racing Commission, escorted by Derby Colonel Anne Rush, dressed for the part in formal black suit, white shirt, big black felt hat and flowing black string tie, headed the parade of the contenders — each state president led by her jockey wearing a jockey cap, white shirt and string tie, and a diagonal sash bearing the state's name in two-inch letters.

With $275,000 in by the end of her first year in office, Marguerite began looking for a temporary location in Washington, and a way out of the lease in New York. Still, the headquarters and membership campaigns dominated the pages of the magazine. By March, she was able to announce: "Goodbye Broadway. The move to Washington is under way." The new headquarters would find its first home on the twelfth floor of the Du Pont Circle Building "in the very heart of Washington, with a commanding view of the Potomac." The next month, it was: "Welcome to Washington at Cherry Blossom Time."

Marguerite accomplished what she did with the enthusiastic backing of over 160,000 clubwomen. She entertained them with gimmicks and hoopla — and praised them when they succeeded. She pushed the staff constantly, motivating hundreds of club leaders, writing thousands of personal letters, and talking every day with bankers, realtors, lawyers.

Occasionally, there was criticism as well as praise. Her attraction to the limelight annoyed some women. Some thought she talked about money too much, they said. Sarah Hughes was like a sister to her, but they differed over the extent of BPW's involvement in international affairs. Few understood Marguerite's vision of BPW as a powerful political force for women in America.

Although Marguerite had few confidants in BPW, she sometimes shared her feelings with Sara Creech, a florist who lived near Miami and stayed clear of club politics. She admired Creech, an idealist who ran a successful business, lived with her mother, and devoted her spare time to helping migrant workers in south Florida. After the July board meeting Marguerite wrote Creech. "There is no one who understands so well as you do that my heart is with the 'little' member who is eager to learn and to do, and not concerned with the fine art of dismemberment, or the vain pursuits of how she looks to others."

Occasionally, she complained to her fellow officers, as she did in a letter written in the midst of the headquarters move: "The going is pretty thick, to put it mildly. I don't want to lose my bread and butter job either (perish the day) so that the nights and Saturdays and Sundays seem to shrink. Will interview two possible people at noon — for office manager, and secretary. Have advertised for an accountant too."

In a year and a half, Marguerite had done what they said couldn't be done. She had raised close to $300,000 in cash, replaced the entire New York staff, and moved the headquarters. Now, with only four months left, she was determined to set up a tax-exempt BPW Foundation.

Since BPW's legislative activities made the federation itself ineligible for the advantageous 501(c)(3) tax exemption, a foundation would have to be incorporated separately. Such a foundation could solicit tax-deductible contributions to finance the research she knew needed doing. She had nurtured the idea for a long time.

Soon after her election, she told Libby Sachar what she was thinking. A practicing lawyer and chair of BPW's finance committee, Sachar easily grasped the advantages. Although she thought of herself as an individualist, not an organization person, she shared Marguerite's hopes for women.[4]

Immediately, Marguerite had Clara Longstreth at work doing the background necessary to setting up a foundation like the one she envisioned. She herself began talking with Allan Higgins, the

Boston lawyer who had founded the American Bar Association Foundation, and Cecil Kilpatrick, a longtime Washington associate and expert on corporate tax law. She named a foundation committee of four lawyers, and by the time the officers met on October 22, 1955, she had the recommendation she wanted.

> That the Federation establish a Foundation for the purpose of acquiring and operating in Washington, D.C. a suitable and adequate national research center and clearing house devoted to the interests of business and professional women; to provide headquarters for the National Federation of Business and Professional Women which would enable the Federation to serve its members and other working women efficiently.

The BPW Foundation would be the first of its kind, a center and a clearinghouse for research on women, a resource for scholarship on the history of women and women's organizations in America, a resource for Congress and scholars. With permission to get the best legal and real estate advice she could find, Marguerite set out to finish the job.

She wrote legal advisor Hazel Anderson a few days after the October 22 meeting, her enthusiasm only slightly dampened by the grueling commitment she had made: "I really feel that this is a great look into the future. . . . I know that I cannot personally reach that far. . . . As long as I have you and a few similar loyal friends, I will manage."

Amid the fundraising and the foundation work, Genevieve Riley resigned as executive director to be replaced by Helen Hurd, a woman whose intelligence, dedication, and friendship would prove invaluable. Formerly head of the department of sociology at Rutgers University and now dean of students, Hurd was an experienced administrator and journalist — and an active member of BPW in New Jersey.

Impressed with Hurd's background, Marguerite wrote her fellow officers: "I think it is quite a matter of prestige for us to be able to secure a college dean from one of the leading universities. . . . It is my conviction that she has both brains and ability. The only improvement that my observation could suggest. . . would be that she might be a little more clothes conscious." To Hazel Palmer, she described her as "completely poised, educated, nice-appearing, though not pretty." As an intelligent companion and co-worker,

Hurd would never disappoint Marguerite, despite her absent-minded disregard for appearances.

By the end of February, the Business and Professional Women's Foundation had been incorporated. Throughout the spring, Marguerite worked with Higgins and Kilpatrick and people they all knew at Internal Revenue, hoping to secure tax exemption before her term ended in July. At the same time, she was fending off complaints from members who objected to her setting up the foundation without a vote by the national convention.

In March, she received an unexpected call from the West German government inviting her to be one of seven U.S. lawyers to tour West Germany comparing their judicial and legal systems with ours. It would be a month-long tour of nine major cities, beginning April 13. She hesitated, thinking there was too much work to be done. But Helen Hurd and her good friend and office manager, Isla Benedick, convinced her that "the honor should not be sacrificed."

In addition to scheduled activities, she met with BPW leaders in Bonn, Munich, and Berlin, wrote postcards to the executive committee and the national board, and corresponded regularly with the BPW staff. Exhausted after sixteen hours en route from Frankfurt to New York, and another two hours of waiting in New York in 90-degree heat, she returned to bad news. Viola had suffered a heart attack during her absence.

Although it was already mid-afternoon on Sunday, she called Isla and Helen to meet her at BPW headquarters where for three hours they worked on correspondence and made arrangements for the Miami convention. With 2,000 already registered, it was sure to be the biggest in history. Her convention was going to be a celebration of those women, all they had done and all they were going to do.

After unpacking and sleeping for a few hours, she caught a 3:00 A.M. flight for Corpus Christi. She arrived to find her mother breathing oxygen and sitting in a lounge chair. Although there was little Marguerite could do, she stayed until Friday. Viola was recovering but she would never be well again. In October, she would write Billye Russell, a Houston friend: "Mother is not well. . . there is nothing that medical science can do but fight to keep the end postponed; for as the doctor tells me, 'your mother's heart is just worn out.' "

Just days before the convention in Miami and the end of Marguerite's term, BPW received a favorable ruling from Internal Revenue. The foundation would be exempt from paying federal income tax; it would serve as a vehicle for raising money for research and education; contributions would be tax deductible by donors. The foundation would hold title to the property and provide suitable headquarters for the federation. In a year, the tentative ruling would become permanent. BPW would save a lot of money and be able to raise more. All she had to do now was go to the convention and enjoy it.

For Marguerite, the lavish Miami Beach convention began on Wednesday, June 27, with an all-day executive committee meeting at their convention hotel, the elegant new Fontainebleau. On Saturday, Vice-President Richard Nixon, en route to the Philippines, paid a surprise visit to a board of directors meeting. Photographed at the microphone, laughing with the vice-president, Marguerite's picture appeared in newspapers all over the country. In a *Miami Hearld* story, reporter Arline Thompson called BPW's president "A tall dynamic Washington woman with the fast, summarizing mind of a lawyer, the enthusiasm of a housewife, the carriage of a model, and the appearance of a smart career girl."

The Sunday night program opened on a theme of "achievement jubilee," with a parade of silk flags from every state setting the tone of the up-beat, patriotic affair. Marguerite wanted each of the 3,000 women packing the vast Miami Beach Auditorium to be as proud as she was. They had more members than ever, over 170,000, up 5,000 in one year. The federation had entered a unique moment in its history.

Exhilarated with what they had done, she painted an optimistic picture of the next twenty years. The Foundation Research Center would become "one of the world's most important sources of information," providing large grants for research, vocational guidance, studying the laws. It would become an invaluable resource to industry, government, and labor unions. BPW would offer courses "on television, on recordings, and in person" to prepare women to enter the work force. More women would be in public office, accepted as a matter of course. BPW's legislative experts would be consulted by all branches of government. World peace organizations would seek the advice of a new generation of trained women. By 1976, working women would be getting equal pay for equal work. Women were indispensable to the country's prosperity; it couldn't be denied.

Her speech ended with a reprimand and a challenge. Since women out-voted men, why didn't they take advantage of their political power? Why did they go on avoiding influence and responsibility? In the fight for suffrage, Susan B. Anthony and Elizabeth Cady Stanton had shown them how to work together. It was time for action, and BPW was an action organization.

For Marguerite, the festivities were marred only by an undercurrent of criticism of the foundation. At the business session on Monday, Dr. Margaret Cussler, the first recipient of a foundation research grant, was received with enthusiasm. But when Marguerite followed Cussler's remarks with a triumphant explanation of the foundation's tax-exempt status, she was astonished at the sprinkling of ill-informed questions amid the congratulations. Most of the women had never heard of a tax-exempt foundation. What authority did she have, they wanted to know, to transfer their headquarters money to "this new organization"? Why had the foundation been set up without being submitted to the convention? Did tax exemption mean they would have to stop lobbying for ERA?

It was simple, Marguerite explained patiently. The foundation was a holding corporation. More importantly, it was a way to double the federation's money since the foundation (unlike the politically active federation) could solicit tax-deductible contributions to carry out the educational and research work of the federation.

In consideration for receiving headquarters offices, plus a tax-exempt status bonus for its money, the federation would assume building operation maintenance costs — a bargain indeed. The officers elected by the federation were the officers of the foundation. The federation office remained in complete control. They were free to continue lobbying; it was not being changed.

What she didn't say was something only a few of them were farsighted enough to realize, that they had pushed ahead because they feared delays and confusion such as had long encumbered the Lena Madesin Phillips Building Fund. They had seen an opportunity to move the federation ahead, and they had taken it. It would have taken years to persuade the membership to undertake the establishment of a foundation — and to assuage the insecurities of women who knew nothing of taxes and finance.

Finally, her patience worn thin, Marguerite handed the gavel to vice-president Hazel Palmer and stepped closer to the microphone. Moving rapidly, her head pushed forward, she looked even bigger than she was.

She didn't know what she was going to say until she began. "We have given you the Foundation without subtracting one iota from the purpose for which you gave these funds to establish a national headquarters — I have no apology to make. NO APOLOGY. I am PROUD of it."

The BPW and the foundation were going to move women forward. She had never been prouder.

[5]

Rising Tide

"**W**hy," Marguerite asked Louis in a letter written just after the convention, "do people so complicate their living? . . . When the routine of office begins to crowd in upon one, the mind's eye turns back to the outdoors, to riding down the channel with the wind whipping through the hair, to the smell of salt air, to the interest in bird life."

The remembered pleasure of her trip to Bird Island with Louis signaled a new time in Marguerite's life. She relished the freedom of setting her own schedule, renewing old friendships, writing long personal letters, enjoying untroubled nights and weekends with Harry. As she wrote Sara Creech a few weeks after the convention, "It seems heavenly to awaken in the morning without that crushing load of realization that there is so much more to be done that I can hope to do. . . My law work is something of a joy and an anchor. It will become a pleasure, now that it need not be mixed up with something else all day long." She wrote on the same theme to Genevieve Riley.

I can close up my desk at 5:30 and go home and without
pressure and without guilt, spend the evening with Harry — just
broiling a steak, listening to the television, going to bed early. In
fact, I am developing a new complex — of just wanting to do
nothing every evening. Too lackadaisical to want to go out at all!

She summed up her feelings of the past six months in her answer to the faithful Harry Crozier's annual holiday letter: "It has
been a great relief to escape from the swift current of twenty-four-
hour pressure. The two years were wonderfully productive of progress, and gave me much to remember. Glad I did it: glad it is over."

But beneath the relief she was still troubled by an urgency that
told her the time had come to step up the fight for women's rights.
Like some others, she sensed discord brewing beneath the quiet
surface of American life.

In 1954, during the first year of Marguerite's presidency of
BPW, the Supreme Court had ruled in *Brown* v. *Board of Education of
Topeka* that separate education for black children was not equal education and launched a civil rights movement that would challenge
the country's definition of democracy and produce the most radical
reassessment of "equal rights" since the Civil War. Late in 1955, a
seamstress named Rosa Parks sat down in the front of a segregated
bus in Montgomery, Alabama, rather than stand in the back after
a long day's work. Around that incident, Martin Luther King, a
young Baptist minister, organized the year-long economic boycott
that became the first success of an exploding black rights movement.

Immediately, Marguerite was interested in the orderly, non-
violent tactics of the fledgling movement. In October 1956, less
than a year after the bus boycott began in Montgomery, she wrote
lawyer Billye Russell in Houston, encouraging her interest in ERA
and concluding: "If women had the sand that some of our minority
men's groups have, or mixed [men and women] minority groups,
we would have this amendment enacted in short time."

After several years of watching women refuse to heed the lessons of black activism, she would sound even more impatient, as
she did in a letter to BPW associate, Helen Kokes.

It is almost unthinkable that women themselves do not have the
conviction and determination which is evidenced every day in our
newspapers, of the racial groups, who are getting their rights de-

clared in every shape and form. Our own sex is indifferent; doesn't want to be bothered being informed or thinking about such hard facts, I fear. If we could get all women together, the ERA would pass Congress with a breeze.

Her belief in aggressive political action for women grew through the 1950s and early 1960s. At the same time, her understanding of "women's issues" was expanding beyond the narrow concerns of professional women. Now her speeches argued for public child care, equal pay for working women, and job training for older women — as well as uniform jury service and ERA.

By the mid–1950s, Marguerite had stopped blaming women for their own problems. Bad laws, obsolete customs, and institutions that discriminated had to share the responsibility. In a 1955 interview with the *Los Angeles Times,* she called on business to raise its sights, acknowledge the contributions women made to the economy, and provide equal opportunity. Speaking to the Louisville BPW Club a month later, she asked for a much deeper commitment on the part of women themselves. The advancement of women was a spiritual challenge as well as an economic one. Enlightened women had a responsibility to all women.

Even as she felt the country begin to move in the direction she longed for, she sensed trouble in BPW. The leadership lacked unity and resolve. There were still rumblings against the foundation. President Hazel Palmer and executive director Rose Liebbrand seemed to sympathize with the complaints.

Marguerite's growing displeasure with the "ladies' club" style of some BPW clubs shows in a letter she wrote to Grace Daniels (a BPW colleague with whom she was often outspoken in her criticism) upon her return from the Rhode Island state convention in the spring of 1957.

> . . . I have come to where "I HATE SKITS." They are so boring and pointless. . . I cut my proposed talk exactly in half; let them see my laying aside one page after another. . . After an asinine skit, I just couldn't steam into anything and put it across. . . this was a time when I let my disgust defeat my own "message."

By the fall of 1957, the new officers had purchased a huge red brick building on Massachusetts Avenue to house the federation and the foundation. By then, there were indications of disharmony between Marguerite and BPW's current leadership. Although a brass plaque on the building identified her as the foundation's "incorporating president," she sat in the audience unacknowledged when the building was dedicated in September. Her irritation shows in a letter to a BPW friend in Alabama:

> . . . The dedication is over. It was wonderful to realize at last there is a national headquarters. The former national presidents had their names called out for introductions from among the audience where they had found places to sit. . . Speakers on the occasion were all men: Secy of Labor, Chairman of U.S. Chamber of Commerce who immediately afterward went on Television against Equal Rights.

A week later, when her loyal D.C. Club named her the "Professional Woman of the Year," her acceptance speech included a tribute to Lucy Moore, the ideal woman boss. Moore's example and awards like this one proved, she insisted, that "women do support women." Although her diary calls it a *red letter day*, a note written to Vi the next afternoon displays both her discouragement with the national BPW organization — and her abiding happiness at home.

> It is more satisfying to be honored, when you are not holding such a high position as national president, by the home clubs. . . I am of course dropping off BPW work as rapidly as I can.
> Harry has put one of those little packaged ham butts weighing about 3 or 4 pounds on to simmer, with peppercorns, comino seed, bay leaf, and it smells wonderful. And I took time to put an apple pie in the oven. . .

Free of BPW responsibilities, Marguerite had time for old friends like the Scotts, the Hunttings, and Louise Wright. She worked on Flake and Rawalt genealogy, spent time with Harry. But she must have missed the involvement, and she sounds lonely in a letter she wrote to Sarah Hughes in October, ". . . come again for another of those little visits which we used to have in the apartment." At seventy-three, Harry was listless, complaining of an annoying numbness in his hands.

On October 16, 1958, Marguerite wrote the last of her birthday letters to Viola. On April 2, her mother died at home in her sleep and was buried two days later on Good Friday. Ironically, Marguerite, who wanted so much for herself, had wished also to be more like her mother, who had wanted so little. Now she knew she would never be any more like her than she was. There was no way to make up for the fact that her own life had been so much fuller than she thought her mother's had been. Now she had to give up the hope of repaying Viola for all she had given.

Her letters in the following months repeat a refrain: Viola had "always been happy and sunny." To a Rawalt cousin, she added: "It was a sad day for us, yet coming at the time of Easter Resurrection we were reminded of eternal life."

For the rest of Marguerite's life, Good Friday would be a deeply personal day for remembering those she loved who were dead. On Saturday, March 29, 1975, she wrote her good friend, Isla Benedick, "Good Friday, yesterday, is always an emotional day for me, for mother was buried on Good Friday. I think of family, and of my role in it, think of the crucifixion; think of Harry."

Just two months after Viola's death, a situation developed in BPW so unpleasant that Marguerite's gravest premonitions paled by comparison. By accident, Dorothy Brimacombe, national treasurer, discovered a letter from Internal Revenue proposing to revoke the foundation's tax-exempt status, apparently because Hazel Palmer was trying to deed the BPW headquarters from the foundation to the federation.

Brimacombe and first vice-president Grace Daniels were irate. What was wrong with Hazel, they wondered. She was a lawyer. She had no authority to do what she had done. Something had happened to Hazel, they told themselves, and blamed executive director Rose Liebbrand. Without consulting anyone else, Liebbrand and Hazel had ordered new lawyers to draw up the deed in May. Indignant and astonished, Daniels insisted that everyone involved, including Liebbrand, Hazel, and the lawyers she had hired, meet in Washington with Marguerite and the lawyers who had set up the foundation.[1]

On Sunday, June 22, the day before the much-dreaded meeting, Marguerite returned from a BPW state convention in New Hampshire to find Harry in bed. He had fallen in town and injured a hip.

Early the next morning, she took Harry to Walter Reed Hospital in time to arrive only a few minutes late for the meeting at BPW headquarters. She found the national officers plus Rose Liebbrand and five lawyers already in conference. John Boice and South Trimble were there to explain their role in Palmer's attempt to deed the building to the federation, an act which was contrary to the terms of the foundation charter and bound to endanger its tax status. Allan Higgins, Eugene Thomas, and Cecil Kilpatrick came to represent the law firms that helped Marguerite set up the foundation.

By mid-afternoon the facts were clear. Although Palmer's lawyers had advised her against deeding the building to the federation, they had drawn up the deed at the insistence of Liebbrand. In doing so, one of them had spoken with people at IRS, who promptly sent the warning that Brimacombe discovered early in June.

Now they were all blaming one another. Hazel denied any intention of undermining the foundation and agreed to sit down with Allan Higgins on the spot and draft a letter disclaimer to IRS.

Marguerite made her own position clear in a nine-page letter to the officers of the federation (who also made up the foundation's board of trustees). She was indignant and shocked by the unprofessional behavior of Hazel Palmer and her lawyers. She was horrified that the foundation's existence was being threatened by "misrepresentations, twisting of facts, insinuations. . . or fraudulent intent."

"I could have wept," she added before ending the letter with a veiled threat. Unless Hazel and the other members of the executive committee who were nominees for election did everything possible to alleviate the trouble at IRS and spoke strongly in favor of the Foundation and Research Center at the national convention in Seattle, she would expose the whole episode on the floor of the convention.

She had done what she felt she had to do, but the unpleasantness rankled. The knowledge that what she stood for and believed in had been surreptitiously attacked and deliberately betrayed by people she trusted for reasons she did not understand left her with an almost paranoid heartsickness. The knowledge that she might not have been able to defend what she had created, the horror that the foundation could have been lost and with it the work and trust of all the women who had believed in it and made it possible — she wouldn't get over it easily.

When the time came, Palmer spoke enthusiastically about

plans for the foundation in her address to the national convention, and — as Marguerite wrote Sarah Hughes later — "on the record, all was fine."

Grace Daniels was elected president and recent problems went unmentioned. Off the record, Marguerite added: "I was out there to protect interests; a story unbelievable developed two weeks before Biennial. . . . Grace Daniels and Dorthy Brimacombe saved the day by tying right into the mess they found. . . . the most astounding and depressing revelations I ever want to know in BPW."

Despite her disillusionment, Marguerite began working on a forty-year history of BPW, and continued her travels to regional and state conventions. But, for the most part, the next two years were devoted to Harry. Both the unhappiness of BPW and her growing concern for Harry's health prompted a gloomy letter to Vi late in the summer:

> I begin to realize that all of us have relatively short years of being active, ahead of us. . . . as life continues so rushed in every way, and I have come more and more to resent it, and to feel tired of it all. . . . And these thoughts remind me soberly that I am not so full of energy and ability to continue the drive as I used to be. And we are all getting older at the same rate. If we don't seize what time is left for a little living, we won't have any good times together.

"Why this?" she concluded, "[I] hardly know."

Soon afterwards, they learned that Harry was suffering from an enlarged aorta and that an operation to replace the artery might prolong his life. Without hesitation, Harry decided to risk it. No need for Marguerite to go home and think about it, he said. He wanted a few more years with her.

On September 11, two days after the operation, Marguerite wrote Grace Daniels: "My sweetheart has pulled successfully through a second night. Each hour and half day and day counts now. . . . I am at this point living for the value of each hour — as you know."

For months, letters to acquaintances as well as close friends recorded "my sweetheart's progress." On Thanksgiving, perhaps feeling the awesome weight of Harry's need for her, she wrote her niece, Louise, "I can imagine how busy you are all day; that is hard work of the variety I am not trained to take. I can face trying conferences, telephones, people pulling at me — but children and their constant needs would be out of my capacity."

After a trip with Harry to Corpus Christi for Christmas, Marguerite dug in with Grace Daniels to secure the future of the foundation, to clear up the trouble at IRS, to make the tax exemption permanent and final. Gradually she became more active in Zonta International, a service organization for businesswomen to which she had belonged since the 1940s. Every year, she and others struggled to come up with something women could do to break the logjam on ERA.

Still, for now, Harry remained at the center of her life. A year after his operation, she wrote Vi: "Harry is well. Begins the day by breakfast with me. Then the Dave Garroway [*Today*] show. . . . He does the shopping thru the day, gets something enticing to eat and plans the supper which is practically ready when I get home." A few months later, to Margie Neal she added: "Harry is well — and more serene than I. . . . He is still the fulcrum of my existence."

Lyndon B. Johnson had come to Washington from Texas a few years after Marguerite. He too had gotten there the hard way, propelled by monumental energy and a fierce desire to control his own destiny. He knew first hand the marginal poverty of poor whites and farmers. As a teacher in a rural high school, he saw even greater deprivation among Mexican Americans. He wanted to do something about those things — and he wanted to get to the top.

Marguerite met Johnson in 1933, when he was a young aide to her congressman, Richard Kleberg. By then, he was already a devotee of Franklin Roosevelt, his thinking marked for life by the Depression and the New Deal. Marguerite and Lyndon Johnson had many friends in common and over the years saw one another frequently at Texas State Society meetings and other gatherings of Texans and Democrats. Although she admired Johnson, she was more at ease with his wife, Lady Bird.

Three years after they met, Marguerite was secure in her job at IRS and Johnson had won a seat in Congress. In 1948, he was elected to the Senate. Five years later, his unwavering drive had made him a powerful, though not universally popular, Senate majority leader.

Within a few years he was running for president. Without a machine, without much national support, he reminded Marguerite of Pat Neff. Still resenting the political establishment's resistance to his southwestern ways, he agreed to run for vice-president with John F. Kennedy, a charismatic northeastern Catholic. That they were a strange team, Marguerite agreed with her brothers: but, she insisted, Johnson was a Texan and, though a northern Catholic, John Kennedy was better than Richard Nixon.

In August 1960, before the election in November, she wrote her nephew Wally:

> The Republican nominee would be far worse than another Eisenhower — he is Tricky Dicky of the first magnitude. His entire record is one of opportunism. I cannot feel that there is the remotest sincerity in him, and that clearly he would be the tool of the highest bidder, which is always "big business." Therefore the choice leaves me no choice whatever. I stay with the party. Lyndon Johnson will still have a commanding position in the party and in national affairs. I have observed the open-mindedness of Kennedy, his getting facts from big brains and then making up his own mind. The fear of Vatican domination is not the big bugbear it was years ago I feel, and hope most voters will agree. That has been exaggerated, too.

Because the Hatch Act prevented federal employees from participating in political campaigns, she could do very little for the Kennedy–Johnson effort. When India Edwards asked her to work for Johnson before the Democratic Convention, all she could do was call close friends around the country. Although she could lend her support to organizational meetings in Washington, her name could not appear on campaign literature. Still, when Kennedy and Johnson were elected in November 1960, she received a letter of appreciation from Mrs. Johnson who credited the success of the Democrats in Texas to "many good Texas friends like yourself whose support 'hatched up' the victory."

With Johnson's election, Marguerite recognized her last chance for a political appointment. Since January 1958, she had been assistant head of the civil division at Internal Revenue. She had no reason to expect to be promoted to the top position; that was reserved for a man. At sixty-five, she thought Johnson's election to the vice-presidency gave her one more chance to do something new and worthwhile.

By January, she was deeply mired in an effort to get herself appointed to the Foreign Claims Settlement Commission, a presidentially appointed body that examined and settled claims made by Americans when their property was seized in foreign countries. She felt her tax work at Internal Revenue qualified her to make such decisions and work with large amounts of money. As an appointed commissioner rather than a civil servant, she could be involved in party politics, give speeches, use her organization contacts for the Democratic Party. Harry was healthy again, and she was ready for something new.

At 9:30 A.M. on January 16, Ralph Dungan, assistant to the director of the Democratic National Committee, ushered her into his office. Looking at her resumé and letters of recommendation, he seemed astonished by all she had done. Things were going well between them; and then he said, "And now for the $64,000-question. How old are you?" She told him the truth and saw the astonishment on his face — and knew it was over. Now, they thought she was too old.

Although forewarned by all her experience and intuition, she was disappointed when the appointments to the Foreign Claims Commission were made — all of them men. A few days after getting the news, she wrote her brothers a rare letter of complaint about her work: "It is good to have a good job continuing, but I am mighty tired of the constant volume and strain of it."

A month or so after the appointments were made, there was an unexpected call from a Johnson aide in the White House. "Who," he wanted to know, "is this woman lawyer who got on the Foreign Claims Settlement Commission?" Didn't Marguerite know her, he asked; her name was Lavern Dilweg. Marguerite had never heard of Dilweg, who — like all the others — turned out to be a man, a former congressman from Wisconsin.

On Sunday, March 19, at a Texas State Society luncheon at the Mayflower Hotel, Lyndon Johnson greeted Marguerite, "What," he asked, "happened to that appointment you wanted?" She smiled, knowing such things had to be said with a smile, "A man got it." Although Johnson urged her to try for something else, by then she had already made up her mind. She had tried off and on for twenty years to get the kind of appointment available to successful male lawyers. She had done all she knew how to do — and failed.

If Marguerite hid her indignation, Margie Neal did not. Three years later, in May 1964, she was still railing against the Kennedy–Johnson administration's unfairness to her friend and to all women:

> . . . I am pretty mad that the administration doesn't seem to be doing anything for you. I realize he (Lyndon) is making "hay" while appointing big women to office. . . that is not you personally. You have done enough in emancipating women throughout the country that *this* administration, if not those before, should have proudly proclaimed it to the nation. . . . I am so proud of you and wouldn't Governor Neff be proud if he were alive!

Marguerite and her friends were not the only people disgruntled with the new administration's poor record for appointing women. John Kennedy had attracted many activist women to his campaign by promising to promote equal rights and appoint women to high positions in government. Women celebrated his victory and waited, as always, expecting that promises made to them would be kept. By mid-March only nine women had been appointed to significant positions — with none in the cabinet and none on the White House staff. Doris Fleeson of the *Washington Evening Star* summed it up, "it appears that for women the New Frontiers are the Old Frontiers."

Eleanor Roosevelt agreed. Having supported Adlai Stevenson in the primaries, she came to the Kennedy camp late and reluctantly. Nevertheless, she remained a political symbol too powerful and respected to be ignored; when she requested a meeting with the young president, it was granted immediately. "Someone," she told the press, should present a list of capable women to "Mr. Kennedy" because, she said, "men have to be reminded that women exist. This is still a man's world." On March 13, 1961, they met at the White House and she told him of her concern and handed him a three-page list of women qualified for high level jobs.

Within a few weeks of Mrs. Roosevelt's meeting with Kennedy, Marguerite wrote Minnie Maffett in Texas, complaining of the administration's poor record and adding, "It is time for another national meeting such as the one in 1944 or 1945, at the White House — you were there I well remember, for I was deeply impressed."

Although they themselves didn't know it yet, a few crucial women had begun to think the same thing: it was time for women leaders to get together and start telling the truth to the men in power. That idea was about to launch a women's movement that none of them could have predicted. Believing in 1961, as she had in 1945, that both women and government had a responsibility to themselves and to each other, Eleanor Roosevelt would become the symbolic hub of a radically ambitious and highminded experiment in democracy — in which the disadvantaged would attempt to get the government to willingly reform itself to their advantage.

Esther Peterson was another essential ingredient in the stew that was brewing. She was Eleanor Roosevelt's good friend and, as director of the Women's Bureau at the Labor Department, one of the highest-ranking women so far appointed by the new administration. With roots deep in the labor movement, she came to the administration with an established reputation for commitment to the welfare of working women — and opposition to the Equal Rights Amendment.

In an April 16 interview with *Washington Post* reporter Marie Smith, Peterson confirmed her opposition to ERA and spoke of plans for putting together a committee of the "best brains in the country" to try to resolve the ERA conflict and find out what women needed most.

Marguerite was leery of Peterson's "summit discussions" and chagrined that BPW had invited her to speak at the national convention in July. Nevertheless, when Peterson announced a May 5 meeting of women leaders at the Women's Bureau, Marguerite went to represent NAWL.

In later years, Peterson could claim to have been awed by the tall, outgoing Marguerite whom she knew by reputation for her strong opinions and influence in national organizations. "She was," she remembers, "so brilliant and had all those degrees and everything; and, although I was opposed to it, I knew we couldn't disregard ERA." [2]

Despite whatever trepidation she may have felt, she approached Marguerite after the meeting and offered to discuss their differences. Marguerite's reply was to the point: "I can not understand how the Women's Bureau can be opposed to ERA when the candidate, now President, John Kennedy gave such a candid endorsement of it. The members of the outstanding groups to which I belong are distinctly puzzled and look to me for an explanation."

A letter Marguerite wrote the next day to Rebecca Bowles Hawkins, president of NAWL, ends with another description of Esther Peterson.

> . . . When one woman asked why, if Government contracts demanded no discrimination on race, they could not also interdict discrimination on sex, [Peterson] replied "Frankly, I think racial discrimination must come first!" But she didn't say that discrimination on sex should ever come. I do not intend to fight a duel, but do think we should stand firm on our ground and speak out.

The letter to Hawkins gives other details of the meeting as well:

> . . . The labor representatives were principally interested in problems. . . such as "day-care"; effects of automation; retraining for new jobs; etc. But two or three times, the mention of "protective" laws was made, with counter mention of the Equal Rights Amendment. No discussion developed and I remained silent.

Soon Marguerite had new worries over the convention coming up in a few weeks in Chicago. President Fannie Hardy, an Arkansan with political ambitions, had invited Orval Faubus, Arkansas's notorious segregationist governor, to give the convention's opening address. How, their critics asked, could an organization committed to equality honor a man like Faubus, who just a few years before had used the Arkansas National Guard to keep nine black children out of Little Rock's all-white Central High School?

By then a spontaneous black rights movement was sweeping the country, dominating the news and spearheading a countercultural revolution that many activist women were going to join. In February, sit-ins at a segregated lunch counter in Greensboro, North Carolina, had triggered demonstrations across the country. A decade that would disrupt all the old alignments had begun.

Although Marguerite saw parallels between racial and sexual discrimination and immediately recognized the brilliance of civil rights strategy, her identification with that movement would remain slim. Unlike many younger women who would identify with both black rights and the women's rights movement, her deepest identification was not with oppression but with womanhood — in all its strengths and weaknesses.

Her behavior in the Faubus incident was characteristic and carefully thought out; what she most wanted was to protect the federation from criticism and bad publicity. But her friends, Isabella Jones and Libby Sachar, were deeply disturbed on another level. For them, there was an inherent similarity in all discrimination. They remembered an early attempt to disassociate the first BPW clubs that took in black women and wondered where the membership really stood on racial discrimination.[3]

When the time came, Faubus spoke briefly while demonstrators carried signs that said BUSINESS WOMEN, WHY ENDORSE JIM CROW? The next day, Isabella Jones asked the meeting to strike Faubus's speech from the official record. Although the motion failed, the debate gave Libby Sachar a chance to denounce Faubus to the press. For two days, newspaper and television reporters dramatized the conflict.

Amid the turmoil, Marguerite received a secondhand message from Fannie Hardy — something about being hostess to Esther Peterson who was scheduled to speak the next morning. She was arriving that night and someone had to look after her, see that she got there, had what she needed, and take her to breakfast. Since Marguerite knew Peterson and no one else did, Hardy wanted her to do it.

Sometime after midnight, Marguerite swept into the suite she was sharing with Washington friends, Frances Myers, Vera Emery, and Thelma Pease. "Listen," she said, "you are going to have to get up early and help me clean up and give me one of these rooms so I can entertain Esther Peterson for breakfast." Long accustomed to their friend's "wheeling and dealing," they agreed and went back to sleep.

Thanks to her "quartermaster corps," when Esther Peterson showed up on time the next morning, the rooms were in order and breakfast was on the way up. They were going to try to bridge a gap older than they were.

Esther Peterson arrived wearing a nautical-looking cotton dress trimmed in navy. As if ready for work, she had pushed her sleeves up to her elbows; the large orchid sent by BPW perched incongruously on her shoulder.

Bringing out the notes for her speech, she declared: "I've come to face my enemies and I'm scared to death. I've come to say why I believe what I believe. I intend to uphold my views on these labor standards laws." She was planning to do what Marguerite feared most, make a pitch for protective labor laws that would widen the long-standing breach between ERA supporters and women from the labor movement.

Almost thirty years of legal and organizational work had taught Marguerite to look for the point at which two opponents could agree. When at her best, she raised compromise to the level of art; and, when the stakes were high, her patience was limitless. "You will not make any friends with that speech," she told her guest. "I wish we could find some other basis. . . something we all agree on. I hope you won't go so strong on some of what I see here."

Finally, they were working together, talking at last about the problems that had kept two large groups of women apart. Each knew where she stood and where she could compromise.

It would be years before ERA helped women at the bottom, Peterson said. Cases would have to go to court and there would be long delays. In the meantime, the women she was talking about would lose the little protection they had from laws that make it illegal for them to work long hours at jobs that are too hard for them — and poorly paid.

Marguerite held her ground. In the long run, ERA would be good for all women. "Protective" laws kept women from being promoted and from getting the best jobs. If they couldn't work overtime, they couldn't rise to the top. The laws themselves were discriminatory. It was discrimination, not ERA, that kept women at the bottom. ERA was the quickest way to get rid of discrimination.

They saw it differently, and Peterson said she would oppose ERA until there were strong minimum wage and equal pay laws. Her voice rising, she added, "I've always thought ERA women weren't with us on the equal pay question — didn't care about it. Some of you have businesses and you yourselves pay women less than men. As soon as you come along and support us on that and see that your poor sisters and your black sisters are taken care of, I'll join you."

Time was running out, and they were not going to agree on the priorities: which should come first, ERA or equal pay legislation.

Sorting out their disagreements and looking for common ground, they had laid the foundation for a lasting — though often adversarial — relationship. Years later, Peterson would say, "With that conversation, Marguerite Rawalt introduced me to the thinking of women I had no contact with. I really didn't know what they thought. I just knew we had always disagreed. But she accepted me. She was an honest woman, who could see broader issues — maybe the only one — and she listened to me and my reasons for why I thought the way I did. She helped me to draw my circle wider." The relationship worked both ways. Marguerite's own already wide circle was about to widen again.[4]

Without time to change her script, Peterson ad-libbed important changes in her speech, stressing her hopes for women in the future rather than BPW's failure to support blue-collar women.

Except for her encounter with Peterson and meetings with old friends, the Chicago convention had been a bitter one for Marguerite. BPW's stubborn political inertia and naivete' grew more and more frustrating.

In addition to the uproar over major speakers who opposed ERA and civil rights, there was a bitter squabble over changing the national officers' term from two years to one. The change was voted on despite fierce opposition from Marguerite and others who thought the longer term necessary to anyone with serious ambitions to lead the organization.

To Marguerite, BPW seemed to be moving further and further away from the future she and her executive committee had envisioned. No longer able to deny it, she told her friends, "I left the convention with bile in my stomach."

Libby Sachar left the convention a day early, "sick in the heart." She too was convinced that BPW would never become a progressive political force for women. She and Esther Peterson shared a cab to the airport and took the same flight home. Sachar poured out her disappointment. Although she had been president of the New Jersey BPW and served on Rawalt's board, she wasn't used to working with large groups. She didn't like this kind of frustration. She didn't understand the political myopia of women afraid to act and speak out even when the moral choice was clear — as it had been in the Faubus incident. They were scared to death they might look unladylike.

Peterson, speaking out of long and thoughtful experience, had a different view of things. "Libby," she said, "I don't think you understand what a leader is. A leader moves ahead but not so fast that the others can't keep up."

Understanding Peterson's definition of leadership, Libby Sachar went home, resigned from BPW, and devoted her energies to her family and a growing law practice. She was an idealist, a thinker. In the future, she would make her contribution as an individual. A few years later, when Marguerite asked her to help get the National Organization for Women off the ground, she sent a check. "Maybe I was wrong," she says now, "but after 1961, I left it to Marguerite and the others." [5]

For the next few months, Marguerite was busy with tax work. She played canasta at night, celebrated Harry's birthday with friends, and plugged away at organizational jobs. In a letter to her nephew Wally, she complained of an emptiness in her life. "Until this day," she added, "when September comes round, I feel the urge to enroll in school for another course — something that lets my mind reach into new fields."

With retirement just a few years off, she was discouraged with politics and club work, tired and close to depression. Her letters overflowed with complaints about the ignorance and apathy of women. "Too many fine clubs are not more than do-gooders. . . . too few women realize the realities. . . . We have to find new channels, and KNOW what we are doing. . . . And I think that the sands are running out on our growth unless we do act with VISION into the future."

Suddenly, in December, a surprise came amid the gloom and sent her mood skyrocketing for the holidays. She was about to be catapulted into a new career for which — unknown even to herself — she had been preparing all her life.

Late on the evening of December 7, 1961, after months of silence, Esther Peterson called to ask if she would be part of a group to study the legal status of women. "Of course," she said, wondering at the lateness of the call. She had agreed to do something like that at the Chicago meeting in July.

By Thursday, December 14, it was in all the papers. By executive order, John Kennedy was creating a Commission on the Status of Women to study economic and legal conditions and make recommendations directly to the president. Eleanor Roosevelt would chair the commission, the first of its kind ever to be established in any country, a handpicked group of eleven men and thirteen women, including cabinet members and representatives from industry, education, labor, and women's church groups — as well as a few independent activists and experts. Marguerite was one of them.

As soon as she saw the list, she knew she was the only ERA supporter included. She was elated just the same.

One of her deepest beliefs — that people can come together and resolve even their bitterest differences — was about to be tested. She supposed she owed the appointment to Esther Peterson, but Lyndon Johnson and his special assistant, Liz Carpenter, had been instrumental in setting up the commission. Both knew her qualifications.

Although the president hoped to avoid a confrontation over ERA, Peterson had insisted on a pro-ERA voice. It would be a mistake, she insisted, and defeat the purpose of the commission to ignore the viewpoint of women like Marguerite.

"My philosophy," she explained later, "was to get the power structure together and make some changes. We needed to take an objective look at the Equal Rights Amendment. We also needed to burst the bounds of the narrow and anachronistic thinking that having a Women's Bureau in the Department of Labor 'took care' of women. Members had to be part of the power structure. . . . I didn't want to leave out any important group." [6]

Still elated after Christmas, Marguerite wrote BPW president, Katherine Peden: "This is news. It is progress. It has been in the making for some months, beginning one might say with the visit of Mrs. Roosevelt to the White House. . . . I am proud to be the 'lawyer' on a 25-person team."

Deeply and personally disappointed in BPW, she couldn't resist comparing its accomplishments with her hopes for the commission: "On this commission, I am sure it will not be necessary for me to insist upon a survey, upon information first, as to what laws exist which discriminate. This was my dream for the BPW Foundation to do — to be the first to assemble, to get money and make a nationwide survey, of what laws do exist in all the states."

Spurred by new dreams, she wrote many friends. The idea that local organizations should provide the commission (or some authorized agency) with surveys of discriminatory laws in the states stayed high on her list for a long, long time. Eventually, she would have to admit that the traditional women's clubs were not to be the prime movers in a new wave of feminism.

Although it would be two months before the commission met and almost two years before its work was done, it was announced with words that account for Marguerite's enthusiasm. The executive order creating the commission emphasized many of the things that concerned her most — employment and wages, taxation, labor laws, legal and political rights, education and training.

A few days after the president announced that he was going to make the government a "showcase of equality," the Civil Service Commission ordered all government departments and agencies to give specific reasons in cases where women were bypassed in favor of men for federal jobs and promotions. CSC Chairman John Macy was appointed to the president's commission and instructed to investigate the need for reform in the Civil Service — particularly regarding a regulation that allowed agencies to specify by sex when requesting names from CSC's register of qualified applicants.

Not all the signs were that good, and Marguerite knew where the problems lay. The commission was by its nature conservative, inclined to a protective attitude toward women, and opposition to ERA was entrenched. Katherine Ellickson, an AFL–CIO employee adamantly opposed to ERA, was to be the commission's executive secretary.

Despite hints of problems to come, Marguerite was riding a tide of optimism. A week before Christmas, she and Harry had a cocktail party and decorated the house with two Christmas trees. Snowed in the next weekend she went on a cooking spree and invited Louise Wright and her new husband, George Stewart, in for a pork roast dinner.

Her holiday letter to her family describes a white Christmas and a traditional celebration with the Scott family, then ends solemnly: "In today's world with the Communist shadow, it is more important than ever to remember that Christ was born and that we are Christians. It's the only thing we can cling to as we contemplate nuclear possibilities."

Instinctively, Marguerite sensed that the commission signaled the beginning of a new and demanding time for her. Spurred by fresh possibilities for action, she considered retiring early to work full-time for the cause to which she had already committed so much. After Christmas, she wrote Margie Neal about it.

> Margie, I wish I had the courage to quit working for the government salary and spend my time on things that carry no salary. That has always been what most would call 'my weakness.' I am committed to writing the history of the National Federation. . . . I want to write the family genealogy and story. . . . then there are things like this Commission on which I would like to be free to put much time and thought. . . . want to do so much more. How can anybody in the world say they wonder what to do with their spare time? Or that life has nothing to intrigue them? All I fear is that the ailments of the body will overtake and stop.

The members of the President's Commission on the Status of Women met for a swearing-in ceremony in the Fish Room of the White House at 10:00 A.M. on Monday, February 12, 1962. President Kennedy came and stayed just long enough to tell them they were dealing with a "matter of great national and international importance."

After lunch in the White House dining room, the group was bused across town to the Maryland Avenue office building where they began immediately to discuss federal employment practices, the first on a list of six topics chosen for them by the Women's Bureau.

The long day ended with a reception given by Vice-President and Mrs. Johnson at The Elms, the house they had bought from Washington's flamboyant hostess Pearl Mesta. Standing in front of a fire in the living room, Johnson welcomed the commission, praised Mrs. Roosevelt, and coined a feminist slogan that has often been attributed to other people: "I believe a woman's place is not only in the home, but in the House, and in the Senate and at the conference table." Nancy Tribush, star of the musical *Bye Bye Birdie*, provided the entertainment, ending her performance with *It's Great to Be a Woman*, dedicated to the Johnson's two daughters, who had come in from school to meet the members of the commission.

Soon Marguerite was swamped with invitations to speak on the status of women and the work of the commission. On February 19, she told the Zonta Club of Hagerstown, Maryland, about the commission — and began a "speaking tour" that was to last more than ten years. Before it was over, she had talked about "the legal status of women" in almost every state and to groups that went far beyond her own circle of professional women's clubs.

The commission set out to study six areas of discrimination:

1) employment under Federal contracts,
2) Federal social insurance and tax laws,
3) Federal and state labor laws,
4) legal treatment of women in terms of political and civil rights, property, and family relations,
5) services — including education, counseling, training, and child care,
6) employment practices of the Federal government.

Along those lines, they were divided into committees and given almost two years to work together — gathering information and bringing in experts — before coming up with recommendations to be presented in October 1963.

Marguerite described the two-day organizational meeting in a long, detailed letter to Massachusetts lawyer Suzanne Shallna:

> ... Mrs. Roosevelt is an able presiding chairman, and kept actively in the chair. ... I was not invited to take a chairmanship, and it is well, for I can hardly do it with my present very demanding job.
>
> The Equal Rights Amendment was referred to. ... It was not necessary to bring it in. ... I felt then that the record of that meeting MUST contain some sort of rebuttal, and I gave it in the most objective manner I could command. Later, it is sure to come up. I hope the men on the commission will be open-minded. ...

As she told Shallna, she would serve on the Civil and Political Rights Committee, which would be chaired by Congresswoman Edith Green from Oregon. Each committee would be headed by two commission members with about ten additional members to be selected by the Women's Bureau.

Although Marguerite was soon impatient with a committee that, for months, had no membership and no agenda, she was in no position to take the lead away from the congresswoman — nor was she ready to do that. Instead, she began on her own, trying to connect women to one another, putting them in place to do what needed doing.

She made lists of suitable women to serve on the committees and submitted them to the Women's Bureau, hoping to get a sprinkling of ERA supporters appointed. Both her enthusiasm and her impatience show in a letter to Helen Hurd, whom she wanted on one of the committees. "BPW is still TALKING a big storm of cooperation. . . My Heavens, Helen, it takes them two weeks to DO what you would do in one afternoon. Let me know that I may submit your name, and which area, or which two areas. Are you in position to do a stint of a few months if that developed?"

Finally however, since Edith Green did not call a meeting of the Civil and Political Rights Committee until the last Monday in May, there was little Marguerite could do but wait out her irritation. By constantly pressuring Katherine Ellickson, the commission's staff director, she had gotten two ERA supporters appointed to the committee: Katherine Peden, president of BPW, and Mrs. H. Lee Ozbirn, president of the General Federation of Women's Clubs.

Three men had also been appointed — a union representative, a legal scholar from Columbia University, and Frank Sander, a lawyer from Harvard whom Marguerite liked immediately. Florence Kerins Murray, a Supreme Court judge in Rhode Island, added another potential voice for ERA.

Pauli Murray was an impressive black woman lawyer on the committee. A senior fellow at Yale Law School, a writer, a scholar, a civil rights and labor activist who had known Eleanor Roosevelt since the 1930s, she was bone-thin with light brown skin and an intensity that matched Marguerite's own. But she was fiercer, less outgoing, more intellectual, less inclined to spread herself thin. Marguerite envied Murray's scholarly credentials and the opportunity to study the law, which she herself had finally had to forego. She had never worked with a black woman lawyer before, never really known one. For different reasons, they were both outsiders. Both were strong-minded and wanted things done their way.

Green had appointed Edward M. Bershstein, a law professor from Purdue University, to be the committee's staff assistant. A young lawyer named Mary Eastwood came from the attorney general's office to observe and assist in writing committee reports.

Intimidated by the Women's Bureau, Bershstein soon left and turned the technical work over to Eastwood, a quiet, beautiful woman in her thirties with the pale coloring of her Scandinavian ancestors. She had never heard of the Equal Rights Amendment and had learned nothing about discrimination against women in law school. She hadn't known the Supreme Court still refused equal protection to women and was stunned by what Marguerite told the committee about legal discrimination.[7]

As staff assistant to the Committee on Federal Employment, Catherine East could — and did — attend the meetings of all the committees. A career civil servant who worked for John Macy at the Civil Service Commission, East was a stocky, capable woman in her early forties, divorced with two daughters to raise. Soon she was obsessed with the work of the President's Commission. Like Eastwood, she had been unaware of the need for ERA or the discriminatory effects of protective labor laws. Sitting on the sidelines, listening to Marguerite debate her committee and the commission, she became convinced that women would never get fair treatment without the Equal Rights Amendment.[8]

Catherine East became a linchpin, keeping everybody informed, introducing women in government to volunteers and activists, xeroxing and mailing out every bit of information she could find about women. Witty and genial with a hint of a Southern accent, she was everybody's big sister — and a one-woman research team.

For their second commission meeting, Eleanor Roosevelt invited the members and their families to spend the weekend of June 16–17, 1962, at the Roosevelt Estate in Hyde Park, New York. Marguerite flew up after work on Friday and checked into the Dutch Patroon Garden Hotel Court not far from the estate and was up early enough the next morning to take Mrs. Roosevelt's nine o'clock tour of the Roosevelt home and grounds. Stirred by the beauty of the Hudson River landscape and Mrs. Roosevelt's revelations about family life among the Roosevelts, Marguerite was suddenly struck with wonder that her own life had brought her to such a moment.

John Macy proudly reported that the Civil Service Commission was eliminating discrimination in government employment. Job eligibility according to sex had been almost totally banned, he said. Carlisle P. Runge, assistant secretary of defense for manpower, came to receive the commission's recommendation that the

Department of Defense remove limitations on the number of colonels, captains, lieutenant colonels, and commanders in the women's division of the Armed Forces. But the commission's greatest political satisfaction came when Deputy Attorney General Nicholas Katzenbach read a letter from President Kennedy accompanying Attorney General Robert Kennedy's reversal of a 1934 opinion that left officials free to fill civil service jobs according to sex.

The commission's long Saturday ended with a buffet dinner at Val-Kill, the gray stucco structure that had once been a furniture factory and was now Eleanor Roosevelt's retreat on the rural outskirts of the estate.

Marguerite drove the few miles from her hotel to Val-Kill in a rented car she shared with Margaret Mealey, executive director of the National Council of Catholic Women. Mealey was a plump, friendly woman whom Marguerite liked despite their disagreement over ERA. Absorbed in conversation, they missed the turn into Val-Kill.

Arriving late, they found their hostess standing at the end of a long table serving chili to a few other stragglers. Thinking their hostess looked tired, Marguerite offered to relieve her at the chili bowl. "No, indeed," Eleanor Roosevelt drew herself up, "My dear, you are my guest. It is my pleasure to serve you." The moment's awkwardness was relieved by a Roosevelt cousin who came through and insisted on getting two beers out of the refrigerator for the latecomers.

On Wednesday, Marguerite met Edith Green to discuss their plans for the Rights Committee. At Marguerite's suggestion, it had been agreed at the last meeting to call on the women's organizations for information pertaining to discriminatory laws. Almost a month had passed and neither the committee nor the Women's Bureau had acted.

A few weeks later, she wrote Esther Peterson complaining of foot-dragging and urging her to face the explosive issue of the Supreme Court's refusal to protect women — as it protected men — from discrimination under the Fourteenth Amendment.

Long accustomed to taking the lead among women, Marguerite would never get used to the considered pace of the Women's Bureau and the inefficiency of the committees. She went to the BPW conference in Los Angeles in July with nothing new to report, but returned to find an equal pay bill about to pass Congress.

The first women's victory for equal pay was met with snide re-
actions from the press that set Marguerite's teeth on edge. A
woman with a salary equal to a man's still wouldn't pick up the
tab, humorist Art Buchwald insisted. She had rather squirrel away
her money against the day when her man is flat broke, and she
could "bail him out in exchange for a walk to the altar." The spoof
went downhill from there. Marguerite wondered if the pointless
ridicule would ever end. She had come to a point in her own thinking where it was no longer possible to laugh it off.

Late in August, her committee met at last and broached the
conflict between ERA advocates and the supporters of protective
labor laws for the first time. The American Nurses Association and
AAUW presented the protective argument while spokeswomen
from BPW and the National Woman's Party defended ERA.

Pauli Murray didn't like laws that discriminated against
women any more than Marguerite did, but she thought women
should go through the courts — the way blacks were doing — rather
than try to amend the constitution. She wanted the commission to
recommend test cases under the Fifth and Fourteenth Amendments
as a compromise between ERA advocates and supporters of the
protective labor laws.

The Fifth Amendment, applicable to federal laws, said no one
could be deprived of life, liberty or property without due process of
law. Under the Fourteenth Amendment no state could pass a law
that deprived any person of life, liberty or property without due
process of law; nor deny anyone the equal protection of the laws.
Murray argued that if women were granted equal coverage under
the Fourteenth Amendment, a separate equal rights amendment
for women would not be necessary. Anyway, she concluded, ERA
didn't have a chance in Congress any time soon.

Marguerite was leery. The courts had been ruling against
equality for women for almost 200 years. It was going to take more
than a long-winded legal brief to change that.

For two tiresome days, October 1–2, the full commission met
again, this time without the leadership of Eleanor Roosevelt who
was hospitalized in New York. It was the first they knew of her illness.

Although the newspapers found much to report, by Marguerite's standards the commission accomplished little. Pauli Murray

presented her conclusion that a test case in the Supreme Court rather than the Equal Rights Amendment was the best way to attack discrimination. Marguerite was flushed and angry before Murray concluded. As she saw it, Murray had been allowed to present her case directly to the commission without full consideration by the committee. She hadn't been appointed by the president but picked by some secret method at the Women's Bureau. Neither Marguerite nor Edith Green had been told that Murray was to present her argument to the commission.

The cards were being stacked against ERA, and Marguerite feared they would not be able to hold together without Eleanor Roosevelt, a longtime supporter of labor whose forty-year opposition to ERA had just begun to soften. In a speech made to the Lucy Stone League in the spring of 1961, she had said, "Many of us opposed the amendment because we felt it would do away with protection in the labor field. Now with unionization, there is no reason why you shouldn't have it if you want it."

Mrs. Roosevelt was already weak and ill when she entertained the commission during the summer at Val-Kill. On November 8, 1962, she died of a rare bone marrow tuberculosis. A week later, President Kennedy announced that the chairmanship of the Commission on the Status of Women would remain vacant: "It is my judgement that there can be no adequate replacement for Mrs. Roosevelt." Esther Peterson and Richard Lester, a commission member and chair of the department of economics at Princeton University, would share the duties of the chair.

Beginning with subcommittee meetings in November, Marguerite became acting chair of the Committee on Civil and Political Rights. Edith Green had scheduled a planning meeting and then gone to Oregon to campaign for reelection to Congress. Marguerite's frustration at staff delays and committee inaction shows in a letter written hastily to BPW President Minnie Miles.

> . . . About the Commission on the Status of Women. . . . the area in which we are interested, that of Civil and Political and Contract Rights, headed by Mrs. Green, has not turned a peg. A professor [Bershstein] was brought here from Purdue as technical secretary — but he was not able to get off the ground, and is now transferred elsewhere. Mrs. Green has been away running for Congress, and no one else has had authority to move.

One more time, she asked BPW to sponsor a survey of discriminatory laws through the foundation: "BPW could be of invaluable assistance — this is a prime need. . . As a group standing for the Equal Rights Amendment, we have reason to be concerned."

Marguerite couldn't study the laws of every state, but she was becoming an expert in the federal law as it applied to women. There were two major positions on the commission: 1) that because women were childbearers and physically weaker than men, they had to be protected by special laws that prevented employers from requiring them to work long hours and do heavy physical work, and 2) that women were so consistently discriminated against under current laws that it would take either an amendment to the Constitution (ERA) or new Supreme Court rulings to set things right. Although she had known from the start that making any progress for ERA on the commission was going to be hard, she was determined to try.

On November 29, she wrote Dorothy Brimacombe.

> Mrs. Roosevelt's death was a very real loss to this work. I am despondent over the outcome, especially in the area which Mrs. Edith Green and I, as commission members, are working. . . . It had been proclaimed in the beginning that the commission would come to grips with the problems, and that it was not to be a whitewash committee. Mrs. Green has been tied up with running for reelection, and the duties of a congresswoman. It is her [belief] that Equal Rights Amendment *should be* aired and considered.

On December 18, she talked with Esther Peterson insisting that the conflict over ERA not be "swept under the rug." It wouldn't be right, she said, and it would be bad for the administration. Finally Peterson relented — it would have to come.

From the beginning Marguerite believed in the commission's potential. Now she considered it part of her job to represent the commission in all her organizations and — as before — she complained often of the conflict between her work for women and her paying job. A letter describing the first full commission meeting to her family in Texas strikes a familiar note, "Harry remains balanced and sane. I continue in my whirling dervish act of trying to do entirely too many things."

Early in January 1962, a few days after Marguerite and Harry returned from their Christmas trip to Texas, something happened to Harry that banished for a while all thoughts of the commission. In mid-afternoon one Sunday as he walked home from a shopping trip in town, two strangers grabbed him from behind, knocked him down, and took his wallet. He had stopped at the store and cashed a big check, he remembered. They must have seen him.

Marguerite came home later in the day and found Harry slumped in a chair, pale as death. The incident brought on a mild heart attack, the doctors told them later. The police came but could do nothing.

Late that afternoon, Harry fell again in the apartment. And on Wednesday Marguerite came home to find him in bed, his face and head bloody. Although he was released from Walter Reed Hospital with a few stitches and a broken rib, they both knew something was wrong.

In describing those two bad weeks in January to her family, she added complaints about her job. On January 6, she had become assistant director of the Refund Litigation Division, the highest position any woman had ever held in the Chief Counsel's Office. She was pleased, but the work was difficult and there were new responsibilities.

Soon she was turning down opportunities to speak on the work of the commission, the one thing she didn't want to give up. Her letters beg for understanding. Late in January she refused an invitation to speak at the annual convention of the YWCA, and wrote its president, Eleanor Freeman.

> Eleanor: the report of the commission must be ready for the printers by August 1. The Committee on Civil and Political Rights, on which I serve, has bogged down, and to me it is a crucial area. I am asked to give special effort, and we have planned some special meetings — they take one full day each time. Prof. Sander of Harvard, and an attorney [Pilpel] come down for the day. There are some other reasons; my environment has "closed in on me" like fog — and I have to be excused.

Her worries over Harry and work and the commission were interrupted for a few days in the middle of a grim, cold February when the women of the D.C. BPW Club gave a luncheon at the National Lawyers' Club and honored her for "distinguished achievement and leadership in women's activities." They had a way of knowing when she needed something. Despite ill health, Harry "broke precedent" and not only went but sat at the head table.

Lady Bird and Lyndon Johnson sent a telegram.

ELEANOR ROOSEVELT ONCE SAID,
"A WOMAN MUST DO WELL, OR SHE HURTS ALL WOMEN" . . .
YOU HAVE DONE WELL AND HELPED ALL WOMEN.

Amid the troubles and the respites, Marguerite became permanent acting chair of the Civil and Political Rights Committee — and faced the first crisis of a new phase in her activist career. She was ERA's only advocate on the commission, and her own committee was hopelessly divided.

On March 8, the committee met and set up an agenda that followed Marguerite's lead on everything except the Equal Rights Amendment. Pauli Murray still thought going for a Supreme Court ruling under the Fourteenth Amendment was a workable compromise. Finally, they agreed on compromise wording to be submitted to the commission at its final meeting on April 23.

> In view of the promise of this constitutional approach, the Commission *does not take a position* in favor of the proposed Equal Rights Amendment at this time.[9]

Marguerite went home relieved, thinking she had salvaged ERA since their recommendation left the door open should the constitutional approach in the courts fail. Not knowing the final struggle on the Commission was yet to come, that night she wrote in her diary, *One of the hardest days of my life — Felt so much depended on me.*

Tired as she must have been when she got home, she wrote her heart out to her "dear friend Vadae" [Meekison], a lawyer, a friend of Florence Allen's, and one of her many encouragers.

> . . . Bless you for such a fine letter. It brought me memories of your loyalty to me, and to women, and inspiration to keep on giving out energy for those who little know and less care as I think when I get very tired. And this evening, arriving home about 6:00 after an emotionally grueling day, I have again read your good letter and derived strength, and something of the answer of why I keep going thru such pressured experiences.
>
> So, dear, you gave me an answer. Your own life of doing has seen so many such instances. And I am one of your disciples who well remembers the complete example of courageous standing for

what you believe which I have seen in you on more than one occasion.

Perhaps in an attempt to get some kind of relief from the solitary responsibility she felt for the women who depended on her, Marguerite described the meeting over and over in letters to women she thought would understand. She knew some would see the "Fourteenth Amendment approach" as a defeat for ERA and for women. To Ruth Hartgraves, who lived in Houston and was president of the American Medical Women's Association, she admitted her own reservations about the constitutional approach. "Of course, looking at the 1960 case of Miss Allred and her endeavor to enroll at [Texas] A&M, and the Supreme Court's refusal to take the case, I can entertain no shred of optimism of a 'test' case."

With the growing realization that she had probably done the best that could be done, her spirits lifted. A few days before the commission was to meet, she wrote her family an exuberant description of Washington among the cherry blossoms. Harry was better, she told them. "Next week is Easter — a time of rejuvenation in spirit and in the world of nature. Isn't it glorious to be able to experience it?"

On the first day of the meetings at which the commission was to come up with its final recommendations to the president, Marguerite was flabbergasted to find many members determined to disregard the Civil and Political Rights Committee's compromise wording on ERA in favor of a clear statement against the amendment.

Throughout the first day of meetings, she fought singlehandedly to prevent the group from taking a vote she was sure would go against her. Finally, a statement suggested by the Justice Department was accepted over the one recommended by her committee. It began,

> . . . in view of *the fact* that a constitutional Amendment does not appear to be necessary to establish the principle of equality, the Commission believes that constitutional changes *should not be sought* unless, at some future time, it appears from court decisions that a need for such action exists.[10]

It was as close to anti-ERA as they could come. The recommendation left not a shred of hope.

Sitting dejectedly through hours of commission business the next day, Marguerite waited. Finally a casual comment opened the door and she said what she had waited to say: "Of course after yesterday's defeat, I should be glad to see nothing printed about what my committee did." Their decision had closed the door on ERA. By changing a few words they could leave that door open. She wanted the word "now" inserted in the last line of the statement they had adopted and the words "should not be sought" changed to "need not now be sought," so that the crucial sentence would read "the Commission believes that constitutional changes 'need not *now*' be sought."

They respected her. Her suggestion was fair. And she had waited until they were all exhausted. Margaret Mealey, executive director of the Council of Catholic Women, broke the ice and seconded the recommendation despite her opposition to the amendment.

It was a small, hard victory but the addition of the word *now* saved ERA from a terrible blow. In years to come even the National Woman's Party would acknowledge what Marguerite had done.

A long letter written on Thanksgiving Day explained the context of the victory to Catherine Agagnost, president of NAWL.

> The commission does not say there is no need for a constitutional amendment. Over my dead body would that have been done, altho I might tell you I was the one and only voice on the Civil and Political Rights Committee, present and talking and voting, when the final recommendation was made. There was a compromise adopted for first a test case, in light of which the Commission did not NOW take a position on ERA. Had that committee taken a position at the time we voted, it would have been a stand against it. I went home feeling victorious in having averted that — and largely the compromise was in plain fair-dealing deference of the men law professors to the opinion which I expressed, with cited cases. . . . I knew the final recommendation would be disappointing to Equal Rights proponents — who could not know the alternative.

Spearheaded by BPW's Virginia Allan, state (or governor's) commissions on the status of women were forming across the country. With Esther Peterson's help, Allan and BPW President Minnie Miles talked with President Kennedy and got his endorsement of the project. Now Peterson wanted Marguerite to go to Puerto Rico in May to speak at the BPW convention there and try to set up a commission.

She had much to talk about now that the commission work was ending. For four days she was a celebrity, treated to tropical meals and entertainment. She toured the pineapple and sugarcane fields and visited the Superior Court and the Catholic University of Puerto Rico in Ponce, one of the oldest cities in America. The night before she left, the mayor of San Juan, Don Felicia de Gautier, included her in an island festival they were having and gave her the keys to the city. She returned to Washington renewed in spirit and able to tell Esther Peterson that the governor of Puerto Rico and his lawyer wife had promised to set up a state commission.

In the spring of 1963, while Marguerite struggled with the commission, a little known New York journalist named Betty Friedan published *The Feminine Mystique,* and triggered a change in women's thinking like nothing anyone had ever seen. Suddenly women who weren't lawyers and didn't belong to women's organizations, who had never worked and never heard of the Equal Rights Amendment were up in arms. They wanted the same opportunities men had. They were tired of low pay and limited roles, tired of always being seen as somebody's mother and somebody's wife.

At the same time, a civil rights bill floundered in Congress, and violence spread across the South. In May, thousands of protestors were arrested and jailed in Birmingham, Alabama, while television audiences watched demonstrators clash with the police — and police dogs and fire hoses. Six weeks later, civil rights leader Medgar Evers was shot and killed in Mississippi.

When President Kennedy reluctantly supported a civil rights bill, Martin Luther King complained that although Kennedy might have done "a little more" for blacks than Eisenhower, "the plight of the vast majority of Negroes remained the same." Now civil rights leaders were planning a massive march on Washington to show Congress just how strong they were.

On June 14, Flag Day, Marguerite wrote in her diary, *2 pm, Negro "Marchers" came to Dept. Justice.* But most of her thoughts during June were for Harry. Their neighborhood was going black. White people were afraid. It was hard for her to forget that Harry had been mugged by two black men.

For the next ten days her diary is almost empty of obligations but sprinkled with notes about Harry and his health. Sunday, June 23, *With Harry, Not out all day tho beautiful day.* June 27, *HS not eating — not well — went to bed early.*

Two days later, on Saturday, she took Harry to Walter Reed Hospital for the last time. He was weak with a numbness in one leg. By nightfall, the leg was blue and cold. The doctors diagnosed a recent heart attack and a blood clot in his leg. On Saturday, they operated to remove the clot and reported that although Harry stood the operation "valiantly," it was not the success they had hoped.

Harry's condition worsened throughout the week. Marguerite spent Friday, July 4, with him, trying to get him to eat, wanting to know he recognized her. The next morning he barely knew her and by midafternoon he was dead. On a hunch that her friend might not have had anything to eat, Irene Scott brought lunch and was there when Harry died. Louis came to be with her.

There were chapel services at Fort Meyer and burial with full military honors at Arlington Cemetery. A few days later, she left with Louis for a week in Corpus Christi.

She returned early Thursday morning. *Entered apartment about 7:00 am. No one to meet me in front, no one at home — heartbreaking.*

Alone all weekend, she was back at work on Monday. After work, she met Mary Eastwood for a final look at her committee's report to the Commission, glad to have something compelling to do.

Much of August and September were spent alone. She wrote many long letters describing Harry's death and her loss. To Louise Wright, her first friend in Washington, and the one who had introduced her to Harry, she wrote: "This is the hardest of letters to write to you. Brother Harry is gone, Weezie." The words repeat themselves over and over. *Harry my dear comrade. My pal. My friend. Brother. Partner.* The longest, most intimate of the letters went to Libby Sachar, whose mother died about the same time.

> . . . Harry was at my side when mother left us. Those two were my complete friends and my partners, and none others can replace them. But I remember the many little trips over this part of the country we three had together. . . . And travels to and from Texas, and those happy memories help so much.
>
> Yes, Libby, I have lost a partner in every sense of the word, and in every phase of life except only my professional. The necessity of returning to heavy office duties tomorrow will prove a blessing, although I dread it, as you would know. . . . While I had

planned to go to Dallas [BPW's national convention] I had no enthusiasm for it.

And to Harry's sister Helen, a nun in Ohio.

. . . Harry was ill only a week. The Lord was no doubt merciful in taking him when he did, for a gangrenous condition was developing in his ankle and lower leg. No more pain for him. Just a big emptiness for those of us here. But he will be waiting for us, I know.

A month later, Marguerite told her family, "friends are good — maybe too good." But she was getting along all right and beginning to be interested in what was going on around her.

She was fascinated by the "March on Washington" planned for August 28, in support of the civil rights bill before Congress. There was talk of violence, riots. Federal office buildings were closing for the day. "A favorite question around here," she wrote her family, is "what are you going to do on the 28th?"

When the day came, 250,000 people (100,000 more than expected) poured into the city on behalf of the civil rights bill and the needs of poor people. Marguerite watched on television while Martin Luther King moved the marchers with words that were famous as soon as they were spoken: "I have a dream that one day on the red hills of Georgia the sons of former slaves and the sons of former slaveholders will be able to sit down together at the table of brotherhood. I have a dream. . . ." It was peaceful, religious almost. No violence, no riots.

Two weeks later, on October 11, Eleanor Roosevelt's birthday, the commission presented its handsomely bound, 86-page report, *American Women,* to the president at the White House.

The report called for action on all fronts, from the president, Congress, state legislatures, local governments, private business, foundations, and the entire educational system. Full partnership for men and women was the theme of *American Women.* "An invitation to action" was their message to the president.

They wanted to end discrimination in the work force, in jury service, in politics, in property rights. They wanted women to be educated and trained to work. They wanted the workplace to accommodate the needs of women: mothers, married women, older women. They called for fair wage and hour laws for men and women in all states and the establishment of a minimum wage. They wanted a cabinet member and a citizen's committee designated to carry out the recommendations of the commission.

President Kennedy immediately set up the recommended Citizens Advisory Council on the Status of Women to carry out the commission's program. Marguerite and twelve other members of the commission accepted appointments. Eventually, there would be twenty-six men and women on the council plus an interdepartmental committee appointed from the president's cabinet. Margaret Hickey, an editor of *Ladies Home Journal* and past president of BPW, was to chair the council.

John F. Kennedy and his Camelot were at the peak of their power — and the end of it. The president had steered the country through the Cuban missile crisis that threatened nuclear war and through the first stages of a minority uprising threatening revolution. Now it looked as if the administration's halting civil rights efforts were going to pay off. Esther Peterson was handling the problems with women. In an expanding, peacetime economy, there was room for everybody.

On November 22, 1963, less than six weeks after the commission presented its report, John Kennedy was shot and killed in Dallas, Texas, apparently by a lone assassin, Lee Harvey Oswald. Marguerite's diary for that day reads simply: *2 pm Pres. Kennedy died in Dallas, assassinated.* The next day's papers carried a now familiar photograph of a solemn Lyndon Johnson being sworn in as president by Judge Sarah T. Hughes. Jacqueline Kennedy stood beside him, stunned, wearing a pink suit stained with her dead husband's blood.

A week later, Marguerite wrote Vi: "The assassination, funeral, all was tragic. Yesterday, I went by Arlington Cemetery to put flowers on Harry's grave. Got in a traffic jam, moving bumper to bumper, a mile and a half long — people driving to the cemetery to visit Kennedy's grave. People were all over that big hill, going and coming."

Having missed her holiday trip to Texas because of an emergency in her office, she wrote the "Rawalt family in Texas" an odd Christmas letter that mirrors the strange mood of a country celebrating the season of hope in the midst of mourning:

Christmas Day dawned bright and clear, with snow on the

ground here. A heavy snowfall two days before made it a White Christmas. I was busy with my Christmas card mail all morning. . . . The broad Potomac was all white and still — ice with the snow on top. No muddy water visible.

We then drove past the Kennedy grave, on the hill below the Lee Mansion. Although it was approaching dark, the gates were open late and there was then a solid three–four wide line of people streaming up the hillside.

Yesterday, Sunday, I did the other thing that anyone alone should do. Not be alone. For I have literally scores of good friends here in Washington who live alone and who are interesting for their jobs and accomplishments. So I invited five of them for brunch at 11:00 a.m. We had a wonderful time, about our travels, our jobs, and getting acquainted, for I try to invite one or two new people into such a group.

Happy New Year to each of you. The year 1964 surely brings hope of better things. As for me, 1963 will never be forgotten for its sorrow, even though it also brought blessings of a new job, appointment on the permanent Citizens Advisory Council on the Status of Women.

Although Marguerite was closer to the White House than she had ever been before, she made no attempt to secure the long-coveted appointment. It was too late for that, she thought; and, in a way, she no longer wanted it. She sensed something coming for women — and waited.

[6]

Cresting

As president, Lyndon Johnson was making big promises to women. When he promised "no stag government," for his administration, Marguerite took him at his word and began organizing women to prepare and submit rosters of women candidates qualified to serve. Things she had wanted for so long seemed possible.

The National Woman's Party was working to get women covered under a civil rights act designed originally to protect black rights. There was hope, too, for uniform jury service and a Fourteenth Amendment test case.

Senator Margaret Chase Smith was running for the Republican nomination for president and railing against the inertia of women. In Congress, Florence Dwyer, Edith Green, Catherine May, Katharine St. George, and Martha Griffiths were active for women.

Martha Griffiths had come to Washington from Michigan in 1954. A member of BPW and NAWL, she had been elected to Congress with the help of Virginia Allan and the BPW clubs in her district. She was a down-to-earth woman, a straightforward politician who worked harder in Congress for women than anyone ever had before. She didn't hesitate to aim her quick wit and caustic humor at her enemies. If women were excluded from Title VII of the Civil Rights Act and it passed, white women would become the only group that employers could legally discriminate against.

In April 1963, Marguerite wrote Zonta International president Maria Pierce. There was a new thrust among women who were, she said, "pushing forward with determination to achieve full partnership as citizens." In June, after the first meeting of State Commissions, she told another friend, "Truly, the cause of recognition of women is on the upward curve." By October, her enthusiasm encompassed the new president's council: "Yesterday and today, the Citizens Advisory Council on Status of Women has been in session. . . . So many great advances are being made for women."

Exhilarated by the winds of change and unmindful of the fact that she was almost seventy years old, Marguerite set a pace for herself that made the pace of the early 1950s seem leisurely by comparison. She had a wider audience; she would go almost anywhere, talk to any group about the "new day" coming for women, the work of the president's commission, the state commissions, outmoded discriminatory laws, the failure of the courts to cover women under the Fourteenth Amendment.

She talked about the "Changing Status of American Women" to accountants in Wilmington, Delaware; to a conference on legislation in Albany, New York; to Zonta members in Detroit, Jacksonville, Alexandria, San Francisco, Charleston; to NAWL members in New York City; to the women of the Chamber of Commerce in Greenville, South Carolina.

When she was made an honorary member of Zeta Tau Alpha sorority for her work on women's issues, she went to Miami and told the women there about a "great onward sweep of public interest and increasing awareness. . . . a tidal wave of interest in what women have been talking about among themselves for twenty years." At home, she spoke on the same subject to the American Federation of Government Employees at the National Press Club — and to smaller groups of all kinds: Zonta, BPW, professional groups, even the Daughters of the American Revolution.

Perhaps, as she suggested in a letter to Louise Wright and

George Stewart, she filled her life this way, in part, to make up for the emptiness at home: "You have not heard from me because I have been so overwhelmed with work and travel and making talks that I can hardly keep myself going. I seem to lose myself that way and make up for the lack of Harry at home to care."

Suddenly, her audiences were different. Her mail was different. Women were listening. They wanted to know more. They wanted to help, and they wanted her to tell them how.

The rewards were coming at last for what she had been doing on her own for twenty years. And, despite the loneliness at the center of her life and a longing for Harry that never left her, the winds of change brought pleasure and excitement as well as new demands.

On February 12, 1964, the Citizens Advisory Council met for the first time in the Fish Room of the White House. The meeting was interrupted when President and Mrs. Johnson invited the council to join them in welcoming Britain's prime minister, Sir Alec Douglas-Home. Marguerite described it in a letter to Zonta friend, Alice McRae.

> So we took part in the formal ceremonies, in front of the door, snow-covered grounds, bright sun shining, soldier guard with flags of nations flying in the breeze, speeches by the President and the Prime Minister (very brief) — and then, came Lady Bird Johnson for a personal welcome to us, each at a time. As someone started to introduce her to me, she said "No introduction to Marguerite necessary — We have known each other for a long time."

In June, the Interdepartmental Committee and the Citizens Advisory Council hosted the first Conference of State Commissions on the Status of Women. With forty-seven states represented, it was a broad, well-informed gathering.

Out of favor since suffrage, the word "feminist" was slipping back into the language. In speaking of the new state commissions Virginia Allan, then national president of BPW, used the word favorably and in its broadest meaning:

> . . . Once World War II was over. . . . The woman who cared or dared to look beyond the four walls of home for satisfaction or interests came to be known as a "feminist" and the contagion of the charge began to affect all of us.

> Now I believe we are coming to an end of this era of antifeminism and are entering a new one in which the 25 million of us

who work will begin to assert a new pride in our abilities and our present and potential contribution.

With the propelling of Title VII and the Civil Rights Act of 1964 (which forbade discrimination in employment) through Congress by a tight network of Washington-connected activists, the new feminism secured a crucial foothold. The struggle to get women included in Title VII had begun late in 1963, when Alice Paul and other members of the National Woman's Party began negotiating with Howard Smith, a conservative Democratic congressman from Virginia, who opposed the bill on racial grounds.

Apparently fearing that a women's rights clause would threaten a bill aimed primarily at protecting black rights, the Johnson administration, including Esther Peterson, opposed the inclusion of women. To the chagrin of many women leaders, Edith Green agreed with them — the purpose of the bill was to prevent *racial* discrimination. Women would have to wait.

When, on February 8, Smith finally moved to amend Title VII to include sex, he did it in a way that brought rounds of laughter from the floor. Maybe he was mocking the entire bill. Maybe he was teasing women for wanting to be like men. From the gallery, where Marguerite sat, it was hard to tell.

The jesting among congressmen lasted until Martha Griffiths put them all in their places, the jocular old racist and the other men laughing with him:

> I presume that if there had been any necessity to have pointed out that women were a second-class sex, the laughter would have proved it. . . . I rise in support of the amendment, primarily because I feel as a white woman when this bill has passed this House and the Senate and has been signed by the president that white women will be last at the hiring gate.

In the end, she played to the emotions of all and the racism of some: "a vote against this amendment today by a white man is a vote against his wife, or his widow, or his daughter, or his sister." Against all expectations, the amendment passed in the House by a vote of 168 to 133. The bill itself passed the House two days later.

By the time the civil rights bill came up in the Senate, Marguerite, Catherine East, and Pauli Murray were at work. East, now executive secretary of the Citizens Council, kept Murray informed while Marguerite wrote women lawyers and BPW and Zonta members across the country, explaining the bill and Title VII, telling them whom to write, what to say.

Backed by a flood of letters and telegrams from Illinois BPW members, Margaret Chase Smith was able to get Senator Everett Dirksen, a Republican from Illinois and the powerful Senate minority leader, to withdraw his opposition to the inclusion of sex in Title VII. Influential Texas women wrote the president. Finally, seeing the support the women's amendment had in the House, Esther Peterson changed her position and worked for it in the Senate.

Early in the spring, Marguerite got in touch with Pauli Murray. She wanted her to write a memorandum to the president. It would be delivered through Mrs. Johnson. Because Murray was both black and a woman, she could speak for all of them.

Always a fast worker, Murray had the long, impassioned document ready in a few days. Civil rights could not be divided up and rationed between blacks and women, she wrote. Civil rights were supposed to be for everybody.

Marguerite had it delivered to Mrs. Johnson immediately, then mailed it to President Johnson and Vice-President Hubert Humphrey. Margaret Chase Smith, Dirksen and others in the Senate also got copies.

After a long wait, Murray received a telephone call from White House social secretary, Bess Abell. The First Lady had done some checking and sent this message: "I am happy to tell you that it is the administration's position that the bill should be passed as it is at present." The carefully worded message was good news. Martha Griffiths recalls sending the president a different kind of message through his aide Liz Carpenter: "If that amendment comes out of that bill, I will send my speech door to door in every member's district who voted against it, and in my opinion, those who voted against it would never return to Congress." [1]

In June 1964, the Civil Rights Bill of 1964 passed the Congress, with Title VII prohibiting employment discrimination against women as well as blacks.

Title VII outlawed discrimination against women in employment in all businesses exceeding twenty-five people and created an Equal Employment Opportunity Commission with broad powers to investigate and review complaints. Unfortunately, EEOC had little power to enforce its findings. Although enforcement was sure to require costly, time-consuming court cases by individuals, the supporters of Title VII were elated.

Marguerite's reservations about Pauli Murray's approach to women's rights had disappeared. She bragged about Murray in letters to friends. She was "a fellow at Yale, a colored woman lawyer who. . . wrote a splendid memorandum supporting the addition of the word 'sex' [in Title VII] and concluding that both Negro and white women were equally affected and concerned." In October, she responded to comments Murray had made to her about the narrow membership on the Citizens Council.

> To you comes a real measure of credit from the ultimate successful passage of the Title VII. . . . your memorandum and your thinking was really fine. I do think we can take a share of credit.
>
> I fully agree that it is important to get unbiased and intellectual representation on the Commission [the Council, sometimes called the "Permanent Commission"]. I had not in fact given it thought, nor have I stopped and looked up the provisions. What about you? Are you interested? I should be pleased to raise my voice in your behalf if you are.
>
> You and Mary Eastwood have contributed much out of your work and talents which I have particularly appreciated.

With the year of intense activity and exhilaration rushing to an end, Marguerite needed a rest. For weeks during the fall, she was slowed down by deadening headaches that came every few days, lasting for hours, sometimes putting her to bed. Although the last months had been full of success, they had been hard. She admitted it twice in her diary at the end of November: . . . *too much pressure.* . . . *over exerted.*

In the spring of 1964, an unexpected vacancy plus her experience had made her eligible for a promotion to associate chief counsel at the Internal Revenue Service. When she spoke of it to Sheldon Cohen, the chief counsel recently appointed by President Johnson, he said she was too close to retirement to be considered. Marguerite knew they began saying that to a woman as soon as she turned fifty. The two men before her had each served only a few years in the position.

Suddenly, she was angry with years of pent-up fury, enraged with the memory of all the times she had been refused what she deserved. Unable to make any headway with Cohen, she wrote the president:

> What do I want? Promotion within my own office. . . .
>
> I do not criticize Mr. Cohen; to one his age, an over-60 must seem like ancient history although not all individuals wither on the vine at that time as witness the Congressional leaders, the Supreme Court, . . . and others.
>
> In the Chief Counsel's office, my career began as Junior Attorney. . . . promotion at snail's pace! to present position as Assistant Director of the Refund Litigation Division, not withstanding no blemishes on the record and praise for performance. It has been reported that the real drawback is "no woman wanted at staff meetings" hence a ceiling on women attorneys.

She didn't expect the president to get involved and he didn't. The letter was simply something she had been unable to do before — and wanted to do now. She didn't get the promotion, but she was too near retirement for the gesture to cost her anything other than Cohen's ill will. In recollection, she says, "I just no longer gave a damn."

Early in August, she learned that she was one of eight women selected by the State Department to go on an exchange trip to the Soviet Union, only to learn within the month that the trip had been canceled. The two governments had not been able to agree on the circumstances of the tour in Russia — and it was off. She described her disappointment to her family and concluded: "When the Indian summer of October comes along, I always get an urge to travel, and probably will accept a weekend or two of speaking invitations."

Instead, she stayed home and saved her energy for a long September weekend at the World's Fair in New York. Alone for three days, she did exactly what she pleased. Her fascination with new inventions, progress, foreign places, had not waned since she and Harry took in their first World's Fair in New York as newlyweds. She wrote about it in another letter to the "home folk" in Texas. "The fair is a fairyland. . . a historical education. . . . a story of progress. . . . nostalgic, and to be enjoyed by one my age." For the first time in a long time, it was enjoyable to be alone.

Nineteen sixty-five began with the inauguration of President

Johnson, whose victory over the conservative Barry Goldwater promised him four years on his own. Over a million people stood in the cold while Johnson vowed to move the Great Society toward a world without hate. Millions of others saw it on television. His words had a religious tone. He promised a holy war against illness, poverty, illiteracy.

Not everybody was as pleased with the president's message as Marguerite was. No one understood what was happening in Vietnam. Blacks, poor people, women, wanted the promises of the Great Society fulfilled. At the same time, a backward pull was setting in. Some said Johnson went too fast, trying to change too many things at once.

Nevertheless, good things were happening for women, and every day Marguerite's own achievements were acknowledged in some new way. Yet, for the most part, the early months of 1965 were unusually solitary ones for her. On the weekends, she worked at home on the BPW history and corresponded with relatives who would be included in her Rawalt and Flake genealogies. She visited with close friends: the Scotts, the Nicholases who lived in her apartment building and had been Harry's friends as well as hers, the Hunttings, the Benedicks. These were quiet months for her; she was planning to retire from the government in October.

In a poignant letter to her two brothers, she said she wanted to "waste some time." She had always planned to retire and travel with Harry. And now he was gone. On July 5, she wrote on her calendar, *2 years ago today, my Harry passed away.*

Then suddenly, beginning in July, she was caught up again, riding the upswing of a still unnamed women's movement. The second National Conference of Governor's Commissions on the Status of Women met in Washington, July 28–30, sponsored by the Citizens Council. Many BPW women were there as founders of the state commissions, former members of the committees of the president's commission, and some women Marguerite didn't know. They weren't all professional women, not all white either.

On Thursday afternoon, 4,000 women gathered on the south lawn of the White House to hear President Johnson talk about the needs of American women — impoverished mothers trying to keep a family together and well-off women whose lives had lost meaning. Vice-President Hubert Humphrey spoke even more solemnly that night at their banquet, talking about national security and defending the military buildup in Vietnam.

U.S. involvement in Southeast Asia had mushroomed, and some blamed the president. The administration was doing the right thing, Humphrey insisted. Defending the people of Vietnam against a Communist takeover was bravery, not villainy as some suggested.

For Marguerite, patriotism was rooted in childhood memories of immigrants overjoyed to be in America. Two European wars had intensified her belief in democracy and the importance of protecting it. She hardly knew what to think of the distant war in Vietnam, halfway around the world among peoples whose lives she could not imagine. But, not liking the idea of Soviet influence spreading across Asia, and distrusting those who called United States attempts to stop it "immoral," she sympathized with the president.

For Marguerite, the next day's meeting would be the important one. A five-member Equal Employment Opportunities Commission (EEOC) had been set up just a month before to administer Title VII. Two of its members were going to speak to the convention, Aileen Hernandez, EEOC's only woman member, and Franklin Roosevelt, Jr., its chairman. Hernandez had been with the Division of Fair Employment Practices in California. A tall, stylish woman with smooth golden-brown skin, her appointment to the commission recognized both a woman and a black.

Hernandez's humor had a sharp edge to it. She liked the challenge of the commission, she said — with its four-to-one balance of power. She questioned the protectiveness of the protective labor laws.

The EEOC, she said, had to consider the problem of help-wanted classified advertisements in the newspapers. Traditionally they had been printed "Help Wanted" — Colored or White, Male or Female. The same newspapers that had agreed to eliminate "Colored" and "White," only jested about the discrimination implied in "Help Wanted — Female." What if a man wanted to be a Playboy Bunny, they snickered. For Hernandez, Title VII was no joke.

Franklin Roosevelt, Jr., was less to the point, calling help-wanted ads a "tricky question." Marguerite leaned toward his sister, Anna Roosevelt Halsted, seated next to her. Couldn't she do something about her brother? "Marguerite," Halsted replied, "I believe you have brothers."

That night Marguerite was impressed with a speech given by Kathryn Clarenbach, head of the Wisconsin State Commission. A straightforward, graceful woman, she spoke in strong, sensible tones, saying more bluntly some of the same things Marguerite had said. Women couldn't change things by sitting around being "ladies."

In August, Marguerite began meeting with a special committee of the Citizens Council to draft a policy statement to EEOC demanding a positive approach to sex discrimination in employment and the elimination of male–female classified ads. Title VII allowed for exceptions to nondiscrimination in cases where a job could only be filled by one sex or the other (bona fide occupational qualifications, called b.f.o.qs). They wanted EEOC to define b.f.o.qs narrowly: only a woman could be a wet nurse, but surely either sex could be an airline attendant.

Six weeks later, Pauli Murray addressed the National Council of Women of the United States, a progressive group headquartered in New York. The reporter who covered the speech for the *New York Times* was struck by one thing Murray said: If necessary, women should not shrink from marching on Washington as poor people and blacks had done.

In New York, working on a sequel to *The Feminine Mystique*, Betty Friedan read the newspaper accounts of Murray's speech and began corresponding with her. In trying to write about solutions to the problems she had described in her first book, Friedan was convinced that women were going to have to organize for action. Women needed a civil rights movement of their own, she said. Murray agreed.[2]

Soon Friedan was spending more and more time in Washington. She met Sonia Pressman, a young lawyer for EEOC, and learned just how negative the attitudes were toward the enforcement of Title VII for women.

Mary Eastwood and Catherine East often met at night with Friedan in her hotel room or in a cafe where no one from the Women's Bureau of the Labor Department would see them. Women with government jobs had to be careful, they told her; but Betty was independent, she could speak out. They wanted her to start an independent action group for women. Richard Graham, a sympathetic member of EEOC, said it was going to take an "NAACP for women" to get Title VII enforced.

"I don't know anything about organizations," Friedan insisted. "I don't even BELONG to them. I'm a writer, a loner." Maybe, she suggested, they could find an established organization to play the role. But Marguerite had already told them BPW wasn't interested, and soon they were making their own list of women in crucial positions all across the country. If Betty would take the lead, they thought it could be done.[3]

On October 16, 1965, Marguerite retired after thirty-three years at Internal Revenue. The work at IRS had satisfied an abiding need for independence and financial security, and she had loved the income and estate tax puzzles that passed over her desk. With job security, paid vacation, and a nine-to-five work day, her "paid job" had often been a reprieve from the less predictable pressures of her work with women and an immensely important personal life. But the office had never been "home" to her; her deepest involvements lay elsewhere. Finally, she had been disappointed that neither her efforts nor her ability had been enough to overcome the resistance to women-at-the-top in government. When the time came to quit, she was ready to go. From now on, the women's movement would be her only job.

Marguerite began her retirement with a long holiday trip to Corpus Christi. Her diary describes huge meals with family and friends — wild duck, venison, barbecue, champagne. A few days before New Year's, she wrote: "My first duck hunt in years! With Louis, in blind, shot six ducks, bringing down two with a shot. Louis had to be 'retriever' wading in arm deep water to get them. The beautiful sight, near sundown, of hundreds of white breasts gleaming in the sun."

She returned to a leisure almost unknown in her life. She began taking Spanish and signed up for piano lessons and wrote long letters to friends. To Agnes Wright Parker, one of the many "cousins" with whom she corresponded, she described her new life, "I am now enjoying the sheer luxury of not having to get up early every morning. How happy I am today to contemplate that, for Washington is having its first snow blizzard for years and years. It has given about eight inches or more of snow, but right now the wind is blowing a gale, shifting the hard fine snow as if it were still falling."

Unexpectedly, during the first week in February, a package arrived from Pauli Murray — pleadings, briefs, information concerning *Gardenia White et al* v. *Bruce Crook et al,* a case that they had all been following in the Alabama courts. Alabama was one of two states in which the laws forbade women to serve on juries. Black men were excluded by custom. In the wake of the Lowndes County acquittal of two white men accused of slaying civil rights workers, Viola Liuzzo and Jonathan Daniels, the American Civil Liberties Union was challenging the constitutionality of the state laws and practicies. Murray and New York lawyer Dorothy Kenyon had submitted a brief based on the arguments developed on the Civil and Political Rights Committee: that jury duty was a right and an obligation of all citizens.

Along with the other documents, Pauli Murray sent Marguerite an outline of the ACLU's argument for getting the proposed Civil Rights Protection Act of 1966 amended to include uniform jury service for women on state and federal courts. Murray's long memo ended on a note particularly gratifying to Marguerite.

> . . . I also believe that on the issue of equality in jury service, we have reached that juncture which caused the women of an earlier generation, frustrated by the disappointing results of the Woman's Suffrage Amendment, to believe that the only way for women to secure equality of status was the passage of the Equal Rights Amendment. As you know, I have never disagreed with the objectives of that proposed amendment.

A few days later, a three-judge federal court in Alabama ruled in favor of Gardenia White, adopting the ACLU argument almost verbatim. The plain intention of the Fourteenth Amendment, it concluded, was to prevent "prejudicial disparities for all citizens — including women."

Had the state of Alabama chosen to appeal, *Gardenia White* would have been an ideal test of the Supreme Court's stance on the equality of women under the Constitution. Although Marguerite and her friends were disappointed (but not surprised) when that did not happen, the Alabama decision still called for celebration. A federal court had ruled that state laws could not deprive women of constitutional rights.

Two days after the ruling, Marguerite wrote NAWL president Mattie Belle Davis, "Sound the tocsin! a Federal Court has ruled that women are within the equal protection clause of the 14th Amendment!" She bragged about the work Murray and Eastwood were doing and complained about the backwardness of her own organizations: "Needless to say I am elated. I wish that N.A.W.L. and B&PW could take some credit."

A few weeks later, she wrote in a similar vein to Dallas activist Hermine Tobolowsky:

> Had two weeks at home in Corpus Christi during the holidays. Even at that time, I was "apprehensive" lest something would go wrong, for right then we were struggling behind the scenes to get the Attorney General to intervene in White v Crook on basis of sex as well as race. Thanks to two other devoted and able women lawyers [Murray and Kenyon], it got done. We were gadflies.

Pauli Murray was just as elated. *White* v. *Crook* was the *Brown* v. *Board of Education* for women, she said. If such a case came before the Supreme Court, it was "unthinkable that it could say any less."

Immediately, the "gadflies" set out to get sex included in the jury discrimination clause of the civil rights bill in the Senate. Since 1957, women had been eligible to serve on federal juries on the same basis as men. Yet, state laws remained a hodgepodge of exclusions and special conditions.

Marguerite operated the way she always had, mounting letter-writing campaigns through BPW, General Federation, women from the commission and its committees, educating as many women as she could, working closely with the women in Congress. Pauli Murray worked through the ACLU and congressmen sympathetic to civil rights, keeping in close touch with Marguerite, Mary Eastwood, and Catherine East.

The little group of women brought together by the president's commission was becoming the nucleus of the kind of coalition Marguerite had dreamed of creating through BPW. Women were coming together as activists, though not in the way she had expected. In high spirits amid the jury duty campaign, she wrote Vi:

> There has been between 4 inches of snow here today. This time big heavy wet snowflakes. They will not stop traffic, but

hang heavy on the trees making them beautiful. Their naked black branches are suddenly covered with white ermine. I love seeing it. I was out today.

Then I bought a little pork roast, and had myself a wonderful browned pot roast and a sweet potato for supper.

In April, Congresswoman Florence Dwyer read in the *Congressional Record* an article Marguerite had written for the BPW and AAUW magazines, "The Right to Serve." She described the *White* victory and concluded: "We cannot stand motionless awaiting other Gardenia Whites to spearhead other case-by-case actions." By the time the bill passed the House, it included a Dwyer–Griffiths amendment protecting women against the "denial of the right" to serve on any jury.

In June, there was a discouraging decision by the Mississippi Supreme Court refusing to accept as precedent the *White* ruling: "The legislature had the right to exclude women so they may continue as mothers, wives, and homemakers." As the women on the president's commission had agreed, the only real solution to such "legal discrimination" was a Supreme Court ruling or a constitutional amendment.

In the short term, it was more important than ever to get uniform jury service guaranteed by law. Marguerite wrote the president, the attorney general, and everybody she knew in Congress. She kept every organization she belonged to informed, saw to it that they passed resolutions and forwarded them to Congress. She wrote articles and made speeches.

Late in the summer, women were astonished and insulted when the Senate rejected the Dwyer–Griffiths amendment along with other "minor amendments." Finally, a filibuster by Southern senators scuttled the entire civil rights bill of which jury service was part.

Meanwhile, displeasure over EEOC's failure to enforce Title VII for women was spreading. For months, women in NAWL, BPW, ACLU, and the Citizens Council fumed. Marguerite was corresponding with hundreds of women across the country about jury service, and soon the letters were calling for pressure on EEOC as well. Elizabeth (Betty) Boyer, a law professor in Ohio, was one who responded.

Marguerite and Betty Boyer had found themselves kindred

spirits at a recent NAWL meeting in Chicago when the two of them left the others at the hotel to go see Correggio's *Madonna, Child and St. John,* at the Art Institute.

Betty Boyer wore good, comfortable clothes and pulled her hair straight back from her face. She was curious about everything and very opinionated. A good talker, she left no doubt about where she stood. She had married and given up a private law practice, then divorced. Her father had taught her to handle money, save it, invest it. It worried her that most women didn't know how to look after themselves. But she didn't do much organizational work and didn't see herself as a political person. She was all energy: a sculptor, a sportswoman, a lawyer, a teacher, and an avid gardener.

In March, she sent Marguerite the classified section of the *Cleveland Plain Dealer.* "Obviously," she concluded, "these ads mean 'equal' to apply to race but not sex."

On June 20, Martha Griffiths denounced the EEOC on the floor of the House of Representatives. If EEOC and Congress thought women would put up with a charade, they were mistaken. Herman Edelsberg, EEOC's executive director, had called the sex provision a "fluke," and said that he and others at EEOC thought men were "entitled" to have female secretaries. "What," Griffiths asked, "is this sickness that causes an official to ridicule the law he is to uphold and enforce?" They had taken an oath to uphold the law, "not just the part of it they were interested in."

Marguerite was equally blunt: "Employers, unions, and newspapers do not welcome any supervision or departure from the old methods of offering higher level jobs to men and the clerical and lesser posts to women under the convenient headings."

The State Commissions on the Status of Women were scheduled to meet a few days after Griffth's EEOC speech, with Griffiths scheduled to speak at the closing luncheon. Unofficially, Catherine East had invited Betty Friedan to attend. Marguerite was chairing a panel that included Pauli Murray and other ACLU members who would discuss *White* v. *Crook* and sex discrimination.

The conference began, as it had before, with greetings from President Johnson, who mentioned the *White* case and credited his administration with equalizing men and women in appointments and promotions.

But, beneath an air of amiability, the women muttered in discontent. Martha Griffiths's EEOC speech was being circulated. The president's words just didn't jibe with what they knew was happening. Added to their disgruntlement over sex-segregated want-ads was the rumor that Richard Graham, a Republican businessman sympathetic to women's rights, would not be reappointed to the EEOC.

For two days the dissatisfaction grew and crystallized around Betty Friedan and Pauli Murray. Women, they kept saying, were going to have to organize for action the way the blacks had done. They would have to demonstrate *en masse* and take cases to court. They didn't want lip service; they didn't want things to stay the same. They wanted change. No government program was going to do that. Nobody was going to give it to them.

Although, as an employee of the Women's Bureau at the Labor Department, Catherine East couldn't back them up in public, she furnished some of the ideas and much of the information that set the little clique on fire. She *knew* what was going on. So did Mary Eastwood. So did Sonia Pressman. Kay Clarenbach shared their concern but still believed they could work through Esther Peterson and the Woman's Bureau.

On Wednesday, the National Woman's Party was refused permission to introduce a resolution to bring ERA under consideration. Late that night, a small group gathered in Betty Friedan's hotel room: Friedan, Murray, Eastwood, Clarenbach, Dorothy Haener from the United Automobile Workers, and Catherine Conroy from the Communications Workers of America. Inka O'Hanrahan, an avid ERA supporter and member of the National Woman's Party, was there from California. There were others, about fifteen in all. As a member of the Citizens Advisory Council and thereby associated with the Women's Bureau, Marguerite had not been invited.

Some of the women gathered in Friedan's room wanted to introduce a motion condemning EEOC's failure to enforce Title VII for women and endorsing the reappointment of Richard Graham. Kay Clarenbach insisted they do it. She knew the women at the Women's Bureau; she knew Esther Peterson was sympathetic. She and two or three others would go to Peterson the next morning and request to present their resolution.

Murray and Friedan despaired. What good would such a request do? The Woman's Party had already been turned down. Even if it worked, all they would have was another resolution. Why couldn't women DO anything, they asked each other.[4]

The dissidents got their answer soon enough. No, Peterson told them, they couldn't present a resolution of any kind. The purpose of the conference was to share information, not take action. She would have no part of it. Murray, Friedan, and East had known what would happen. Now Clarenbach and the others knew. And they were furious.

By then, Marguerite knew what was going on — and she knew parliamentary procedure. When Betty Friedan rose during her session and asked whether the panel could present to the conference a resolution calling for the reappointment of Richard Graham, Marguerite ruled against them, knowing the Woman's Party had already been turned down. The group could, however, express its view in a "sense of the meeting" motion — which she herself would deliver to President Johnson.

During lunch, Martha Griffiths fueled the flame: "The Constitution of the United States includes you, too. . . . You are human beings." Seated at the head table, Marguerite watched two round tables in the middle of the room fill up with the most militant women at the conference. They were not to be placated. Kay Clarenbach had joined the leaders and now the other women were ready to follow.

What should they call themselves, someone asked, and Betty Friedan began scribbling on a napkin. The National Organization for Women. N.O.W. Not "of" women but "for" women. Men were going to join too; Richard Graham was with them, and Phineas Indritz, a talkative, intense man, the only one of them with any experience in civil rights law.

Clarenbach became their on-the-spot coordinator and collected five dollars from everyone who wanted to join. By the end of the day, NOW had twenty-seven members. Anna Roosevelt Halsted heard what they were doing and walked across the room to put her name on the short list. Soon Martha Griffiths joined.[5]

But Marguerite waited. She had planned a long vacation in Europe, ending with a visit with her nephew, Kenneth, and his family in England.

Before she left, she wrote the promised letter to President

Johnson, quoting the "sense of the meeting motion" passed by the state commissions and explaining the attitudes of the women who made it. "All are apprised of the situation in the E.E.O.C. and alert to immediate developments. . . . they hope that the President will make appointments which will result in obeying the letter of the law passed by Congress."

To the president's special assistant, Bill Moyers, she wrote more plainly: the administration was losing credibility with women.

The women gathered in the Statler Hotel were not the only group disillusioned with the Great Society's unmet promises. The civil rights movement was growing more militant, developing a violent edge. August 1965 saw devastating riots in the Watts ghetto of Los Angeles. By the end of the summer of 1966, ghetto uprisings had broken out in almost every major city in the country. Seven dead, 400 hurt, some 3,000 arrested, and more than $5 million lost to vandals, looters, and arsonists. An incomprehensible tide of discontent was swelling — against poverty, discrimination, the war in Vietnam — against authority — against discontent itself. No one seemed to be in control, and people were blaming the president.

Marguerite returned from Europe in September to find jury reform plowed under in the Senate. The idea of an activist women's organization seemed to have taken hold. She had a letter from Pauli Murray dated August 9. "We're not building a mass organization, but trying to get key women around the country who can move quickly on matters like Title VII, jury amendment, etc." A copy of a letter Betty Friedan had sent to a Dr. Anne Steinman carried the same message,

> The idea, for the moment, is not to set up a big bureaucratic organization with lots of members, but rather to get together women and men who share our purpose, and who can work effectively to stimulate the action that is needed. . . . there is no organization that exists to do this.[6]

Catherine East and Mary Eastwood told Marguerite that NOW needed her. There were already hundreds of members and mail coming so fast they couldn't answer it all. A New Yorker named Muriel Fox was handling the press. Kay Clarenbach managed things and Friedan made the headlines. But none of them knew anything about organizations. They were all prima donnas.

They needed her experience, her knowledge of procedures.[7]

Marguerite joined immediately, and Mary Eastwood wrote Kay Clarenbach: "There are two people here who are musts for the executive board — Marguerite Rawalt and Phineas Indritz. They perhaps more than any others have been following NOW's statement of purpose for a long time, and most effectively." [8]

A new phase of Marguerite's life had begun, and — like all the others — it began with work. They had cried out for an action organization and they were going to get it; but first they must have an organizing meeting, write by-laws, elect a board. Without procedures, the whole thing could fall apart. There were so many things these new women didn't know — about the state labor laws, ERA, the Fourteenth Amendment. Mary and Catherine had learned from her. Now there were many more who wanted to learn.

On October 5, Betty Friedan, Kay Clarenbach, Mary Eastwood, Phineas Indritz, Marguerite and a few others met in Washington to plan an organizing meeting for the 300 members they expected to show up at the Airline Motel on October 28–30. To Agnes Pfeifer, a Zonta friend, Marguerite wrote: "I spent part of yesterday participating in an exciting new organization, N.O.W., by leading women who want an independent group to work for status of women and speak out for action — and no more run-around in Congress! Betty Friedan, the writer, was here — women in Congress — etc."

Soon she was recruiting her friends. She wanted the top people, lawyers, the few stalwarts left in BPW. She wrote Judges Sarah Hughes and Burnita Matthews. To Libby Sachar, Helen Hurd, and Emma McGall, all from BPW, she sent a single long letter describing the founding of NOW and asking them to join:

> . . . Dr. Clarenbach is chairman of the Wisconsin Commission. Many Wisconsin women have joined, including Erma Romanik, former legislative chairman and Mabel McClanahan, president-elect of BPW. Mr. [Richard] Graham will take a part, and two other men who have been working with us. Martha Griffiths. Anna Roosevelt Halsted. They recently had a planning meeting in D.C. and called me in. I joined and agreed to make the organization known to a selective group. They are not out for numbers as such, but for those who will be willing to speak out, for women's rights. Betty Furness and Betty Friedan are members.

. . . Anyway, I hope you may see your way to line up with N.O.W.

On October 12, amid plans for the organizing meeting, Marguerite received a letter from Velma Mengelkoch, an industrial worker in California. She and some other women were suing North American Aviation because the company used state maximum hours laws to limit the number of women they employed and refuse them promotions. Mengelkoch said she had two children to support; she needed the overtime and she deserved a promotion. Her court-appointed lawyers weren't doing anything for her. Someone had told her about Marguerite and NAWL. Could they help?

That night, Marguerite called Phil Silver, Mengelkoch's lawyer in Los Angeles. By the next afternoon, she had talked to interested lawyers in Washington, some on the phone, some in person, and collected sixty dollars which she mailed to Silver. She also sent a copy of the Murray–Eastwood article on women and the Fourteenth Amendment. She wanted to file a brief in the case, the first to test the hours laws under Title VII. It could, she thought, become the Fourteenth Amendment test case they were looking for. That night, she wrote Mengelkoch:

> Your gallant spirit is more than appreciated. You still have support and backers, you have them here, when the word can be spread around. It seems to many of us that you are indeed the bearer of a banner of importance to all women, and the possible medium of a most important decision and a far-reaching one.

In the meantime, NOW had to set up a board and get ready for its first general meeting. Kay Clarenbach had agreed to chair the board and Betty Friedan would be the first president. Marguerite met with them the night before the organizing meeting began on Friday, October 28.

Already obligated to serve as parliamentarian at a Zonta regional conference in Saddlebrook, New Jersey, she would not be able to stay for the weekend. Mary Eastwood understood what had to be done. She had brought in several other lawyers, including Caruthers Berger, a lawyer at the Department of Labor. Berger had a slow Mississippi drawl and a loud voice. As a member of the Woman's Party, she was already an avid ERA supporter. She was tense and dogmatic. When she took a stand, she brooked no arguments.

Marguerite got home on Sunday night and woke up the next morning to newspaper headlines that annoyed her. Troubles in Asia dominated the front page. Heavy losses in Vietnam. A gruesome photograph of a civilian wounded in the fighting. LBJ in Malaysia. A few years ago nobody had ever heard of those places.

And the want-ads. The *Washington Post* was among the worst. No explanation, just "Wanted, Men" and "Wanted, Women." Pages and pages for the men — engineers, biologists, architects, all the good jobs. For women, almost nothing, one page, clerical jobs, service jobs.

Then she saw it, a story about the NOW convention. They had done it. The papers were taking it seriously, an ACTION organization for women.

Marguerite stayed in her bathrobe half the day, calling people, getting the details. They had a board of twenty-four women and men and five national officers — men and women, black and white, union, business, academic, prestigious, and unknown.

In her absence, Marguerite was named to head their legal committee. Guided by Mary Eastwood, the organization had agreed to take on the Mengelkoch case and support other discrimination suits under Title VII.

All over the country women were being discriminated against, despite Title VII. Aileen Hernandez, the only woman member of EEOC, was resigning in frustration and going back to California. She had been elected executive vice-president of NOW but couldn't accept the position until she left EEOC in mid-November.

Soon Marguerite was bombarded with letters from women wanting to join NOW. Others wanted help with discrimination in employment.

Her response to longtime Zonta friend, Nancy Wood, is typical of the letters she wrote to clubwomen: "NOW is getting off to a fine organizational start with good publicity. . . beginning without money for staff, office, etc., but with determination to get something done."

The tone of a letter to California BPW member Cravens Douglass was less gentle: "I can say they [NOW members] are setting out to do what I wish BPW were doing — and that is to be really active in legislative and administrative matters. . . . and there is SO MUCH going on right now. Women must act or just give up for all

time, frankly. . . . I have joined and hope to see this group SPEAK
OUT and TAKE SOME PUBLIC ACTION."

Within a few weeks, NOW had written letters to the president,
EEOC, and Attorney General Ramsey Clark. They wanted the
Civil Rights Act of 1964 amended to cover women in housing and
in Federal (as well as private) employment. They asked for support
for an equal jury bill. They wanted the Justice Department to intervene on behalf of Velma Mengelkoch.

On November 22, Marguerite, Betty Friedan, and Kay Clarenbach marched into the EEOC office and told the commissioners
they wanted the two vacancies on the commission filled by women.
Furthermore, they wanted a decision on the employment of female-
only airline stewardesses and new guidelines for classified ads,
quidelines on retirement, pensions, and maternity rights, help with
the Mengelkoch case.

The next day, Elizabeth Shelton reported in the *Washington
Post:* "Neo-Suffragettes on the March. Mrs. Friedan is Fighting for
Women's Equality NOW."

Then they met with John Macy at the Civil Service Commission. Although he too had been a member of the president's commission, women had gotten nothing from him. They wanted more
women judges and a civil rights bill that included equal jury service. They wanted an interview with Lyndon Johnson and his attorney general.

Marguerite was exhilarated. At last, women were demanding
what they wanted and needed, "tying right into the problem," as
she put it. She was very, very proud. This was what she wanted.

Immediately she was meeting with Caruthers Berger, Mary
Eastwood and Phineas Indritz, her "legal committee," and by the
time she left for Corpus Christi, on December 18, they had written
a seventeen-page "Petition to the EEOC." When Betty Friedan
was hauled into court that Christmas Eve to testify about Aileen
Hernandez's involvement with NOW, the little group in Washington considered it harassment. The airlines knew how much money
it would cost to hire male flight attendants and pay women and
men the same salary.

Marguerite returned from Texas determined to write the de-
finitive Fourteenth Amendment brief for the Mengelkoch case. Her
letters burned with enthusiasm: "Mengelekoch case. . . has all the

potential of becoming a landmark case on women under the Fourteenth Amendment. . . . NOW will file an amicus brief. . . . The attorney general is being urged to intervene, as he is authorized to
do."

In January, when friends in Zonta wanted to nominate her for
district "governor," she declined:

> . . . we are going into a wave of the future in the emancipation of
> women. . . . And I find myself personally involved in so much of
> it. My mail contained five letters of immediate need. And my
> telephone has rung four times with calls pertaining to the law
> case in California, to next week's meeting in Chicago of NOW. I
> know if you knew what I am to do you would readily agree this
> must take precedence for service to women in Zonta and beyond
> it. Mrs. Philip Hart, wife of Michigan's senator, just called me on
> a matter of concern in legislation and in the NOW group. I have
> to do something about it. A motion must be drafted and sent to
> Los Angeles, with letter of instruction, asking the court for leave
> to file an amicus curiae brief — and I am the person who must
> draft and sign it.

While Marguerite and Mary Eastwood worked with her legal
committee, filed incorporation papers for NOW, met with members about legislation and set up a local chapter, Catherine East
was becoming a one-woman clipping service, reading everything
she could find about women, copying it and mailing it to her network. Though still not a member of NOW, East remained at the
center.

Suddenly the tiny nucleus of women was exploding, its influence covering the country like a mist. No one could have predicted
it — and no one could control it.

When Pauline Fyler, executive director of Zonta International, sent Marguerite an account of a California dean's ideas on
educating women, she was indignant.

> [The dean's] approach to the education of women so infuriates
> me that I dare not reply. The idea of placidly educating women
> into an acceptance of the lower rungs in the economic world is
> tragic. The world needs scientists, engineers — and if a brain is
> qualified to do such work, it should be encouraged, not smoth-
> ered because it is a female brain. I wish you would send this letter
> to J. Maria Pierce, along with this memo if you wish. Egads!

Suddenly, it was all right to be angry and outraged at things she had accepted in silence for so long.

Soon Marguerite was spending every spare minute on the Mengelkoch brief. Many nights and weekends, she and the members of her little committee met at Mary Eastwood's office and worked long hours, sometimes debating a point of law for days. Sex discrimination law was new. In terms of precedence and experience, they groped in the dark. As Marguerite explained it to a friend a few months later, "All of us are working folk, and must do this as an added 'patriotic' duty — but do it we will."

On January 27, Marguerite wrote Evelyn Whitlow, a NAWL associate who lived in Los Angeles, asking her to represent them as local counsel for Mengelkoch in the California courts. How did they go about filing the brief they were writing? Did they need permission? From whom? Was there a deadline? It was impossible to do it all from Washington. She needed to know immediately.

At the same time, Marguerite was doing all she could to bring different kinds of women together for women's rights. Along with others, she established and served on the first D.C. "State" Commission on the Status of Women. With the help of Jane Hart (wife of Senator Philip Hart) she set up a local chapter of NOW. Then she began putting together a small, independent group of established women. By January, she had organized it, invited thirty women to join, and named it the Washington Forum. They would meet once a month to discuss issues of concern to women — to exchange ideas and for the sheer pleasure of it.

The group was handpicked from a generation of women who had succeeded against the odds and still cared about what happened to other women. As her work with NOW became more distracting and more far-flung, Marguerite would need that, a bedrock of women who understood her and whom she could trust. Catherine East and Mary Eastwood joined as did Kathryn Heath, a longtime activist and historian for women at the Department of Health, Education, and Welfare. There were several lawyers, including old friends like Annie Perry Huntting, Evelyn Boyer, and Judges Joyce Capps and Reva Beck Bosone, former congresswoman from Utah, and now solicitor of the Post Office.

But she hadn't (and really never would) given up her belief that there was a place in the women's movement for the traditional clubs, and in May of 1966, she had accepted a two-year term as president of the D. C. State Federation of Women's Clubs.

Early in 1967, she tried to describe her new commitments to her family:

> . . . This month has been a killer-diller of activity. Today is no exception. I got up at dark, to have my breakfast and read the paper and then to this typewriter before another day passes. My telephone begins at 9:00 a.m. or earlier and sometimes I could tear it from the wall. I am sure that yesterday I had no less than thirty conversations. My name has been in the newspapers several times this month because of the activities which take all my time.
>
> Last month I organized a new exclusive club called Washington Forum, of thirty women in key posts in government and business. Luncheon meeting, to exchange information of public affairs. It has had much publicity.
>
> This is lots of "I" — but that is what I want to hear from all of you.

By the time NOW's first executive committee and board of directors met in Chicago in February 1967, Marguerite had convinced them of the need to set up a tax-exempt NOW legal defense fund to finance discrimination cases. At her recommendation, Grace Cox, a New York lawyer and NAWL associate, was appointed to investigate the matter. At the same meeting, Betty Friedan selected three Washington women — Caruthers Berger, Mary Eastwood, and Morag Simchak — to study the pros and cons of the Equal Rights Amendment, thinking they might be able to come up with "modern" wording for a constitutional amendment — and give it a chance in Congress.

On Sunday, March 19, the Sunday magazine, *This Week*, featured the encounter between NOW and John Macy at the Civil Service Commission in a lead story on the "Women's Revolution." Like much of the reporting Marguerite saw, the tone was snide. Didn't women already have equal rights? Weren't they just piggybacking on civil rights legislation? But the writer, Thomas Fleming, described their complaints against EEOC fairly and listed correct statistics on the low-status, low-pay jobs held by most women. And he did a fair job of describing NOW's reasons for supporting Velma Mengelkoch. Already NOW had things to be proud of. The administration's new civil rights bill included equal jury service, largely because of pressure from NOW and the Citizens Advisory Council. In direct response to NOW demands and the publicity surrounding it, EEOC had scheduled public hearings on discrimination in employment.

Marguerite's NAWL acquaintance Betty Boyer, read the story that same day in Novelty, Ohio. Maybe Fleming was mocking them. Maybe not. She saw Marguerite's name in the article and agreed with the things NOW was doing. By late afternoon she had written a letter to Friedan and offered to organize Ohio for NOW.

Betty Boyer's life was settled, peaceful. She had a house in the country, a wildflower garden, a teaching job she liked. She had an independent income and many interests. She loved to sail and ski. She had plans to travel and write historical novels when she retired.

When she was young, she had married and given up a good private law practice. Then divorce had called for adjustments. Now she was happy again. She hadn't expected to make new commitments at this stage in her life. "I was in my garden," she remembers. "I put down my hoe and went inside and wrote that letter to Betty Friedan. Like Martin Luther, there I stood. I could DO no other. I did it in loyalty to all those women who had been cut off at the pass. My own mother, even. There were many women like me that year." [9]

Within a few months Boyer had organized several Ohio chapters and enrolled hundreds of Ohio women in NOW: older women, professionals, other lawyers, women she knew, her own nieces, friends of friends. Criticism of NOW had already begun, and she wanted women they couldn't "lay a glove on."

For months after the NOW board met in Chicago, Marguerite, Phineas, Caruthers, and Mary worked on the Mengelkoch brief, trying to prove that the state laws of California denied women opportunities to which they were entitled under the Fourteenth Amendment. They were all working too hard, bolting a sandwich or going without supper too many nights a week, some of them writing, others doing the research, still not knowing for sure what kind of deadline they were under. The work was slow and tedious and the weight of their inexperience heavy. They were in new territory. No one else had experience either. With nowhere to turn but to themselves, they carried the burden of history and an overwhelming sense of responsibility. At times, it seemed as if the future of all women lay in their hands.

But by April 1, Marguerite could write Betty Friedan that they had a forty-to fifty-page brief they could be proud of. "There had been night meetings," she wrote, "photocopies distributed between us by hand, telephone calls, hours and hours in libraries researching, especially by Caruthers Berger and myself."

All the while, letters poured in from other women needing legal assistance. Marguerite's letter to Friedan ends with a cry for help:

> The two pleas which you sent to me from individuals, are just beyond my capacity to go into, and I cannot find anyone else who has time to do it. I have brought them to attention of others on my Legal Committee. Our only suggestion, repeated by Phineas with deep concern: we simply must get a paid *executive secretary.*

For Marguerite the pressure continued to build — the importance of the Mengelkoch case, the lack of funds, the limited time, the growing demands from hundreds of women who needed legal help. Her letters to Friedan repeat a frustrated, sometimes confused, refrain: "I must have relief. . . I can't do it all. . . It must be done. . . How can we do it? I am constantly berating myself since these things must be done, since [litigation] is our ultimate and major goal. . . I constantly feel frustrated, berating myself."

If she didn't lead them into court with the discrimination cases who would, she asked herself over and over. Always she came up with the same answer: since there was no one else to do it, she must.

For the next ten years, she would seldom have time to indulge either her doubts or her fatigue. Now, of necessity, she turned her attention to EEOC hearings brought about mainly by the demands of NOW and other women's groups. In addition to preparing her own testimony against protective labor laws, Marguerite was busy recruiting testimony from NAWL, BPW, and General Federation leaders. She wanted "expert testimony" and she wanted the audience packed. Still pleased a few days later, she wrote her co-workers in NOW: "Hearings were excellent. . . . We were all GOOD."

In mid-July, Marguerite returned to Washington from a three-week tour of the South Sea Islands to face endless rounds of NOW decisions. After talking with Alice Paul and others from the Woman's Party, Mary Eastwood and Caruthers Berger (appointed by

Friedan to study the issue) began calling for immediate and une-
quivocal endorsement of ERA.[10]

Marguerite had reservations. In the light of recent NOW publicity, she thought the possibility of a rejection of ERA by NOW
would be too devastating to risk. Furthermore, ERA endorsement
was sure to alienate labor union women like Dorothy Haener, who
was moving the UAW leadership toward ERA as fast as she could.
She wanted NOW to choose its priorities carefully. For the time
being, she thought the court cases should come first, then ERA.
Later they could take up even more controversial, less crucial issues.

Although Marguerite's committee work on the Citizens Advisory Council had convinced her that abortion should be decrimin-
alized, she had serious reservations about NOW's endorsing legal-
ized abortion. She was even more leery of those supporting lesbian
rights. For her, sexuality was a private matter, not a legal one, and
certainly not a "women's issue." Her argument was always the
same — women activists should define their territory precisely and
postpone controversial issues. They had their hands full with job
discrimination, low wages, poor representation on the bench, on
juries, and in Congress.

While NOW struggled to keep its balance, the country seemed
to be losing its own. Each day was stranger and more tumultuous
than the day before. On Easter Sunday, 1967, 10,000 young people
congregated in New York's Central Park to celebrate love. In San
Francisco, a similar crowd chanting "tune in, turn on, drop out,"
cheered LSD guru Timothy Leary. The love people, the drug people, the peace people, the people opposed to the war in Vietnam.
Suddenly the country seemed to be rejecting all the things Marguerite valued most: education, hard work, thrift, responsibility,
citizenship, patriotism. When the "Women's Strike for Peace"
brought hoards of women to the steps of the White House, she considered them "peaceniks" rather than activists for women.

Extremists were drifting into NOW as well, and radical
"women's liberation" groups unaffiliated with NOW sprang out of
the discontent of women in leftist political groups and peace and
civil rights organizations. Small groups, loosely connected to one
another, surfaced across the country, mainly in New York, Chicago, even Washington — objecting, it seemed, to everything.

Suddenly, the women's movement Marguerite had longed for was not what she had envisioned. Increasingly, she was convinced that activism for women would have to focus on legal rights and reform in order to have any hope for success. A fragmented movement was sure to sink in a sea of confusion.

A letter she wrote in September to a woman in California who wanted NOW to support her right to smoke at a job where men smoked reveals Marguerite's position:

> I might add the personal, purely personal, reaction, that the NOW, being so new and in the growing stages, and building a public reputation, should direct its main thrust upon legal discriminations in priority to others. Perhaps in time, we can reach to all sorts of personal privilege discriminations. Would the mounting of a campaign to permit women to smoke at their desks create the kind of public image which would build strength into an infant organization? Much as I may sympathize with personal liberties being observed for men and women, there must be priorities established where we have not the means as yet to resist all discriminations.

By late summer, Velma Mengelkoch had fired her lawyers, and NOW had taken over. Evelyn Whitlow in Los Angeles would be local counsel in California and would file NOW's Fourteenth Amendment brief.

In August, a Georgia woman named Lorena Weeks, who had been denied a promotion by Southern Bell Telephone Company, sued under Title VII and lost in the district court. Weeks was told the job she wanted was closed to women even though she had more seniority and more experience than the only other applicant, the man who got the job. Southern Bell had won in trial court by hiding behind a thirty-pound maximum weight-lifting regulation applied to women only.

Marguerite had made up her mind: NOW *had* to take certain cases even though there was no money for them and no way of getting it. She would be responsible for the Weeks case herself, she said.

A similar case, *Bowe, et al.* v. *Colgate-Palmolive Company*, had been lost in the Indiana federal court, leaving employers free to keep separate seniority lists and pay categories and enforce weight-lifting maximums against women only. The legal committee wanted that case too. Explaining the *Colgate* case to Friedan, Marguerite wrote, "I do not see how NOW can fail to go forward on it. It is an extremely important case." If the defeats were allowed to stand, there would be little chance of protecting women from employment discrimination under Title VII. Regardless of the hardships, they had to go on.

In October, they read about Jane Daniel, a woman given a ten-year sentence for armed robbery under a state law that required longer sentences for women than for men — since women, it said, took longer to rehabilitate than men. According to the Pennsylvania Superior Court, the distinction did not deny women equal protection of the laws as defined by the Fourteenth Amendment. When the Department of Justice refused to intervene, Marguerite and Phineas Indritz began working on the case jointly for NOW and The American Veterans Committee, for which Indritz served as general counsel.

In mid-September, the NOW board met again in Madison, Wisconsin. Alice Rossi, a sociologist Marguerite knew from her work on the Citizens Advisory Council, and Ti-Grace Atkinson, from the New York chapter, were assigned to study NOW's position on the legalization of abortion.

Atkinson was a graduate student at Columbia, a beautiful woman in her twenties, her Louisiana accent sprinkled with the Marxist jargon of the student peace movement. Her feminism seemed peculiar and farfetched to Marguerite. Women should set out to abolish power — not share it — Atkinson insisted. Leadership was oppressive.

Atkinson and others, including Betty Friedan, wanted to reduce NOW dues for students, and make membership free for anyone who couldn't afford to pay. To women like Marguerite and Betty Boyer, it was all too strange. What were they going to do for money?

As soon as Marguerite got home from Madison, she began writing friends in NOW, urging them to attend the November meeting. ERA was sure to come up for a vote, and they couldn't risk defeat. She, Eastwood, East, Berger all agreed: if it came up, it had to pass. They would have to talk Alice Paul, Mabel Vernon, and others from the Woman's Party into joining NOW. ERA was at stake.

On Saturday, November 18, 1967, the National Organization for Women held its first annual convention in Washington's Mayflower Hotel. Expanding in all directions at once, at a rate no one could have predicted, it could shatter into a million pieces along any one of the myriad cracks in its unstable surface. A week earlier, Marguerite had written NAWL veteran Grace Cox, begging her to come to the meeting, "I am not pessimistic, but. . . . Our NOW is growing and growing fast, and we must guide it through these initial stages."

The struggle over ERA raged for two days behind the scenes. The labor union women begged for a delay. Kay Clarenbach wanted to grant it. Most of Saturday night was spent talking and arguing in Betty Friedan's room. Finally, it was all fought out on the floor of the Mayflower's Chinese Room.

Marguerite sat at the front, serving as Betty Friedan's parliamentarian. She had agreed to do that with the understanding that she be allowed to enter into the debate. Caruthers Berger made an impassioned plea for ERA. Dorothy Haener and Caroline Davis argued against it. Women in the unions needed another year; they were making progress.

Phineas Indritz made enemies by telling them the truth they didn't want to hear: ERA didn't have a chance in Congress anytime soon. They should invest themselves in the courts where they had a chance. Berger was outraged. The debate went on and on.

When it finally ended, ERA was number one in NOW's "Bill of Rights." After the vote, the meeting room became a motley sea of faces, all ages, sizes, races swarming behind a row of suffragists from the Woman's Party, there in hats and white gloves to cast their votes.

Finally, the "Bill of Rights" outlined an ambitious agenda for the volatile movement, calling for immediate action on the Equal Rights Amendment, equality in employment, maternity leave, tax deductions for home and day care, child-care centers, equal and unsegregated education, equal job training opportunities and allowances for women in poverty, the right to control their own reproductive lives.

Women students had shown up in unexpected numbers. Aroused by new possibilities, they associated feminism with a multitude of private and political causes: peace, sexual freedom, even anarchy. They came particularly to cast their votes for abortion rights — "a woman's right to control her own body."

After it was all over, Marguerite described the conference to Evelyn Whitlow. "Wonderfully able" women were there. "We really made strides — voted to endorse the Equal Rights Amendment as a first item. Other endorsements in many fields, some of which did not interest me as much." She had reported on the Mengelkoch case and three of the plaintiffs in the Colgate–Palmolive case told their own story to the convention. "Everyone was enraptured and educated."

The price for what they accomplished was high. The union women resigned from the board. Dorothy Haener was particularly disappointed.

Betty Boyer, a former president of the League of Women Voters as well as the recruiter of NOW's earliest members in Ohio, went home in despair over the abortion vote. She remembered how excited she had been during the summer when she had gone to Washington and talked with Marguerite and Catherine East about getting NOW going in her state. In August, she had written to tell Marguerite how she and thirty other women had celebrated the chartering of the state chapter on her back patio.

> We have a good start with several leading women profs at Kent and Ohio State, and the college girls and younger business & professional women are really taking off on it. We are also pleased at the cordial & cooperative attitude of the younger men, when they are approached on a factual basis. . . . It is obvious that only a very exceptional earner can any longer support his wife in both idleness and security! [11]

The conservative, established women she had recruited in Ohio would be appalled at the abortion stand. So was she: a new life was a "sacred trust." Boyer's young niece, who had come to the convention with her, was horrified to think what her parents would say.

Just as Marguerite and others feared, the *Washington Post* emphasized NOW's stand on abortion and, quoting from the "Bill of Rights," added: "NOW supports the furthering of the sexual revolution of our century by pressing for widespread sex education and provision of birth control information and contraceptives, and by urging that all laws penalizing abortion be repealed." In an interview, Ti-Grace Atkinson said, "the abortion stand seeks to free women really from their own notions of themselves as 'slaves' to their reproductive processes."

Marguerite's friends began complaining early the next morning. Those who hadn't attended the meeting didn't like what they read in the papers. Those who had, thought the convention had been stacked with students and radicals.

Marguerite didn't like the tone the younger women were taking either and, by Wednesday, had mailed a long letter saying as much to Betty Friedan, Kay Clarenbach, and Inka O'Hanrahan. Alison Drucker, NOW's student representative on the board, had given a report no one could hear and now there were all sorts of rumors about what she had proposed in the name of NOW. Why, Marguerite wanted to know, hadn't the Drucker report been printed and distributed like the others? Where was the organization going? Who was calling the shots? Things were happening too fast. She didn't know what was going on.

Like Betty Boyer, Marguerite was angry to be put on the line with the women she had recruited — for things about which she knew nothing and over which she had no control. She wondered if they were excluding her deliberately.

The letter to Friedan makes her philosophical position clear. The movement had to be organized and guided. ERA and litigation were too important to be undermined by irresponsible influences. She could continue to give her time only so long as she knew what was going on and had a voice in the decision-making.

> . . . While I am for having university women in our midst, in fact emphasizing this as most needful, I do feel we should exercise control over how this movement is implemented for the sake of our own effectiveness. I do not want to see NOW in the midst of student rioting on campuses, or quoted as supporting some of the leftist doctrines read every day. When it does, I wish my name off this letterhead.
>
> If the tail is going to wag the dog, I shall not continue to expend such effort on employment litigation.
>
> Morning Post, just as I knew it would after hearing our conference, headlined abortion and Ti-Grace Atkinson's statement. And today at Board of Trade annual luncheon, honoring our new Mayor and City Council, with 1,000 business and professionals, I sat at a table with nine men, one of whom, a fellow lawyer, asked me whether I was involved in this organization. I was immedi-

ately on defensive, trying to establish the legal discriminations
which men should help us erase.

Friedan's answer is a touching attempt to bridge the gap between Marguerite and women younger than she by two generations:

> . . . I make a special plea to you, Marguerite, whose service as
> head of our legal committee and whose magnificently intrepid
> counsel generally has been so invaluable through NOW's forma-
> tive first year, to make a real effort to understand the importance
> to NOW of the young women and students who are so eagerly
> joining our ranks and volunteering so much time and effort. They
> share your concern with sex-discrimination in employment and
> in the laws, and it is their support that makes NOW such a vital
> new force to be contended with and that will give unfinished
> business (such as the equal rights amendment) a new, young and
> urgent image. Some of the issues that concern them as much as
> employment discrimination and the equal rights amendment
> seem to irritate you; but to them, and I must admit increasingly
> to me, these two kinds of issues are in effect indivisible in terms of
> the purposes of NOW. To be blunt, the New Woman whom
> NOW speaks for (you and I were New Women before our time
> but they, the younger ones, are going to be New Women en
> masse) insists on an honest confrontation of the sexual implica-
> tions of full equality for women in truly equal partnership with
> men, and sees these sexual issues not as irrelevant but as indis-
> pensable to true equality in employment and the body politic. . . .
> we are truly a three-generation movement. . . and this is our vital
> strength.

Sensing the depth of Marguerite's uncertainty over the role
she played in a movement being swept along at a speed beyond
their control — perhaps beyond their understanding — Inka
O'Hanrahan wrote her a long letter of sympathy and encouragement. She didn't think the organization would be damaged by the
abortion issue; the news coverage in general had been good. Marguerite had not been intentionally left out of important decisions.
They needed her desperately. "We all feel strongly about the purposes of NOW and how vital this organization is in its yeastlike
function. . . . Rest assured, dear, that I shall do everything in my
power to keep you happy and to keep us all sailing along harmoni-
ously and effectively." [12]

Despite growing concern over "radical and irresponsible" elements in the movement, nothing shook Marguerite's commitment to the Title VII cases. In order to continue that work, she walked a precarious line between total commitment and doubt. She justified her position repeatedly in letters to Betty Boyer: "NOW is the only organization taking sex discrimination cases to court, the only group able to take political action."

Under Marguerite's guidance, NOW appealed the Weeks case. They could not, she said, have wished for a more straightforward test of sex discrimination under the Civil Rights Act of 1964.

Lorena Weeks, a small, gentle woman in her thirties, had worked for the telephone company in Wadley, Georgia, since her senior year in high school when she took a job as a telephone operator to support an orphaned sister and brother. Through her union newsletter, she had learned about Title VII and had not hesitated to apply for her boss's job when he retired as switchman. Stunned by the reaction of both the company (the job was closed to women) and her friends and relatives (why did she stir up trouble, take a good job away from a bread-winning man?), she had appealed to EEOC. She was then assigned a local lawyer, who lost her case in court and assured her she would soon lose her job as well. Her husband thought she was causing trouble. Her children were embarrassed.

She was near despair when the NOW legal committee, gathered in Caruthers Berger's apartment, called to say NOW would take the case if Weeks would promise to stick with it until the end — despite the harassment that was sure to come. They would represent her and there would be no legal fees.

With encouragement from a sister-in-law, she agreed to their terms. She was a religious person, she said. This was something she was called to do. She knew how hard women worked. Now that help had come, she would not turn her back on it. Immediately she joined NOW and began working with Marguerite and Sylvia Roberts, a NOW lawyer in Baton Rouge, Louisiana. Soon she had joined a BPW club in nearby Lewisville. Still, she found only a few women in the tiny Bible Belt community to sympathize with what she was doing.

Increasingly frustrated with EEOC's refusal to respond to women, NOW organized the first national demonstration for women's rights since suffrage. Thursday, December 14, 1967, was declared a National Day of Demonstration with EEOC offices targeted all over the country. New York NOW members carried stacks of classified ad sections bound with red tape.

Marguerite took her turn before the main office in Washington between 12:00 noon and 1:00. Mary Eastwood appeared in the next day's *Washington Post,* wearing a tailored wool coat, her blonde hair falling over one eye. She looked young, innocent, determined.

A letter from Marguerite to Christine Krutchko, a BPW member interested in NOW, describes the event.

> Picketed the EEOC yesterday — about fifteen to twenty in picket line — white and Negro women; a catholic priest; older women and younger ones. Two high school boys came and asked to join, saying they couldn't understand why women did not have the same opportunities. . . . I am working very hard in this [organization] as I find it the only medium that is in ACTION.

A few days later, Marguerite left Washington for two weeks in Corpus Christi. In a January 3 interview with Nita Peterson of the *Corpus Christi Times,* she talked about the failings of EEOC and NOW's work in the courts, emphasizing the Mengelkoch and Daniel cases. That afternoon, she left for Chicago to get herself admitted to the Seventh Circuit Court of Appeals in order to appeal the Colgate–Palmolive case. Leaving Texas despite thick fog, she missed connections all along the way and arrived in Chicago in sub-zero weather a day later than she had planned. "Just the same," as she wrote the plaintiffs in the case, "at 9:30 the next morning, I taxied thru the cold to the courthouse — and lo, I can now sign papers. With Caruthers doing the brunt of the work, we will give it all possible."

Exhilarated by her hairline finish in Chicago, Marguerite returned to a nest of NOW challenges. During the first few days of 1968, the legal committee filed its brief in behalf of Jane Daniel and worked on the Weeks case. The incorporation of the legal defense fund in New York seemed to be on its way. They were making plans to sue EEOC to force it to comply with its own rules. Then, amid the first inklings of success, the board met in Pittsburgh on January 27, and faced divisions that ran so deep they threatened to tear the leadership apart.

Betty Boyer had returned to Ohio from the November convention to face complaints and outrage over the abortion plank. In self-defense, she polled the women she had recruited. Even those who agreed in principle thought the abortion vote had been "rammed through." They wanted an organization committed to the earliest objectives of NOW — elimination of discrimination in jobs, wages, and education. She had promised them that.

Boyer had a strong sense of right and wrong, and she wasn't timid about it. She felt a "moral obligation" to form a new organization in Ohio to be what she had promised NOW would be. Late in January, she wrote the national board saying that an appearance in Cleveland by Martha Griffiths scheduled for March under the sponsorship of NOW had been turned over to a nonpartisan group, mostly non-NOW members.

A few days later at the board meeting in Pittsburgh she resigned as president of the Ohio clubs and chair of the national membership committee and said she would resign from NOW's board if requested to do so. Incensed, Betty Friedan accused Boyer of using her position in NOW to set up a rival organization.

At the end of what Marguerite called "intensive debate" and what Boyer termed a "shouting match," nothing had been resolved. The exchange dramatized an ideological gap they would never be able to bridge. NOW was built on diversity and with it came gaps in culture, generations, race, politics. For years, they would struggle with the question, "What is a women's issue" and try to define themselves in terms of the answer.

Recalling her own distress over the abortion vote, Marguerite agreed with Betty Boyer that NOW wasn't run like other organizations and got off the track often enough. But, she insisted, they should stick with NOW as long as they could. It was through NOW — and only NOW — that women were making themselves heard in the courts and in Congress for the first time. Finally, Boyer agreed to stay on the board and retain her position on the nominating committee.

Despairing over the administrative bobbles that still held up the incorporation of a NOW legal defense fund, Marguerite agreed to take over the task herself. In an attempt to expedite matters, she suggested that an unwieldy eighteen-member legal defense fund board be replaced by an "incorporating board" of only seven members: the president and vice-president, two New York lawyers, and three of the four members of the legal committee — herself, Phineas Indritz, and Mary Eastwood. Caruthers Berger was not included.

Berger was smart and committed — but uncompromising. She resented authority and didn't know how to share responsibility. And she had never forgiven Phineas for being opposed to NOW's endorsement of ERA. Since both were government lawyers, neither Eastwood nor Berger could sign the NOW cases. Berger thought Marguerite got all the credit. Now she felt doubly slighted.

Not knowing how to handle the rift she had created in her committee, Marguerite stepped up her own work on the pioneering litigation fast developing in Weeks, Colgate, Mengelkoch and Daniel plus the Pittsburgh Press and the EEOC mandamus suit. With sheer force of will, she tried to placate Berger and hold the committee together, wanting them all to sacrifice themselves to the all-important sex discrimination cases.

At an age when most people are well into retirement, Marguerite was putting in eighteen-hour work days and long weekends. Occasionally, her diary still recorded a precious Sunday, *at home all day*, but even those were apt to be devoted to NOW correspondence and telephoning. Her demands on herself and others were unremitting.

Throughout the spring, Mary Eastwood was a binding force on the committee. She would work anytime, anywhere, with either Caruthers Berger or Marguerite or both. When Berger talked about contacting the plaintiffs and taking "her" cases away from NOW, Mary objected. She respected Marguerite and Phineas. On the other hand, she agreed with Berger, the "new feminism" mustn't tie itself to old-fashioned procedures.[13] Work and more work. Details and more details. Marguerite seemed unable to take the ultimate chance and let the cases go.

That spring, the whole country seemed to be falling into chaos. Draft protesters and anti-war demonstrators had followed blacks into the streets. Almost every big city in the country was threatened by ghetto riots and campus rebellion.

By March, disgruntlement with Johnson's strategies in Vietnam and his advocacy of civil rights had reduced his administration to a shambles. Peace candidate Eugene McCarthy was attracting the young in droves. Betty Friedan was backing him and ruthlessly attacking the president's policies. Suddenly Robert Kennedy was also running for the nomination.

Unexpectedly, on Sunday, March 31, 1968, Lyndon Johnson called for a reduction in bombing in Vietnam and announced his decision not to seek reelection.

A few days later, Marguerite and Irene Scott found their friend Annie Perry Neal Huntting dead from a heart attack in her Virginia home. She had died on Saturday night alone. On April 4, Martin Luther King was killed in Memphis, Tennessee, shot by James Earl Ray, a white man with a long police record.

Marguerite spent the afternoon of King's death at the funeral home with Annie Perry's family. The next day she wrote in her diary, *. . . a funeral, a riot.*

Martin Luther King's death had triggered a rampage of riots, arson, and looting in hundreds of cities across the country. Washington was the worst hit. Buildings within blocks of the White House were on fire. Before it ended, over 20,000 people were injured and close to 3,000 arrested. Fifty thousand soldiers were called out to restore order.

On Saturday, Marguerite wrote Margie Neal a long letter about Annie Perry and added,

> . . . Within two hours after returning from her funeral, traffic up 16th Street was bumper to bumper, offices being closed, curfew imposed and people trying to get home. One riot center of looting and burning is about twelve blocks from me, on 14th Street. The traffic thinned a little about 5:30 before dark, and I got in my car and went to Maryland with friends who had been ordering me to do so. Several others telephoned urging me to get to their homes. Today troops were on duty on the street. What has our country come to?

The next afternoon she finished a letter she had started to her family on Saturday: "I am back home. Streets are quiet, and word is that troops are on hand, no fires today. So I will remain at home. . . It must be over. . . Don't worry."

By the next Sunday, Easter, the streets were quiet. Marguerite woke up to a fair, unseasonably warm day and wrote Willis and Anna again. "Trees are half leafed out, and beautiful, flowers blooming, pink cherry blossoms at their height. One week ago we were hiding in our homes so to speak."

Stirred by the beauty of the day and the sense of order restored, she picked up the phone on an impulse and called Lorena

Weeks, whom she had never met. They were both about to leave for church. Weeks for Baptist services in Wadley, Georgia; Marguerite for the National Cathedral. Have faith, Marguerite told her. She was helping all women. They were counting on her and she could count on them.[14]

Marguerite's spirits were high throughout April. The report from the Task Force on Family Law and Policy, which she had chaired for the Citizens Advisory Council, was going to press. Over 80,000 copies of the original president's commission report, *American Women,* had already been distributed, and it had come out in translation in Italy, Japan, and Sweden.

The Family Law and Policy Report was more forward-looking and sure to be influential — as well as controversial. It called for the revision of all domestic relations laws based on the concept of marriage as an economic partnership. It recommended the repeal of laws that made abortion a criminal offense and restricted access to birth control devices and information. Illegitimate and legitimate children should have the same rights, and custody in divorce cases should be determined by the interests of the children. The Task Force on Labor Standards was recommending major reforms in labor laws that applied to women only. For the first time ever, a government commission was calling for radical changes in the legal treatment of women.

Despite the difference in tone and the impeccable credentials of Council and Task Force members, their women's agenda mirrored NOW's Bill of Rights and the aims of the moderate women's movement in general. At the same time, polarities within the movement were growing. Influences among the "women's lib" element continued to challenge the reformist goals of the majority. In October, a group called New York Radical Women was organized by women dissatisfied with their role in the leftist Students for a Democratic Society (SDS). The system was the enemy, they said, men were the oppressors, women the victims.

The identification of women with oppression set Marguerite's teeth on edge. Women were not an "oppressed minority." They were a majority. They were *part* of the system. They *were* "the people." Women were entitled to equality.

The Marxist lingo alarmed her, and she didn't like women portraying themselves as victims. She didn't see what they could gain from it. The women she most admired had devoted their lives to showing women how not to be oppressed. What, she wondered, would Lucy Moore have thought? Burnita Matthews? Florence Allen? Lena Madesin Phillips? These new people sounded as if there was something wrong with making it, succeeding, getting some of the good things men had always had.

The influence of the Radical Women was rampant in the New York chapter of NOW. There seemed to be nothing too outrageous for the support of its president Ti-Grace Atkinson who constantly challenged the national leadership. On March 10, the *New York Times Sunday Magazine* carried a feature story, "The Second Feminist Wave," exposing the extremes within the new movement.

On June 3, when a twenty-eight-year-old New York actress named Valerie Solanas shot pop artist Andy Warhol, Ti-Grace Atkinson dubbed her a "feminist heroine." Solanas had written something called the SCUM (Society for Cutting Up Men) Manifesto in which she advocated removing all men from positions of power (one way or another). Claiming that Solanas was being "prejudicially treated" by the courts, New York civil rights lawyer and NOW member Florynce Kennedy called her one of the "most important spokeswomen of the feminist movement." The *New York Times* and papers across the country identified the case with NOW. When Atkinson claimed the NOW legal committee was backing Solanas, Marguerite was horrified. Attending a General Federation convention in Boston, she watched the publicity go from bad to worse.

Back home, she learned that Mary Eastwood thought there might be a sex discrimination issue in the Solanas case. If so, they should consider helping. After all, a double standard for sexual and emotional behavior discriminated against women even when there was no law at stake, she thought. For Marguerite, Solanas's poor taste and the bad publicity for women ruled out the possibility of NOW involvement. It certainly ruled out the possibility of her becoming involved.

Betty Friedan stood firmly with Marguerite. She wanted no part of their "anti-male, anti-social posture," she said, and wrote Faith Seidenberg, "I want all of you to realize that what is involved here is something very sick. . . . The New York NOW executive committee members tell me that Ti-Grace is now doing a study of the Amazons." [15]

At the end of the month, Marguerite wrote Betty Boyer:

> . . . NOW is surely having indescribable inner tortures. . . . I have been ready to give up more than once, I can tell you.
>
> I intend to hold on in hope that we will learn to act as an organization very soon. There are other women, like you and me, who stand for equal rights and have long worked in other groups, who make it my decision to hold fast for a while longer at least.
>
> . . . perhaps some day our energies may be turned constructively.

The inner tortures of the country seemed endless as well. On June 4, Robert Kennedy won the California primary and seemed headed for the Democratic nomination for president. A few days later, like his brother, he would be dead from an assassin's bullet.

Ghetto and campus uprisings spread throughout the spring and summer. A thousand poor people camped in a "Resurrection City," set up between the Lincoln Memorial and the Washington Monument. On May 18, Marguerite wrote her brothers and their families,

> Of course you are reading daily of the Poor People's March on Washington. We hear nothing else here.
>
> It is discommoding business, keeping people anxious of course. The really poor of course are well intentioned. The danger is the criminally inclined and communist-inspired who take advantage of the situation, just as they did when Martin Luther King died. Everyone is angry about why those in authority don't do more.

Fearing more violence in the city, she was planning to leave the Sixteenth Street apartment where she and Harry had spent most of their life together. Many of her friends had already left the city.

In August, the Democrats nominated President Johnson's vice-president, Hubert Humphrey, and adopted a hawkish Vietnam plank that turned the anti-war demonstration outside the convention into a bloody, nationally televised clash between protesters and the Chicago police. Mary Eastwood watched the convention in Marguerite's apartment, just blocks from the White House, later describing it in a letter to Pauli Murray as "bloody Chicago in living color." [16]

By fall, Ti-Grace Atkinson had lost her hold on the New York club and organized a radical group called first "The October 17th Movement" and later "The Feminists." They were the women outside the mainstream, they said, "the young, the black, and the beautiful."

For a while, Mary Eastwood became more interested in the radical groups and less accepting of the conservative methods of the Washington women who were still her friends and with whom she worked closely. Her work with the Citizens Advisory Council, the Woman's Party, and the NOW legal committee had deepened her commitment to women's rights. She saw new horizons. Women in New York, on the West Coast, and in Chicago were straining at the old definitions of women's rights. They talked about the social, sexual, and spiritual liberation of women. There seemed to be no end to where they were going — what they had to do.

Soon the discord on the legal committee was mirroring a rift widening throughout the movement. On September 7, Women's Liberationists picketed the Miss America Contest at Atlantic City, throwing girdles, bras, high-heeled shoes, hair curlers, and false eyelashes into a "freedom trash can" — to the glee of the national press and the consternation of old-line women's rights reformers. Headline coverage for a thing like that! What a sedate celebration it had been in 1937, when BPW paraded on that same boardwalk to endorse ERA.

Three days later, NOW members and nonmembers staged an extravaganza in front of the Colgate–Palmolive building in Manhattan to protest the company's weight-lifting and seniority regulations. Women danced on the sidewalks around an "open-air toilet bowl" contributed by sculptor-writer, Kate Millett. Wearing Bermuda shorts, lawyer Florynce Kennedy told reporters, "It's a groovy swinging means of protest, and sometimes you accomplish something. But even if you don't, it's better than making a better jelly."

A company official answered with the kind of condescension they had come to expect: "We didn't realize that women wanted to carry around 50 to 100 pounds. I seriously doubt if the women picketing know what it's all about. . . we still love the ladies."

Late in September, Marguerite complained to Kay Clarenbach. Every night the news on television brought new "NOW problems, crisis, unpleasantness. Too, too bad. I am sick of it."

But not all the news was bad for the legal rights side of the movement. While feminists of various persuasions demonstrated against the Miss America Contest and Colgate–Palmolive, a California court became the first to rule that Title VII superseded state laws limiting weight-lifting and overtime by women. Furthermore, NOW's mandamus suit had forced EEOC to rule out segregated want-ads. And the work of the legal committee on the Jane Daniel case brought a big victory in the Pennsylvania Supreme Court.

Late in August, an article by Elizabeth Shelton in the *Washington Post* featured Marguerite and the NOW cases: "Fightin' Marguerite Rawalt Is on Law-Path for Women's Rights." Marguerite told how the NOW Legal Defense and Education Fund had been modeled after the NAACP Legal Defense Fund. "The women's rights movement is very analogous to the racial rights movement," she said, acknowledging a similarity that she had sometimes wanted to deny. The Mengelkoch case, she added, could result in a "landmark decision similar to the school desegregation decision."

When the NOW national board met in Louisville, Kentucky, on September 14–15, the legal committee troubles finally came to a boil. Mary Eastwood demanded that the board vote immediately to place Caruthers Berger and another Washington lawyer, Sylvia Ellison, on the defense fund board, and Marguerite insisted the NOW board had no authority to act for the defense fund, a separate corporation.

When it was all over, the board voted with Marguerite. She agreed to remain as chair of the legal committee and general counsel. But, finding it impossible to work with Berger, she withdrew from the Colgate case, which had already been briefed. She would retain responsibility for the Mengelkoch and Weeks cases.

Communicating with Caruthers Berger was no longer possible. "When I found myself shouting back at someone I was trying to work with," she told a friend, "I knew it was time to stop." She couldn't work with Berger and maintain her self-respect, she added. Her diary for September 14 records simply, *A most unhappy NOW Board meeting;* and the next day, *Retd DC same plane as Berger, Eastwood.*

Deeply disturbed by the conflict, Marguerite hoped the troubles were over; but, by the end of the month, it was clear that they were not. Mary Eastwood, Caruthers Berger, Sylvia Ellison, and Ti-Grace Atkinson were incorporating a defense fund independent of NOW and had talked Velma Mengelkoch and the Colgate plaintiffs into transferring their cases to them.

Marguerite's mailbox was a "nest of thorns." Friedan and Clarenbach thought they should try to appease Berger in order to keep the cases. As Marguerite saw it, Berger and Eastwood had gone in secret to the plantiffs in order to blackmail the board into turning the legal committee over to them. Such behavior was not to be tolerated.

"Compromise for the sake of compromise is a mistake," she wrote Clarenbach and Friedan. She had been working with the law and women's constitutional rights since the 1950s; her rationale was the basis of all their arguments. "True I haven't raved about it [her work]. I just did it." No. She was not willing to try to work out yet another "compromise" with Berger and Eastwood. The briefs had been filed. Let them have credit for the decision. There were, she concluded, enough sex discrimination cases to keep them all busy for the rest of their lives.

Writing from California, Aileen Hernandez sent a long letter to Friedan, O'Hanrahan, Clarenbach, Rawalt, and Eastwood. They were at the heart of a movement, she said, begging them to settle their differences before the December 6 national convention in Atlanta.

> The brilliance of our briefs and the willingness of everyone concerned to spend long, long, uncompensated hours. . . deserves three (if not more) cheers formally at this National Conference. . . .
>
> We need all those beautiful brains working together and in the kind of harmony that everyone says women cannot maintain. I don't believe that and I hope that in all our actions we try to "do in" that horrible stereotype. Let's begin again on December 6th as if none of the problems were irreconcilable and work to find a way of restoring that positive image of action that we had a year or so ago.

By December, Eastwood and Ti-Grace Atkinson had incorporated a legal defense fund called Human Rights for Women, and Marguerite and what was left of her legal committee had new cases to consider. A woman named Jan Dietrich was suing World Airways for a job as a jet pilot. Kathy Kushner, a woman jockey, had won the right to ride in competition only to have her races boycotted by male riders. They were pioneers and the kind of women Marguerite thought NOW should be working for.

On October 7, Sylvia Roberts had argued a good case for Lorena Weeks before the Court of Appeals in New Orleans. Later in the month, the American Newspaper Publishers Association sued EEOC in an attempt to stop the desegregation of classified ads. In November, the district court approved new regulations calling for consolidated male/female want-ads.

On November 5, Marguerite learned that Betty Boyer had incorporated a second activist organization for women to be called WEAL, the Women's Equity Action League. She wanted Marguerite to be on the national advisory board because of her work in the courts and because she thought WEAL needed to work closely with NOW. Attracted to the promise that WEAL would concentrate on discrimination, especially in employment and education, Marguerite accepted the invitation. There was room, she thought, for an organization with clearer, more traditional goals than NOW.

[7]

Continuing

Marguerite returned from her Christmas 1968 visit to Texas ready to make her last great effort for women. She had come full circle, back once again to the Equal Rights Amendment — the bedrock of her philosophy of equal rights. Everything else was, as she had learned so many times, "piecemeal, stopgap, temporary." She still hoped women would get beyond that in her lifetime.

Amid the new efforts, rewards for three grueling years in NOW were beginning to come in. The *Reader's Digest Almanac* for 1969 recognized NOW's work and named Marguerite and Betty Friedan "outstanding women" for founding the organization and leading it into the courts under Title VII.

On March 4, NOW won its first unmitigated victory for women under Title VII when the Fifth Circuit Court of Appeals ruled that Lorena Weeks had been denied a promotion because she was a woman, not because she lacked any necessary qualifications as an individual. The language of the ruling was clear: Title VII rejected "romantic paternalism as unduly Victorian and vests individual women with the power whether or not to take on unromantic tasks. . . . The promise of Title VII is that women are now to be on equal footing.''

Eventually Weeks would be awarded the job she wanted plus $31,000 in back pay and commuting expenses. The case was a death knell for the labor laws against which women like Marguerite had struggled for so long, that had shackled women, limiting their chances for higher wages and promotions in the name of protection.

As soon as she got the news, Marguerite sent out a "Flash Bulletin" to the NOW membership and sent the story to many women's publications including the *Women Lawyers' Journal.* Working together, women had opened doors for themselves that could never be shut, she said. Some day it would no longer be necessary to go to court to permit a worker, "even a female worker," to hold any job she was capable of performing.

Starting in mid-March, the *Baltimore Sun* gave NOW its due in a carefully written five-part series on "The Female Revolt," by Vera Glaser, Washington correspondent for Knight Newspapers. NOW made the papers again when the Plaza Hotel refused to allow the members of the national board to eat lunch in its Oak Room. The rule was "Men Only" for lunch. Marguerite, Kay Clarenbach, Betty Friedan, and others marched with posters declaring "Plaza Discriminates."

On May 7, wearing a short white dress and her hair piled high on her head, Marguerite joined other NOW members in a nationwide equal rights demonstration in front of the White House. Her handmade poster declared, U.S. CONSTITUTION PROTECTS MEN ONLY. The three-year-old daughter of another NOW member held a tiny banner: WHEN I GROW UP, I WANT TO BE A HUMAN BEING.

For the first time in months, Marguerite was having fun, mugging for photographers, chanting slogans with the others as they marched. Since 1966, women's rights had left little room for the pleasures that had once so enriched her busy life. But new friends couldn't take the place of the old ones. Louise Wright and Hattie Crawford, Annie Perry Neal, Amanda Bradley, Harry. Now she carried the old playmates and mentors in her heart.

From the beginning of the 1960s Marguerite had abhorred the angry, arrogant mood of some of the demonstrators for peace, for civil rights, for women. Over and over, she told the young members of NOW: "We must choose carefully what we demonstrate for."

For her, a march for ERA was in a long tradition of legal rights and suffrage. She thought no one could deny the orderliness and the meaning of their demonstration, the legitimacy of what they asked for. To Helen Hurd, she added, "I have come all the way to thinking that women have got to get into some limelight if we make any progress — take a leaf from the blacks. Truly."

Reflecting on the Equality March a few months later, she told the *Dallas Times Herald*, "I never thought I'd see the day when I'd picket the White House for women's rights, but I've come to that point. . . We've gotten to the place where women have to become militant to get anywhere."

While they marched, First Lady Pat Nixon entertained the State Commissions on the Status of Women inside the White House. Acknowledging the women outside, she told the group, "It's the funniest thing. I don't feel there's any discrimination. I know my husband feels that way." Elizabeth Shelton, a longtime *Washington Post* reporter with feminist sentiments, pulled Marguerite out of the line and repeated Mrs. Nixon's words. Pat Nixon and her husband thought women already had equal rights, Shelton paraphrased.

The words passed down the line and soon they were chanting, "Let Nixon stand Pat. We want equal rights."

On the afternoon of the march, Betty Friedan and others met with Elizabeth (Libby) Duncan Koontz, newly appointed director of the Women's Bureau. Koontz was a black woman, a Democrat, a former high school teacher, and president of the National Education Association. Youthful at fifty, she was winsome, easygoing, full of vitality, with smooth reddish-brown skin and dark — almost black — eyes. They trusted her immediately. As an outsider and a newcomer she might be able to move the Women's Bureau in their direction. She was open-minded on ERA, and she listened to Catherine East. Marguerite knew Koontz's brother, John Duncan, a Washington lawyer and supporter of women's rights. From a long line of civil rights advocates, educators, and artists, the Duncans shared a tradition of hard work, commitment, and social responsibility with the women's rights reformers.[1]

In July, with much support from women in their party, Republican congresswomen secured an unprecedented meeting to discuss women's issues with the president. A month later, he finally appointed a Citizens Advisory Council, made up largely of progressive Republican women. At the same time, he appointed a special Task Force on Women's Rights and Responsibilities to be headed by former BPW president, Virginia Allan. Unlike the conservative commissions on which Marguerite had served since 1961, the new council and task force were heavy with ERA supporters and long-time BPW members.

Having canceled a two-month trip to Europe because neither of her brothers was well, Marguerite spent most of June and July traveling, corresponding with friends and family, and working with Betty Boyer on WEAL's case against the American Newspaper Publishers' Association. Early in June there was the General Federation convention in Cleveland and a two-week visit in Texas. Worried about Louis's refusal to attend to his failing health and Willis's difficulty coping with illness, depression, and retirement, she revealed her concerns in an unusually soulful letter to her nephew Wally and his wife Melody:

> . . . While he [Willis] seems to have adjusted. . . I am wondering about the deep down unseen effects on emotions. This is one of the reasons I so much wanted to visit with him, although visits in our family turn out to be such surface exchanges because of too many people bunched together and a natural reticence. But there can be no more genuine family love and respect I am sure than exists between my two brothers and me. I couldn't have better ones if I had the making, different as they are. And nothing is more satisfying than being together for a time.
>
> [Louis is] the introspective one, who never has a moment alone except when he can drive down the island by himself. We are all living in a cage, if we but stop to contemplate it.

Her sympathy for Willis, confined to a life of physical inactivity by doctors' orders, ran deep:

> Willis is enduring a traumatic experience that none of us can realize. We can't know what goes on inside A MAN SUDDENLY GROUNDED. . . he becomes a virtual prisoner within the four walls of that house and the road surrounding the farm. I grieve. . . Think of it.

She grieved for a brother sentenced to a life so constrained that she herself could have found it unbearable. Occasionally, amid the activities of her life, she was stricken with guilt that she was sepa-

rated from her brothers as they aged and grew ill. Later in the year
she wrote them:

> I wish that I lived closer to all of you — yet my lifetime interests
> and friends are now here. . . and as long as I need to and wish to
> remain active in groups I know and belong to, it would be wrong
> to cut it all to move to another location. Harry and I always said
> that our retirement years would be spent. . . in living where our
> friends were and our interests.

The same letter shows just how happy she was with her life in
Washington. "Three days ago as I drove into the city along the
river road to the Lincoln Memorial, the trees were gorgeous. Big
red oaks with their deep red leaves. The elms were nearly bare,
their black arms reaching to the sky. . . . Many little trees laden
with red berries. . . Today it is raining gently." Her apartment was
luxuriously convenient, the view was grand, she enjoyed a public
television program called *The Lands and Seas*.

After her trip to Texas, she was home only a few days before
leaving for BPW's fiftieth anniversary celebration in St. Louis
where her long-postponed history of the organization was to be presented. Leaving St. Louis, she headed for four days of Rawalt gatherings in Illinois, then returned to the Washington heat and hearings on the WEAL intervention.

Just before leaving for the BPW convention, she had written
Kay Clarenbach and Betty Friedan resigning her place as chair of
NOW's legal committee. She was proud of what they had done in
three short years ("Why didn't they brag about it?"), but she was
worn out with the ideological confusion, the poor communications,
the refusal to set priorities. She would continue her work on the
legal defense fund (still not incorporated), but could no longer
carry the weight of responsibility for court cases.

In the past, she had needed the structure and support of the
established organizations. But since her early years on the president's commission, much of her best work had been done not as organization woman but as gadfly, conduit, catalyst, connector of organizations and individuals. Organizational baggage had too often
been an impediment. She was ready to go to work for ERA on her
own.

The opportunity to begin came sooner than she expected. On
Tuesday, October 8, after a day of NAWL regional conference

meetings, she returned to her apartment and found an emergency message from Virginia Allan.

The Task Force on Women's Rights and Responsibilities was meeting the next afternoon. Its report would be the strongest, most progressive set of demands women had ever made to a president, Allan said. But a few crucial members were shaky on ERA. She wanted Marguerite to talk to them the next afternoon.

No, she said. She was too tired, too involved with the women lawyers. Justice Warren Burger was having lunch with them, and they were invited to the White House in the afternoon. She couldn't do everything; she had to think about herself once in a while.

Allan pressed. Could she come in the morning then? Catherine East said no one else would do. It was the lawyers who were undecided. Marguerite knew the cases, the legal history. They all looked up to her. Suppose a forward-looking report to the president reneged on ERA?

Marguerite relented and arrived at the Labor Department at 10:00 the next morning. Flustered and out-of-breath, she spoke impromptu from hastily prepared notes. Thousands of state laws still discriminated against women, she told them. Only a constitutional amendment would address them all. Even Supreme Court decisions would be piecemeal. A ruling that negated the eight-hour law or weight-lifting limitations would not, for example, do anything about laws discriminating against women in property ownership. Without ERA, women would have to wait a long, long time for equality.

Marguerite had never been more convincing. The group endorsed ERA. Virginia Allan was true to her promise. In December, her task force submitted a report so forceful that the White House refused to release it for months. It did not appear in print until June 1970, and then only after a pirated version showed up in the *Miami Herald,* leaked no doubt by Task Force member Vera Glaser, Washington correspondent for the chain of papers to which the *Herald* belonged.[2]

The report, entitled "A Matter of Simple Justice," echoed Marguerite's argument: women were still denied rights the Constitution promised to "all persons." The report was very specific. Women wanted complete equality.

The closing months of 1969 brought another surprise when the

Seventh Circuit Court of Appeals ruled in favor of the women in the Colgate–Palmolive case. The decision was a strong one. If retained, weight-lifting regulations would have to apply to men as well as women. Separate seniority lists for men and women were forbidden. All the women harmed by the banned policies were to receive back pay. The court blamed the unions to which the women belonged as well as the company for which they worked.

Regretting only the trouble between herself and the lawyers who represented the women at the end, Marguerite refused to claim any fees for the work she had done on the case, and wrote Sylvia Roberts: "I am just so genuinely glad for the decision and the back pay relief to be given to Sue Sellers and the others." All women should rejoice.

For Marguerite, the first few months of the year were taken up with NOW and WEAL business. On March 16, 1970, she filed incorporation papers for the NOW Legal Defense and Education Fund, and a few days later the fund held its first official meeting in Chicago.

Guided by what Marguerite called a "nerve center" of Washington women that included herself, Dr. Bernice Sandler, Catherine East, Martha Griffiths, and Vera Glaser, WEAL began a long, ground-breaking struggle for equal opportunity in education. Early in February, they brought a sex discrimination complaint against the University of Maryland, and later in the year took on the college and university systems of Florida and California as well as all the medical schools in the country.

Then, unexpectedly, on February 26, 1970, Senator Birch Bayh, Indiana Democrat and chairman of the Senate Judiciary Committee's Subcommittee on Constitutional Amendments, announced plans to hold ERA hearings in May — the first action by Congress in almost ten years. A few days before, the Citizens Advisory Council endorsed ERA and urged the president to do likewise. Thanks to the work of women like Dorothy Haener and Olga Madar, the United Automobile Workers Union was about to become the first labor union to endorse the controversial amendment.

With political instincts sharpened to the point of premonition, Marguerite began getting ready for the hearings and the legislative battles to come. She cleaned house, reupholstered furniture, ate dinner with friends, answered letters, reorganized her files. One of her bedrooms had already become an office, with the record of her long fight for women's rights collected in notebooks, filing cabinets and boxes that lined the walls and overflowed into the closet. Degrees and awards hung beside her desk facing a haphazard assortment of photographs of First Ladies, presidents, congresswomen, family members, and old friends. For Easter Sunday, 1970, her diary records, *Hard rain, some snowflakes — all day from 5 am to night — at home working, shifting files.*

Her correspondence took time now and came from all over the country. Students and young women wanted information. No longer pressed by organizational responsibilities, she enjoyed the role of teacher.

That spring she tried to define "women's liberation" for a high school senior who wrote to her from Maiden, North Carolina. She had long been for liberating women from the "old common-law concept of women as chattel, household drudge," she wrote, unlike Sam Ervin, the senator from North Carolina who wanted women to remain outside the protection of the U.S. Constitution. As for the so-called "women's liberation groups," they did not seem to be "realistic about the law."

She spent the weekend of March 13 at the University of North Carolina in Chapel Hill, where she was featured at a "Women and the Law" seminar sponsored by WEAL and a consortium of women's rights and women's liberation groups. She returned elated. Young women were "really the hope of the present and the future," she wrote Betty Friedan. To Sylvia Roberts, she described the event in detail:

> What sessions — I wore myself out. Friday night on Title VII and the other litigation uppermost, and what was done. Saturday morning symposium on every familiar complaint about discrimination... It was most stimulating to me. Two women, each with children, about 30 years old spearheaded it — what fine persons they are.

Still excited a few days later, she sent the same message in a letter to Betty Boyer and WEAL President Nancy Dowding in Ohio. She had told a standing-room-only audience of close to 300 young people about Title VII, the Fourteenth Amendment, and the need for ERA. "Saturday morning symposium and luncheon were terrific — only women present and franker talk."

The letter ended with a description of her efforts to get all "her" women's groups to file statements for the Senate hearings scheduled for May 5–7. Other letters went out to groups that still wobbled on ERA. Individuals were told about the hearings and urged to write representatives in the House and the Senate. Now her mailings went out in quantities, photocopied or mimeographed, carrying simply her own name and bold signature at the top.

In April, she sent a long letter to Mrs. Nixon explaining the need for ERA and urging her to use her influence with her husband. The amendment stood very much as it had in 1923, when the Woman's Party first presented it to Congress: "Equality of rights under the law shall not be denied or abridged by the United States or by any state on account of sex." How, she wondered, could anyone object to that?

Even personal friends and family got accounts of her new work for ERA. "ERA is boiling," she wrote Gracy Nicholas. "Washington has had a bad winter — although to tell the truth I have not the time to concentrate on it. When I have to go, the weather can't stop me."

On April 9, she put on her silver-gray "alaskine" suit and went alone to the Fort Meyer Officers' Club to a party given by Congressman John Young of Texas. His daughter, Gaffney, was representing Texas in the Cherry Blossom Festival. A letter to her family describes it in sumptuous detail:

> . . . Roast beef sliced for making your own sandwiches, hot bacon and chicken liver things, a delicious Texas hot cheese dip. . . . I got into a delightful conversation with a Major and Mrs. Hickey, quite young, and a Miss Foster, secretary to General Besson. . . .
>
> LBJ was sitting on a settee on one end of the room, with two women keeping him surrounded. Nevertheless I walked up and stood a minute and when he looked up, he extended his long arm and said "How are you Marguerite". . . . Then Mrs. Johnson spied me and she is always so cordial. Few minutes later was Major Robb and Lynda Byrd.

But most of the month of April was spent helping other women get ready for the hearings and writing her own testimony. The men in Congress had never heard the truth about ERA. They didn't know what harm was done to women in the name of the law. For years they had heard women rail in vague language against "second class citizenship." Now she was going to tell them about the law, case by case. When she was done, she had a thirty-page typescript that read like a carefully documented legal brief.

On the morning of May 5, the cavernous hearing room on the third floor of the oldest of the Senate office buildings was packed. An overflow crowd lined the wide halls outside. There were suffragists from the Woman's Party, young women carrying babies, women's liberationists, professional women in suits, students wearing trousers and short skirts.

"I am tired of paying into the pension fund to support your widows," Martha Griffiths told the senators. "If I die, gentlemen, while I sit here talking to you, my husband has no survivor rights to my pension." Testimony by Representatives Florence Dwyer, Shirley Chisholm, Margaret Heckler, and several male senators followed. All in favor of ERA. Then Aileen Hernandez, Betty Friedan's successor as president, and two other representatives of NOW told a cheering crowd: "Women are enraged."

Three women from the Washington Women's Liberation Group calling themselves "Emma Goldman," "Sarah Grimké," and "Angelina Grimké," spoke of the viciousness of "male supremacist society" and called for revolution: "Free our sisters, free ourselves, all power to the people."

The afternoon session began with the only opposition testimony of the day, an outdated labor union diatribe delivered by Mortimer Furay of the AFL–CIO Council. Modern industry created stress and fatigue that women were "physically and medically" unable to bear. Since the days of Adam and Eve. . . men and women had been different. Under pressure from Bayh (and a sometimes unruly audience), Furay finally admitted that the United Automobile Workers Union was supporting the amendment.

Marguerite delivered a concise oral statement and filed a written statement that included her long testimony plus three task force reports — her own on Civil and Political Rights and Family Law and Policy and Virginia Allan's on Women's Rights and Responsibilities. No longer nervous, she spoke informally from notes she knew almost by heart.

Through the years, she told the committee, the United States Supreme Court had ruled against women under the Fourteenth Amendment denying them the right to vote, the right to practice the occupation of their choice, the right to equal opportunity at

work. Nevertheless — thanks to Title VII and the National Organization for Women — federal courts were gradually outlawing the
discriminatory state labor laws. Yet, fifty-nine percent of employers admitted they disqualified women on the basis of sex. Since the
Fourteenth Amendment had not opened the doors to equal property rights, equal jury service or equal prison sentences, an equal
rights amendment was the only answer.

Her witty examples brought laughter and applause from the
audience and support from both Bayh and Senator Marlow Cook,
a sympathetic Republican from Kentucky. As she walked to her
seat, the audience stood for a long, rowdy ovation, and she remembered what Lorena Weeks had said to her on Easter Sunday a year
ago: "I was meant to do this."

The next two days of hearings were long and demanding with
statements from a star-studded list of ERA advocates that included
writers Betty Friedan, Gloria Steinem, and Caroline Bird. Betty
Boyer and Bernice Sandler spoke for WEAL and Virginia Allan for
her task force. Marguerite knew most of the women who testified —
and she wanted them all to know one another.

By Thursday morning, excitement and optimism were riding a
high tide. ERA had strong support in the Senate and the hearings
seemed to clinch it. The real bottleneck was in the House where the
Amendment had been locked up in the Judiciary Committee since
1948.

On Wednesday some of the women at the hearings came up
with a plan for getting the House Rules Committee to bring ERA to
the floor by discharging its Judiciary Committee. Rules Committee
Chairman Claude Pepper advised them to try it. By Thursday,
Marguerite and another prominent Washington lawyer, Margaret
Laurence, had drawn up a petition and circulated it in the hearing
room.

The next two weeks were spent getting the signatures of BPW,
Zonta, and NAWL women. By Wednesday, May 20, they had
1,500 names — but by then it was too late.

One of the women had naively mentioned their plan to someone in the office of Emmanuel Celler, chair of the House Judiciary
Committee and archenemy of ERA. In order to prevent action by
the Rules Committee, Celler promptly announced that he would
hold hearings (with no intention of doing so), thus foreclosing action by the Rules Committee.

Marguerite described her frustration to Hermine Tobolowsky, a longtime ERA supporter in Texas: "Of course the Rules Committee idea is killed, dead. Thus it goes, without head or tail, and with new inexperienced ones considering it all so easy." To the officers of NOW she added: "I am just sick to the core over this. If women could only get together — and learn when NOT TO TALK."

Immediately Marguerite, Catherine East, and Martha Griffiths's legislative aide Pat Kelly, were at work on another idea. If enough members could be enticed into signing a "discharge petition," the House itself could dismiss the Judiciary Committee and bring ERA to the floor for a vote. No one could remember who first thought of it. Perhaps Catherine East and Phineas Indritz. It would take two-thirds of the membership. Griffiths didn't think it would work, but they insisted. They had to try it.[3]

The activists wanted Griffiths to introduce the petition during the June 10–11 celebration of the fiftieth anniversary of the Women's Bureau. Guided by Libby Koontz, the Labor Department was going to endorse ERA for the first time. Over a thousand influential women would be in town for the event.

Finally, Griffiths agreed. On June 10, she entered Marguerite's Senate testimony in the *Congressional Record*. The next day she introduced the petition. Within a few days she had seventy-five signatures. Women sitting in the galleries watched her buttonhole the men, joking with them, taking them by the arm and walking them across the floor of the House to sign the petition. She was a member of the powerful Ways and Means Committee. Many of the men were indebted to her. All she wanted was their signatures, she said. Because she wasn't permitted to copy the names, she memorized them, calling women leaders who would keep pressure on those who hadn't signed.

Marguerite was prodding everybody, women from NOW, BPW, Zonta, General Federation, NAWL and organizing her own telephone campaigns, sometimes using the WATS lines in Martha Griffiths's offices at night.

On July 16, she left for two weeks at the BPW convention in Honolulu, with plans for spending a few days in Corpus Christi. Although she would be lobbying for ERA and attending workshops at the convention, she also had plans for island-hopping and enjoying the perfect weather, boat rides, tropical food, and swimming.

An emergency call from Martha Griffiths changed all that. They were nearing their goal on the petition. She wanted telegrams, lots of them — to every member of Congress.

Like carnival barkers, Marguerite and Virginia Allan got the word out, setting up tables in the halls outside the meeting rooms, peddling their wares in the convention hall, at dinner, over drinks by the Hawaiian Village Hotel pool. They made a show of it, calling themselves Rawalt–Allan: "RA for ERA." Using information supplied by Griffiths's office, they dictated the telegrams. When House Minority Leader Gerald Ford signed, Griffiths called again: they were going to get the Republicans as well as the Democrats. With former presidential aide Liz Carpenter there to address the convention body, their luau turned into a rally for ERA.

Later, Griffiths described what she did in Washington while Rawalt and Allan worked in Hawaii. "Every night I called them [Rawalt and Allan] and told them the names of the Congressmen and the people of their states deluged them with cablegrams. The signing business picked up immensely. . . I continued my lonely and tedious way of singling out Congressmen." [4]

Late on July 20, Griffiths called again. The discharge petition was over the top. A most unlikely victory, but they would have limited time to debate the issue on the floor before a vote on August 10. Marguerite had to get back to Washington immediately, Griffiths insisted. No time for sightseeing.

Flying from Los Angeles, Marguerite arrived at her apartment late on the afternoon of Wednesday, July 29. By 8:00 P.M. she was at work with Martha Griffiths helping prepare the congresswoman's remarks and drafting a letter to go to 3,800 club presidents urging telegrams to congressmen who were asked to be both "present and voting 'yes' " on August 10. They had a chance.

On Sunday, August 9, Marguerite wrote Grace Nicholas: "I am working with Mrs. Griffiths, who must carry the argument. . . I am as nervous as if *I* had to make the argument."

Taking her seat the next day in a gallery packed with women's rights activists from all over the country, she was more nervous than if she had been doing it herself. The terrible waiting for the time to pass, watching their opponents manuever. If they succeeded in watering down the amendment, it was all over.

Challenged immediately by Emmanuel Celler, Martha Griffiths began with the combination of facts, melodrama, and wit that had become her trademark. Paraphrasing black suffragist Sojournor Truth, she asked, "Ain't I a person?"

At eighty-two, Cellar had lost none of his glibness: "The only equality is in the cemetery. . . there was as much difference between a male and a female as between a horse chestnut and a chestnut horse."

Griffiths replied, solemnly paraphrasing the information Marguerite had provided: for ninety-eight years the Supreme Court had refused women, as a class, the "equal protection" guaranteed by the Fourteenth Amendment.

Opponents raised every possible question to sidetrack the bill and recommit it to the Judiciary Committee. Did ERA mean all women would be forced to work outside the home, would they have to go to war? Wouldn't the states have to change too many laws? Radical change shouldn't be administered in haste.

Representative Edith Green answered. It was incredible that they were still debating "whether or not the majority of the American people have equal rights under the Constitution. They were not acting 'in haste.' It was high time for 'profound social change.' "

The one hour of clock time stretched into the afternoon. Marguerite remembered thirty years of her own speeches. Over and over she had told women, "when the men know the facts, they will be with us." What if she had been wrong? All those years of effort. Then suddenly it was over, a huge victory, bigger than they could have hoped for: 350 votes for ERA.

Marguerite managed to get to Martha Griffiths amid the mob of congratulators, reporters, photographers. It was time to celebrate. Women had never had such a victory. Marguerite got out the word to the inner circle of workers as fast as she could, Wilma Scott Heide, vice-president of NOW, Betty Boyer, Dorothy Haener, Catherine East, Margaret Laurence. They would meet for dinner at the National Lawyers' Club.

Some of them had already gathered in the lobby when Marguerite arrived a few minutes late, a black chiffon scarf protecting her hair from the late summer breeze. Amid the hugs and laughter, her eyes fell on the ominous bust of William Blackstone, the man responsible for the English Common Law notion of women as "chattel." A woman was a man's property. Everything she had belonged to him, even her children. So much for Blackstone, they laughed, turning his face to the wall and draping his head with Marguerite's black scarf. So much for Blackstone.

A friendly version of the story made the news the next day. But most of what they read was either hostile, condescending, or both. Columnist James J. Kilpatrick called the amendment a "constitutional time bomb. . . . the contrivance of a gang of professional harpies, descendants in zealotry of the late Carrie Nation. . . . the biggest bores in town." William F. Buckley called the action in the House "little short of fiasco." Until now women had been underdogs. "Backlash" was not a word they knew.

At Martha Griffiths's request, the amendment was placed on the Senate calendar the next morning. But leaders like Marguerite and Margaret Laurence knew that, with no Martha Griffiths to lead them in the Senate, ERA could fail.

Recently widowed, Laurence was in the process of selling the lucrative patent law practice she had shared with her husband. A charismatic woman with thick brown hair and a no-foolishness manner, she told them: "I'm not a woman's woman. I don't like the nit-picking that goes on in women's groups. But with a few of us at the top, we can do this." She had spare time, office space, money to back them up. She thought the men in Congress needed to see new faces, a single group with some authority to represent women.[5]

With her laser-beam attention now focused on ERA, Marguerite hardly noticed other things that were happening to the country. In April 1970, U.S. attacks on Cambodia brought another round of anti-war protests. On May 4, while Marguerite prepared testimony for the Senate subcommittee hearings, the nation reacted to the killing of four protesting students at Kent State University. The following weekend, Marguerite and Margaret Laurence rounded up signatures for the foiled Rules Committee petition, and 100,000 demonstrators stormed the White House. In July, New York State put into effect the country's most liberal abortion law while Marguerite, Catherine East, and Phineas Indritz worked with Martha Griffiths on the discharge petition.

In the midst of it all, the media discovered the women's movement. Previous publicity was a ripple compared to the blitz that began in late 1969. "Militant Women" shared the cover of the December 12, 1969, issue of *Life*, with a photograph of the *Apollo 12* moon landing. By spring of 1970, almost every national magazine and broadcasting network had featured the women's movement. *Life*'s September 4, 1970, cover announced WOMEN ARISE, THE REVOLUTION THAT WILL AFFECT EVERYBODY, across the cover that commemorated the fifty-year anniversary of woman suffrage.

Most major newspapers gave headlines to the August 26 Women's Strike for Equality spearheaded by NOW to celebrate the anniversary of suffrage and call attention to the needs of mid-twentieth-century women. Over 23 million American women held full-time jobs; another eight million worked part-time. Yet a woman made only three dollars for every five dollars made by a man doing the same job. Abortion, child care, lesbian rights, equal pay, ERA: their demands ran the gamut as huge crowds of marchers and onlookers gathered in metropolitan shopping districts across the country.

Vera Glaser described the events in Washington for the *Miami Herald* — young women in miniskirts and jeans, older ones in suits and thin summer dresses. Young men wearing Indian headbands, beads, granny glasses. Many men. Many blacks. "The park glowed with glorious blooms, red carnations, white petunias, and, over all, blue balloons marked *Women Are on the Way Up*. It was, she said, "an orderly, sweet-singing, hand-clapping, good-natured march with speeches, red-white-and-blue balloons, and lunch on the grass — more like a church picnic than a drive for women's rights."

Glaser found Marguerite in a huge crowd of speechmakers and listeners gathered at Farragut Square in the middle of downtown Washington. The issue was not women versus men, she insisted, but women versus the law of the land.

There were in fact, two rallies in Washington. The one at Farragut Square was put on by NOW and a motley coalition that included women's liberation groups, peace groups, and labor union women. Since women employed by the government could not participate in a "strike," Federally Employed Women (FEW) sponsored a "sympathy rally" at noon in front of the White House at Lafayette Park. Thousands marched across the city carrying signs: WOMEN DEMAND EQUALITY, FREE WOMEN ARE BEAUTIFUL, SISTERHOOD IS POWERFUL, THIS IS ONLY THE BEGINNING.

At noon Marguerite spoke about ERA to the crowd at Lafayette Park. "I shouted into the microphone," she wrote Martha

Griffiths, "and people really listened, and we got big hands as did others."

In the afternoon she joined other ERA advocates for a workshop at the Senate Office Building and described the "Teach-In on ERA" to Griffiths a few days later. "Young women [attending] almost altogether and they drank it up. Standing two or three deep around the wall. It is really knowledge and education which is needed."

Soon all her efforts were called back to another crisis in Congress. No longer protected by the bottleneck in the House of Representatives, ERA support in the Senate had begun to fall away. A poll announced at the FEW rally showed that fewer than half of the amendment's eighty sponsors in the Senate had remained faithful.

Two days after the vote in the House, Sam Ervin, Emmanuel Celler's counterpart in the Senate, went on the attack. By the middle of August he had scheduled more ERA hearings for September and introduced a "protective" equal rights amendment of his own making. The day after the Women's Equality Rally, Birch Bayh told reporters: "ERA is in serious trouble in the Senate." By the end of the next day, Marguerite had written a long report to women activists calling for a massive write-in–call-in campaign to the Senate. She sent a five-page defense of ERA to every senator and began rounding up ERA proponents to counteract the opposition sure to appear at the September hearings. She described it in a letter to Griffiths:

> . . . I did my Paul Revere yesterday. First to BPW national headquarters. . . a letter went out yesterday asking permission for new president to testify. I called Adele Weaver new NAWL President, who will come Sept 11th. I have just written her request for her as she is campaigning for a judgeship, primary Sept. 8th. Yesterday I got "MY" letter mailed. . . . And this morning, Senator Cook's secretary called to ask whether I could put together specific information including court cases, under various topics, or tell her where to get it. . . . he just doesnt have the high-level or legal help he could use, I see.

A letter sent to WEAL activists that same day began: "Armegeddon again." WEAL must testify in September. This time there would be opposition. Senators Eastland (of Mississippi) and Ervin would be in charge, not Bayh. Betty Boyer responded by return mail: "Isn't this the damndest thing, that the Senate would do this. . . we are getting our wires and letters in. I can just hear that phone ringing and the 'action' in your apartment. . . Take your vitamins!"

Within a few days Marguerite was at work with Senator Cook's staff. She wanted more lawyers to testify. The hearings began on Wednesday, September 9, scheduled to last through Monday. Senator Sam Ervin was presiding in place of Judiciary Committee Chairman James Eastland. For three days they heard only arguments against ERA. But on Friday there was a surprise.

Professor Leo Kanowitz, one of Ervin's favorite authorities, had changed his mind. In the past, he had argued against ERA, insisting that the Fourteenth Amendment should and would be construed to include women. Now convinced that stronger action would be required, that the Congress would have to correct what the Supreme Court had failed to do, he was supporting the version of ERA passed in the house. Phineas Indritz and Catherine East had been corresponding with Kanowitz. Now he was with them all the way.

Shaking a shock of white hair and lowering his voice to its pontifical Southern depths, Ervin badgered Kanowitz with questions and insinuations, reading from the professor's book, accusing him of contradicting himself. Finally, the charade wound down. After one more opposing testimony, Ervin declared the hearings over.

He did not have time, he said, to hear the pro-ERA testimony scheduled for Monday — Martha Griffiths, Wilma Heide, Alice Paul, Marguerite Rawalt, Pauli Murray, and many others. Working together through the weekend, Marguerite and the presidents of the D.C. Women's Bar and NAWL got out a letter to the members of the Senate Judiciary Committee protesting Senator Ervin's "patently biased action" in the selection and scheduling of witnesses. Ultimately the Judiciary Committee refused to take action based on Ervin's one-sided hearings, and Senator Cook heard the remaining testimony on Tuesday.

Despite the frustration of wasted energy and activity that seemed to accomplish nothing, Marguerite was at the top of her form, enjoying the work she had prepared to do for a lifetime. There was still hope that ERA would win on the floor of the Senate. A week after the hearings, she told her niece Ruth, "I have become a pivot of information," and then added, "*YOU* write both Senators John G. Tower and Ralph Yarborough."

In high spirits, she wrote Willis a few days later.

> It is one of those perfect days. Sun bright, cool enough for a
> coat morning and evening, but right now the sun is warm and
> pleasant. . . I just caught a bus at the door and went over to the
> little Virginia village where I keep my bank account, and then
> walked back. A mocking bird or two in the yards along the way,
> talking but not singing full song. Trees have hardly begun to
> turn, though the first leaves are falling.
>
> Tomorrow I shall be in the gallery and any other time I
> think the debate is going on. There will be powerful resistance by
> Sen. Ervin. . . . You gave me my laugh of the day and the pleas-
> ure of knowing that you are watching for news of our Equal
> Rights Amendment. . . . in your report of the new organization —
> no — I had not heard of MAM [Men are Masters].

The enemies of ERA in the Senate immediately attacked the
bill with extraneous amendments. Senator Howard Baker, a Tennessee Republican, secured passage of an amendment requiring
prayer in the public schools and Ervin added another forbidding
the drafting of women. Despite their discouragement, women filled
the galleries to hear endless questions about the effect of ERA on
the draft and separate restrooms. Marguerite was there on Friday,
October 9, to hear Senator Cook defend the unmodified ERA.

Annoyed and close to despair, she described the day to Betty
Boyer and Nancy Dowding. "Senator Cook made one magnificent
speech. Every Senator had left the floor! Not one of the scoundrels
heard it. . . So much to do — and I really don't know what more
there is to do."

On Wednesday, just hours before Congress went home for the
elections, Senator Bayh introduced a "substitute" for ERA which
would extend the Fourteenth Amendment by providing that no one
be denied "equal protection of the laws" on account of sex. After
meeting with Senators Bayh and Cook in Bayh's office, Marguerite
was still leery. She described her reaction to Martha Griffiths,

> When I questioned whether this [the Fourteenth Amend-
> ment substitute] would overturn Supreme Court sex classifica-
> tion theory, they hopped down my throat, of course. I refused, at
> more than one direct question, to say that I could give it sup-
> port. . . knew we would have to give more thought.

Since the Fourteenth Amendment applies only to state laws, she knew the Bayh substitute would not eliminate all legal discrimination. It would just create a new muddle that might end any possibility of getting ERA through in the future. Surely they all knew how slim the chances were of getting an amendment through both Houses during the short session following the October recess.

Everybody wanted to know what she thought. She and others, especially Martha Griffiths and Margaret Laurence, were convinced they had to put together some kind of clearinghouse organization to focus their strategy and handle emergencies like this one. For now, all they could do was keep their fingers in as many dikes as possible.

Immediately, Marguerite's calendar was a hodgepodge of emergency meetings. On Thursday she met until midnight with national officers of BPW. They were all enamored of Birch Bayh. He was doing so much for them. They wanted to approve his recommendation.

But Marguerite was doubtful. Senator Ervin was sure to try to derail the substitute as he had the amendment, so they would get no advantage there. Why, she wondered, was Senator Edward Kennedy, who had always opposed ERA, backing the substitute if it would accomplish the same thing as ERA? Even former advocates of the constitutional approach like Pauli Murray and Leo Kanowitz didn't want women in the Constitution as a special category of citizen. Women are *already* citizens, they insisted.

Coached by Catherine East, NOW was coming out against the substitute. Of course the Woman's Party opposed it. But organizations representing thousands of women — BPW, Zonta, General Federation, NAWL — wanted to hear from Marguerite. The tension (and her need for support) shows in a long letter to Martha Griffiths.

> . . . I have no peace, and my phone keeps ringing to know what we should do. I keep saying that we should get opinions, such as BPW is doing. But Martha, it is going to come back to you AS OUR LEADER and if you have no objection to comments in the making against the amendment, I wish I knew it. I could influence against some of them if it were wise. (P.S. both Virginia [Allan] and I are restive with the namby-pamby approach of our BPW national officers — and more and more inclined to march along with NOW)! . . . if you can give an inkling on whether to let the NOES be heard, I would follow thru with any influence of

mine. YOU ARE VERY SPECIAL TO ME — as to thousands of others.

Talking with other women lawyers only strengthened her doubts. There was nothing in Senator Bayh's substitute to stop the Supreme Court from ruling against women as it always had done. On October 20, she received a letter from Bayh — he didn't want to proceed without the approval of women's groups. He wanted her views as soon as possible. Her three-page reply makes her opposition clear:

> It would not seem there would be justification for submitting to the states for ratification a constitutional proposal that would accomplish but a small part of legal recognition for women. . . . It is not believed that women who have persevered for almost two centuries in their efforts to be recognized as people and persons under our constitution would be willing to compromise for a crumb of recognition and continue ad infinitum, state by state, statute by statute, to work for additional crumbs of legal self respect and self determination.

Spearheaded by Gladys O'Donnell, president of the National Federation of Republican Women, and backed by Harriet Cipriani from the Democratic National Committee, a wide-ranging coalition of women met in the Rayburn House Office Building the afternoon of November 2, to try to reach a consensus on the substitute. Worried that BPW would approve the substitute out of loyalty to Bayh and destroy the united front they wanted to present, Marguerite wrote Martha Griffiths again: "It would be disastrous to have a division, and to have them [BPW representatives] take a different stand. . . . There is too much hero-worship of the Senator."

Marguerite had become the voice of experience among ERA advocates. Presiding over the November 2 meeting of the "Joint Organizations," she guided the long debate. Finally the group agreed to oppose the substitute. Although BPW representatives, having met with Bayh's office separately two days earlier, came prepared to support the substitute, they agreed to abstain for the sake of unity and to withhold comments from the press. Still, Marguerite was disappointed by the defection: "This is really too, too bad," she told a group of past presidents of BPW.

A letter to Sylvia Roberts ended on a more personal, more philosophical note: We have "kept a unity of view, but not without effort and heartaches. . . . the major and largest organizations are turned off by anything that sounds like women's lib. . . . And I stand in between so often. . . We must stand unified. . ."

With Marguerite acting as spokeswoman, representatives of the joint organizations met with Senator Bayh on November 18. She began slowly, trying — as tactfully as possible — to explain the stand they were taking. In a short time, Bayh held up his hand, "Marguerite, I get the message."

Despite their "united front," press reaction was varied. Writing in the next day's *Washington Post*, Marie Smith emphasized the commitment to work for an unadulterated ERA in 1971. UPI headlines cried FEMINISTS GIVE UP, but quoted Marguerite: "Women do not want a substitute for absolute equality of rights. We appreciate Senator Bayh's support, but we made it clear to him there would be no retreat."

Amid the emergency action and plan for a two-week speaking tour and then Christmas in Texas, Marguerite and Margaret Laurence laid the groundwork for a political action committee to fight the carefully organized AFL–CIO opposition. But an organization of organizations wouldn't do. As Marguerite had written NOW activist, Rita Mae Brown, in 1969, "Such an undertaking demands the highest degree of knowledge of the organizations, and the wisdom of Solomon and tact beyond comprehension." [6]

Instead, they wanted a nucleus of informed activists, especially lawyers, with the money and the authority to dispense information and act quickly. Marguerite began by securing ten pledges of $100 each from friends.

On Wednesday afternoon, December 2, Marguerite, Margaret Laurence, and Martha Griffiths met at the home of *Washington Post* columnist Sara Booth Conroy to discuss their plans.

Dr. Estelle Ramey and her husband had joined them for dinner. Dr. Ramey, an endocrinologist and professor at Georgetown University Medical School, had been busy defending women against charges made by Democratic Party activist Dr. Edgar Berman who claimed that fluctuating hormones made women unfit for leadership.

By the time the evening ended, Conroy had agreed to write an article for *McCall's* magazine announcing the founding of the liaison organization they would call Women United and asking for small contributions from individuals. The next day Marguerite began writing friends for contributions.

She returned from her Christmas trip to Texas to find her mail piled so high she had to carry it up the elevator in a grocery cart. The next day there were calls from Senator Marlow Cook's office asking her to help write the speech Cook would use to introduce ERA in the new session. He and Birch Bayh would introduce the same simple wording they had begun with the previous year.

Equality of rights under the law shall not be denied or abridged by the United States or by any State on account of sex.

When states rights advocates had objected to a clause that "empowered" the "several states" to enforce the amendment, the coalition agreed to its removal. The phrase was redundant, the women agreed, since the states already had that power. Finally they also accepted a seven-year limitation on the time allowed for ratification by the states.

By mid-January, they had the approval of most of the traditional women's organizations plus NOW and WEAL for the Bayh–Cook wording about to come before the Senate. In early February, Women United wrote every senator and sent a massive mailing to women everywhere asking for contributions in money and effort.

Only the small but still symbolic Woman's Party refused to join them. Alice Paul didn't like the seven-year ratification period. It might take longer than that. She was alarmed that it no longer called for enforcement by "the several states." On Tuesday night late, February 11, Marguerite got home tired after days of meetings and conferences, hours of helping Martha Griffiths prepare to introduce the Bayh–Cook wording in the House. Before she could take off her shoes, the phone began to ring.

Alice Paul talked and lectured and would not let up. What did Marguerite think she was doing? Why was she working so closely with Bayh and Cook and Griffiths and not the Woman's Party? Paul had already spoken with Senator John Tower of Texas about introducing ERA with the original wording. It looked to her like newcomers had taken it on themselves to change the Equal Rights Amendment. No. She would not support this.

Marguerite wanted her to understand. They had not harmed the amendment. It said the same thing it had always said. But this way, with leaders in the House and the Senate backing the same wording, they could get it through. By striking out "the several states" clause they eliminated one of the arguments of the opposition simply by removing meaningless words. It gave them another advantage. What was the point, she asked, in getting nowhere year after year? Not wanting to lose her temper, Marguerite hung up the phone.

Alice Paul had always considered Marguerite too aggressive, too flamboyant, a *par venu*. She wasn't going to change her mind about that.[7]

Women United was the organization Marguerite had always wanted — small, sophisticated, committed. With a feminist elite and one mission, they could keep the procedures simple. It would, as she described it, be "a convener of organizations when desired; a purveyor of information; workers for passage of ERA. . . . an organization of individuals, a wonderful launching, bipartisan, across the spectrum of organizations."

Seeing her own optimism reflected in the promise of spring, she wrote Willis a typical letter on February 20.

> Am working today and tomorrow as I did Sunday, getting out a big mailing for a new organization we have just formed. May send you a copy.
>
> Today is beautiful and sunny — although it opened with rain. Faintest buds are beginning to soften the lines of the naked tree skeletons which winter brought. Yet, two little oak trees I can see just below still have leaves, dried out and sere hanging on. What was that poem we memorized in high school —
>> *And if I should live to be*
>> *the last leaf on the tree in the spring*
>> *Let them laugh as I do now*
>> *at the old familiar bough — where I cling.*
>
> I feel well. Next week end I go to New Jersey to make a talk to a big gathering of B&P women there, spending the week end with Helen Hurd of Rutgers.

Women United's first job was to get ERA supporters ready to testify before Congress again, this time before a subcommittee of the House Judiciary Committee. Don Edwards, a sympathetic California Democrat, would be chairing hearings scheduled for March 24 through April 1.

Hoping to combat the opposition's maddening insistence that ERA would force women out of the home, onto the battlefields, and into unisex bathrooms, Marguerite used her testimony to explain the probable effects of the amendment. Congress already had "unchallenged power" under the Constitution to draft any citizen, male or female. Men and women alike should be ranked, as men already were, for military service according to age, physical condition, educational and family circumstances. Women, like men, had a responsibility to their country and the right to the benefits, veteran's preferences, and employment and educational opportunities available to citizens who served.

Congressman Robert McClory, a Republican from Illinois, complimented her when she was done. She was especially pleased when he said she had given a "studious, comprehensive, thorough and convincing statement." She had, he added, "forthrightly and courageously tagged segments of organized labor and its leadership," as instrumental in denying women equal rights and opportunities, something he thought most members of the "liberal element" were unwilling to do.

In May, Sara Booth Conroy's article came out in *McCall's* magazine and small contributions from individuals came pouring in. Working with Women United and the Washington Forum, Marguerite reduced her constitutional argument to a simple question-and-answer format in a bright four-page flyer called, *Is a Woman a Person?* Within weeks, thousands of them were in the mail. Soon photocopied "editions" were being mailed out by other organizations. Reprints showed up in newsletters the Washington women had never heard of. *Is a Woman a Person?* was a best seller.

Early in June, Marguerite set out on a twice-postponed "world tour" with the General Federation. By the time she returned six weeks later, she had been sightseeing and shopping in Germany, Russia, Thailand, India, Hong Kong, Taiwan, Japan, and Alaska. In New Delhi, she heard over the radio that destructive amendments added in the House had killed ERA in Congress. She returned to Washington to find nullifying amendments tacked on in both Houses. Committees were stalling. Sam Ervin was leading a filibuster in the Senate.

Bad as it looked, Women United and other organizations refused to let up. They knew support for ERA was spreading. Groups like the American Association of University Women and the American Nurses Association were endorsing it for the first time.

Suddenly, Marguerite was called upon to render a more personal service.

June Norris, a friend since the 1940s, had been passed over for promotion at the Bureau of Internal Revenue. Like Marguerite, she had put herself through law school at George Washington University. Also like Marguerite, she was sometimes called "too hard-driving, too aggressive for a woman." But she had been at IRS for fifteen years, done more than her share of the dirty work and risen slowly to a grade 14, the highest level held by any woman in the agency. When her superior was asked to lower her always-high performance evaluation so she could be passed over (for the third time) for a less experienced man, she was indignant.

Sex discrimination cases were new and no one had ever brought such a charge at Internal Revenue; but Norris, active in women's bar associations and a friend of Marguerite's for thirty years, knew what was happening in the courts for women. Encouraged by her husband, also a lawyer, she had filed a sex discrimination complaint in 1970. When her husband died in July, she asked Marguerite to represent her. She didn't think she could do it alone.[8]

Marguerite was deeply disturbed by the request. June Norris was just one of a million women in distress, but she was moved by her friend's suffering — the death of her husband, her indignation, the belief in a principle for which one finally has to fight.

Still she hesitated. This would mean hearings before the Civil Service Commission. She would be on her feet, a lone lawyer defending a woman against the Federal service system, the very same government agency to which she had been doggedly loyal — despite discrimination — for over thirty years. All that time, she had managed to avoid angry confrontations, to work behind the scenes, to keep her career, her activism, and her personal life separate.

Remembering the frugality she learned on the farm, the insecurities with Jack, the harshness of the Depression, she had protected herself, never allowing her activism to threaten her job. At work, she had kept her emotions under control, remained silent sometimes when the office where she worked mocked her deepest beliefs. She knew the price the crusader paid: bitterness and anger in herself, hostility and rejection from others. She hadn't wanted that. If she took the Norris case, all those old feelings would have to be faced.

She told herself she had too much to do, the law review articles, speeches, meetings, Women United. Grinding stomach pains mounted with the pressure.

Nevertheless, by late August, she had agreed to represent June Norris. They did the work together, meeting at Marguerite's apartment at night, making dinner, working until both of them were falling asleep. Sometimes June came back the next morning to work over an early breakfast.[9]

Marguerite endured the suffocating end-of-summer humidity with rising irritation, outraged by the evidence of discrimination against June Norris. In the meantime, efforts for ERA were getting nowhere. The more support it got, the more entrenched the opposition became.

Late in the summer, her spirits were lifted by a letter from Pauli Murray. They communicated only occasionally now, working for the same goals in different ways. Of the testimony she prepared for the Senate hearings, Murray had said: "I am a woman, a black woman, a black woman constitutional lawyer. Nobody could have written this but me." Each of them was doing what only she could do. Soon Murray would enter General Theological Seminary in preparation for becoming the first black woman to be admitted to the priesthood in the Episcopal Church. The next step in Murray's education was still unknown to Marguerite when she wrote her on September 1:

> I have been missing you for months. Knowing that you were "there" and doing good work, of course, and that, like me, the days were not enough long to keep up with periodic correspondence and friends. I wish you were in my city — I need you right now as I am undertaking a discrimination case in Federal employment — sex discrimination of course. None has ever been won — or reached the court that I can get word of.

By September 29, 1971, the date of June Norris's hearing, the two of them had gathered hundreds of pages of evidence and secured the testimony of nine witnesses, including a former commissioner of Internal Revenue. Still, there were no precedents, and Marguerite's anxiety and loneliness show in a letter to Anna and Willis.

> Hardly a chance of winning it, but we are putting on the best fight that we can. I am weary of all this, and swear this is the last.

I do wish my family did live near. I get homesick for family at times, and especially when I get under tension.

Looking out the window just now — it is almost dark. It is raining gently. Lights are on, but the rain dims the Lincoln Memorial and the Monument. Cars still go to and fro along the highways.

She wanted the men to understand what they were doing. She wanted them to do something about it. Why, she wondered, had she waited so long to tell them?

On Saturday — after the hearing ended on Friday — she wrote in her diary, . . . *let down all day*. A few days later she told Anna and Willis: "It was nerve-wracking. It is strange how one will keep going with seeming calm through three grueling days of that kind, but when it is over, the reaction sets in."

She didn't have time to let down for long, or regret the past. ERA was beckoning. On October 12, the House of Representatives voted overwhelmingly for the amendment without harmful additions.

Yet, despite the efforts of Birch Bayh, Marlow Cook, and others, the Senate refused to schedule consideration of the amendment until February. By October 25, Women United had instructions in the mail to all its subscribers along with a chart listing each senator and how he had voted on the amendment and the crippling additions. The instructions were always the same — see your senator during the holidays, or write, or wire, and express disapproval of those who voted wrong last time. They had watched it work in the House. As soon as the congressmen saw that the negating additions were failing, most of them shifted and voted for the amendment alone. For the first time, women in large numbers knew what was going on in Congress.

After Christmas, the signs were good. In January, Senator Ted Kennedy, who had previously sided with protective law advocates, endorsed the Bayh–Griffiths wording.

A few days later, June Norris learned that she had won her appeal. She had been denied promotions for reasons that would not have been held against a man. Immediately she received the grade-raise she sought. Marguerite described the case to her friend, former Congresswoman Reva Beck Bosone:

. . . [June Norris] was passed over for promotion for three times, each time a man, one of the clique, was promoted. Two of them she trained. It took three days of "trial" before a Hearing Examiner. [IRS officials] were shocked when the finding of discrimination was made — and then adopted by the Treasury. It was promotion to Grade 15. But it took so much out of me — for six weeks I didn't do anything else but study Civil Service regulations, court decisions, etc. etc. Not to mention assembling witnesses. And I am not a cross-examination expert, but with her help, I did a good job.

Norris wanted to call a press conference to announce a woman's first successful appeal before the Civil Service Commission. Women should know they didn't have to put up with discrimination in government jobs. She wanted to carry the case to court and try to get back pay.

Marguerite insisted they accept the victory rather than begin a long court suit for back pay. She would not take the case at the expense of ERA. She had given all she had to give. She remembered when the victories had been few indeed. They accumulated now, but the risks had to be calculated, and the war was never over.

Throughout February, the Senate Judiciary Committee refused to act on ERA. Women United kept the pressure on strategically selected members of the Senate and the committee, which promised to act by the end of the month. The calculations of Women United suggested they might defeat all "killing" amendments and get ERA through if they could get it on the floor of the Senate and keep up the lobbying.

Finally, on February 28, the Judiciary Committee reported out the ERA as originally worded — despite Senator Ervin's solitary efforts to stall and water down the bill. Immediately, Women United mounted the kind of write-in, call-in, walk-in campaign that Marguerite understood best: "This is the last big push! Your letters got it through the House. . . don't stop now. . . . Insist that the President make it 'perfectly clear' he supports the ERA. Make the most of an election year!"

Elated with the sudden success and the central role she played, Marguerite pushed harder than ever, trying to ignore mysterious stomach pains. She could hardly remember when she had accepted the responsibility for this work — and the haunting guilt when anything she might have done went undone. If ERA went through, she might be able to rest, to enjoy the retirement she kept promising herself.

Debate began in the Senate on Friday, March 17, Birch Bayh began with a long speech echoing arguments he had heard from Marguerite — sex should not be a factor in determining one's rights under the law; yet, the Supreme Court had consistently refused to apply the Fourteenth Amendment to discrimination based on sex. "After 200 years of history, the time has come to sound the death knell and signal the end of discrimination against a class of Americans who happen to constitute a majority of the citizenry of this land."

Marlow Cook followed, quoting a letter Marguerite had sent to all the senators in August, explaining the effects of ERA on the draft. All day Monday, Senators Ervin and Bayh argued over the merits of protection and unfettered equality. On Tuesday, Ervin came armed with a barrage of protective amendments, beginning with the draft. Did the senators want women to

> ... be drafted and. . . sent into combat, where they will be slaughtered or maimed by the bayonets, the bombs, the bullets, the grenades, the mines, the napalm, the poison gas, and the shells of the enemy? . . . I have seen the bodies of mortal casualties lying upon the field of battle. . . and have witnessed the beginning of the putrefying process. . . . I have seen the bodies of my comrades mangled and their limbs torn asunder. . . . women will suffer the loss of their privacy and sometimes become pregnant and bear illegitimate children; and the equal rights amendment will prohibit the discharge from the armed services of any single woman for pregnancy or childbearing no matter how often she becomes pregnant or how many bastards she bears.

Only men who wanted to see such things happen should vote for ERA, he concluded.

At last, the times had turned against the long-honored rhetoric of men like Sam Ervin, and that afternoon the Senate rejected the draft amendment 73 to 18. Sensing victory, the women in the galleries began to cheer. For two days, Ervin introduced "protective" amendment after "protective" amendment, losing by a bigger vote each time. With the rejection of each attempt to stifle the "pure" ERA, the women in the galleries roared while the chair rapped for order.

Finally it was over. The *Congressional Record* called the uproar that followed "demonstrations in the galleries." After almost 200 years, a nearly all-male Congress had voted to put women in the Constitution of the United States. Everyone was congratulating everyone. For many of them, including Marguerite, it was a personal triumph, the culmination of a struggle they thought would never end.

A UPI photographer caught Marguerite and Birch Bayh arm in arm beaming at one another. Friends across the country sent her copies of the photograph captioned "He's My Boy" and "From One Equal to Another."

The impromptu celebration overflowed into a meeting room off the Senate floor. Senator Bayh was their hero, and Marguerite promised a "Congressional Jubilee" to celebrate what their leaders had done in Congress.

Late that night she wrote in red ink across the obligations penciled on her calendar for March 22, 1972: *Equal Rts A passed Senate.*

She remembered that heart-chilling day in 1928, when she was told she could not study law at Georgetown University because she was a woman, and the slow realization that the laws themselves denied women the promises of American democracy, denied them the opportunities of choice, prosperity, security. Then the war came and ended and she began to think there was something she and other women could do, would have to do. And then she was doing it, and now it was done. Nike, winged victory, she had seen it at the Louvre. . . so long ago. . . . If only Harry had been there to share the joy. Harry and Mom.

Within days, Marguerite was putting together the Jubilee she had promised. Virginia Allan, recently named deputy assistant secretary of state for public affairs at the State Department, would be toastmaster. Committees were set up, thousands of invitations mailed. Martha Griffiths, Birch Bayh, and Marlow Cook would be "lionized." Marguerite wanted a night they would never forget, a coming together of all the women who had worked so hard for what they all needed.

On April 9, Isabelle Shelton announced plans for the celebration in the *Washington Sunday Star,* calling it the "Equal Rights Bash." The Nixons had been invited. If the president came, she said, he would be "breaking bread. . . with some very nonestablish-ment types whose paths rarely, if ever, cross his." Women from lib-eration groups, the established clubs, BPW, NOW, WEAL, many of them would be crossing paths they rarely crossed.

The "bash" was set for May 10 at the Washington Hilton Hotel. Marguerite and her arrangements committee solicited $100 each from thirty organizations and individuals and began making plans. In addition to the celebration that night, they would hold a workshop in the afternoon to discuss and plan strategy for ratifica-tion of ERA by the states. They were all full of hope.

Marguerite was enjoying herself, planning an event she had dreamed about for over forty years. Then on Friday, April 29, just ten days before the Jubilee, she was called home to Corpus Christi, Louis had suffered a heart attack. Vi needed her.

She turned responsibility for the Jubilee over to Virginia Allan and caught a late flight to Texas. For a week, she shared hospital duties with Vi, writing her speeches in between and somehow find-ing time to shop for silver trays to present to the Jubilee's honored guests. By the next Saturday, Louis was well enough for her to re-turn.

As soon as ERA passed the Congress, the states began ratify-ing, with Hawaii coming in just hours after passage in the Senate. By the end of the summer, twenty of the needed thirty-eight states had ratified. Despite the good start they were getting, the women and men who met for the Ratification Assembly on the afternoon of May 10 knew there was work ahead. They had too much experi-ence to doubt it.

Phyllis Schlafly was attracting attention, railing against the amendment, calling housewives, conservatives, and religious peo-ple together in opposition. ERA would deprive women of freedom and privilege, she said. Did they want to be just like men? Did they want to *have* to work in offices and factories? To *have* to go into com-bat? If ERA passed, men would no longer support their families. Women and children would be destitute. She sounded like a crack-pot — but people listened.

That night, 800 women and a sprinkling of men overflowed the Washington Hilton's International Ballroom. Liz Carpenter was there, Esther Peterson, Betty Friedan, Senator Robert Dole, Congressman Gerald Ford. Marguerite wore a long dress she had bought in the Philippines, pale embroidered ecru with tall "butter-fly sleeves." Someone fastened a big *Jubilee 72* pin to the scooped neckline and she left it there. With sparkling gold loops dangling from her ears, she felt like a girl, and remembered the gold satin dress with cream-colored lace she had worn with Jack.

She spoke of the National Woman's Party and Alice Paul, ill and still convinced that Congress had passed an unacceptable version of the amendment she had written in the 1920s. Without Paul, suffrage would have been longer in coming, there would have been no ERA, no continuity of effort. The torch had been passed; women were no longer the "Sleeping Beauties of American Politics."

Martha Griffiths was their Joan of Arc, Birch Bayh their Lochinvar, and Marlow Cook a Kentucky Colonel. The "Green Berets for ERA" had led their good soldiers to victory. The crowd laughed uproariously as the valiant Senator Bayh struggled helplessly to unwrap the engraved silver tray they had given him.

A month later, Marguerite told the Jubilee sponsors that the affair had been so successful financially that she could return the $100 each had contributed. But they insisted the money go toward ratification, and by August, they had established the ERA Ratification Council. With Marguerite as chair, the council would be the first group to see the need for a centralized strategy in the states.

But what they needed most was a leader, a strong knowledgeable woman to direct them, to call them together, to keep them moving in the same direction, to fight off the growing opposition, to do nationwide what had been done in Washington through Women United. With the energy and momentum she had lavished on NAWL and BPW in the 1940s and 1950s, Marguerite could have done it herself. She knew what was required: constant travel, total commitment, involvement with hundreds of new women and organizations, the patience of Job, the wisdom of Solomon.

A year later she wrote Reva Beck Bosone agreeing on the need for a world conference to unify women: "I could wish I was 40 years younger and. . . had all this experience, even as you [do]." Then together, *we* could do such a thing. . ."

But she was seventy-seven years old, and as the women's movement had grown, she had become more and more attuned to working with small, handpicked groups of women she knew and trusted. Someone else would have to do this.

As she had done so often in the past, Marguerite began looking for the right person to carry on the work she had set in motion. A few days after the Jubilee, she wrote Osta Underwood, current president of BPW, a forceful woman, a lawyer who had joined the organization during the 1940s in order to work for ERA: "I could wish for nothing more optimistic than that you could drop for another year your own professional work and come to Washington as a Director of Ratification. A wonderful spirit of cooperation was developed through our planning for the Jubilee. . . . get togethers should continue here, and should be disseminated as a pattern in the states."

In October, she resigned as chair of the ERA Ratification Council and told a friend, "I have given my share to this."

She had watched the tiny underground movement to which she had belonged since the 1930s become a powerful, turbulent force and then begin to flow into the mainstream of American life. Between 1972 and 1980, a majority of men and women in the United States came to believe that women should have an equal role with men in business, industry, and government.

NOW and WEAL continued to grow in size and political influence; and in July 1971, 200 prominent women had come together to form the National Women's Political Caucus, a bipartisan organization that would raise increasingly large sums of money to expand the role of women in politics. New leaders were involved, journalist Gloria Steinem and New York Congresswomen Bella Abzug and Shirley Chisholm.

A year later, Gloria Steinem and a group of New York writers began publishing *Ms.*, the first nationally circulated feminist magazine. Soon publications like *Working Woman, Savvy* and *New Woman* were attracting a new generation of mainstream, feminist-influenced women in larger numbers than Marguerite would have dreamed possible.

[8]

In The Marketplace

For Marguerite, activism was inherent. Her energy rose in response not to abstractions but to people — what happened to them, what they did, how they acted and reacted, how they responded to her. Despite her half-serious longing for the rocking chair of retirement, she would never be satisfied to sit in the proverbial marketplace dispensing wisdom. Yet during the 1970s, a contemplative strain appeared amid the activism, and she began devoting more time to teaching, sharing her experience with young women, connecting them to the historic and philosophical roots they forgot so easily, passing on the know-how of leadership.

She and others began to see that ERA alone would not be enough. Women were learning to back their own interests with money, information and publicity, learning to use the tools that worked for men. They called it clout. By the end of the decade, Marguerite had incorporated and secured tax exemption not only for BPW, NOW, and WEAL funds, but also for Federally Employed Women (FEW) and the General Federation of Women's Clubs.

After the NOW Legal Defense and Education Fund became fully tax exempt in 1971, she again became an active member of its board. Early in 1973, under the auspices of the forward-looking Division of Women's Studies at George Washington University headed by Dr. Ruth Osborn, she created and began teaching a course she at first called "Sex Discrimination and the Law," drawing heavily on her own experience and emphasizing the history of ERA and the Title VII cases.

A few days before the course began, she testified before the Virginia Legislature, and then flew to Tuscaloosa, Alabama, to debate Phyllis Schlafly at a statewide ERA rally. Disturbed by the growing backlash against women's rights, she wrote former Congresswoman Reva Beck Bosone, "[Utah's failure to ratify] was a bad blow for ERA. . . . But if the University classes get in on the subject of discrimination, they may prove the leavening which will bring change."

In the spring of 1973, she was hospitalized for emergency removal of a long-ignored stomach ulcer. But by August, she was fully recovered, planning a trip to Europe, completing her Rawalt genealogy and, lamenting the Watergate cover-up.

In the fall, she returned to a "Women and the Law" class that had grown to three times its original size — with a waiting list. Despite the problems with ERA ratification, she was increasingly optimistic about the future she saw for women. As she told Debbie Rawalt, a recently married grandniece:

> You know when I came to Washington to study law, I could not be admitted to the Georgetown University Law School because they would not admit a woman to study law. Today, all schools are open to them. I have some young women in my class whom you would love to know and they to know you. All getting their education so they can do things in the world that they want to do. . . . This is the pattern of many young couples today. So the world will be a much better and happier place for all of us in years to come.

A year later she was still enthusiastic about the course, now elevated to the graduate school, and still using it to put the lives of women in perspective for herself. She wrote about it to Debbie's mother, Melody.

> The clock just struck six-a.m. I have been up since four and

have read two more of the four remaining graduate dissertations which I must complete and turn in grades for by Friday. I never sleep long when something is pressing for action — or perhaps it is the farm girl in me, where we got up at daylight. However, it is still dark outdoors, and I look out my office windows on the lights shining along the nearby highway, the Lincoln Bridge, Washington Monument. I am thankful for my comforts of living and for my health. That and family like yours, and what could anyone want besides?

To raise three wonderful children. . . is surely a highly important, if unsalaried job. After they are on their own, you will still be a young woman. Most of my class in graduate work is composed of just such women, who are now getting trained in thinking and self confidence, to go into the work world. . .

So long ago she had postponed her education and her career to marry Jack. For women the conflict between love and work was always there — with choices that had to be made and a price to pay, as she told Ruth Rawalt Hestand's daughter Sandra.

Maybe you wonder why your Aunt Mike did not become a judge. Well, to begin with, I had the desire during my first year at Texas University [sic, The University of Texas] to attend the law school and get my degree in law. Instead, war came along and I fell in love. The result, I lost ten years out of school, before turning the corner and getting back to school in Washington, under my own steam. That is, working as secretary by day, and attending University law school at night. That ten years crept up on me before I could get as high as I would have liked, although I made some sidewise waves holding office in bar associations, even if not as a judge. There is no bar to falling in love — just holding it in check until an education is attained — Well, anyway. . .

Many things happened in 1973 to remind Marguerite of her contribution to making the world a "better, happier world" for women. In town for a symposium at George Washington University, Pauli Murray paid her a surprise visit in the hospital, and they remembered the work they had started together for the president's commission in 1961, how they had agreed and disagreed and hacked out the different roles each would play in a women's rights movement that had grown beyond anything either of them could have imagined.[1]

Now Pauli wanted to become a priest. For Marguerite, activism was a public thing, religion private. For Paulis religion and politics were closely akin, and her battles for civil rights and women's rights had become one. So unalike, with so much in common, together — hardly knowing what they did — they had seen it begin.

A letter from Sylvia Roberts recalled the most trying of all Marguerite's labors for women: the launching of the National Organization for Women, the NOW Legal Defense and Education Fund, the Title VII cases, a personal struggle that had forced her to reexamine long-held values and draw the line between her sense of who she was and her commitment to a movement she helped start.

In August, Roberts wrote: "Our deepest thanks for making the [NOW Legal Defense] Fund a reality. None of us can fully appreciate the extent of your sacrifices, or the hardships of the onerous duties you performed. . . . Of course, there would be no Fund today without your singlehanded efforts under what could only be described as most difficult circumstances."

Nineteen seventy-four opened solemnly with word of Martha Griffiths's resignation from Congress because of her husband's illness. "It is just devastating," Marguerite wrote Pauli Murray, "I suppose we must respect her reasons and join in appreciation of the wonderful contributions she has made to the cause of women's emancipation under the law."

To Griffiths, she sent a message of affection and regret. "A whole pall of gloom is cast over the troops when the word comes down the line that the General has fallen. You have become the five-star General of the Women's Rights Movement in this country. The bright side of it is that you have inspired. . . and trained and convinced so many others in the movement that we will carry on to the best of our ability without our leader in Congress." The list of Griffiths's contributions was long: leadership through the traditional organizations, work with NOW, the courageous battle to get Title VII enacted and then enforced, the historic discharge petition in the House, the drive to get the "Griffiths Equal Rights Amendment" through the Congress.

By early spring, Marguerite was at work with two other Washington lawyers, Sara-Ann Determan and Brooksley Landau, on a brief to be filed by the American Bar Association before the Supreme Court. In 1975, the Court would decide in their favor in the *Edwards* vs. *Healy* case, finally ruling out state limitations on a woman's "right and responsibility" to serve on a jury.

Marguerite's efforts for ERA continued through the Ratification Council, which worked to inform and coordinate local organizations backing ratification. Now her speeches and articles were enriched by her growing knowledge of family law and the possible effects of ERA on family life.

In July of 1975, she joined some 6,000 other women at the World Conference on the International Women's Year in Mexico City. With her never-flagging desire to "do it all," she took in both the official gathering sponsored by the United Nations, which she called "hardworking but essentially dull," and the disorderly but invigorating mass meeting at the Tribune. As she described it to several friends, it was "history in the making — and sometimes in the raw."

> The Tribune attracted thousands of women, and was ultimately opened to anyone who wanted to enter, after a throng of Mexican women charged the doors demanding entrance. . . It was a madhouse. . . But there was the plus of meeting leaders from U.S.A., and women leaders of all other countries, and seeing all in action.
>
> Betty Friedan and a woman from one of the small African countries, really handled an auditorium of very vocal ones, and hammered out a platform of demands in the form of amendments to the World Plan of Action.

When President Gerald Ford established the President's Commission for International Women's Year, Marguerite was appointed to two committees: the ERA Committee jointly headed by Congresswoman Margaret Heckler and actor Alan Alda, and the Committee on the Homemaker and the Laws which Martha Griffiths would chair. Soon she was drafting the rules of order that would govern the state conferences and the National Women's Year Conference planned for November 1977 in Houston.

After Phyllis Schlafly and other ERA opponents complained about the implications of a quasi-governmental body advocating legislation, the ERA Committee channeled its activities into ERAmerica. The high-visibility, independent corporation with the ability to raise money and speak out became the unified lobbying voice of the many groups supporting the amendment. Convinced that the initial publicity and funding made ERAmerica the most effective way to work for the amendment, Marguerite turned her energies in that direction, hoping the umbrella organization could unite the loose-jointed efforts now floundering in the unratified states.

By the mid-1970s, a bitter wave of conservatism had engulfed the country. Only four more states were needed to ratify ERA, but an adamant resistance had set in, especially in the South. Several states had tried to rescind their ratification.

It was tight, too tight. Occasionally Marguerite's frustration shows, as it does here in an angry description of Phyllis Schlafly's address to a gathering of media women at the National Press Club in April 1976.

> Mrs. Schlafly mounted her usual outright lies in a most convincing manner if one did not know them to be misstatements. (Men will desert their wives; wives will have to leave their children and go out to work to support children and husbands; all women will be slogging in the mud in the trenches of the next war; homosexual marriages will be legal — she will not even listen to the U.S. Supreme Court which last week held otherwise [on homosexual marriages]. . . and on and on.)

A year later, ERA's chances looked even slimmer. Lamenting Florida's failure to ratify, Marguerite wrote her good friend Isla Benedick who had moved to Florida,

> The inborn prejudice of legislators, like Sam Ervin's is really showing. Southern men! Of course they love their ladies and must "protect" them. I had hoped ERA would get passed, and I could just sit in a rocking chair. And it isn't that I think it will fail unless I, big I, carry on. Thank goodness young women are learning to know their legal status. But the deadline for the constitutional amendment is March 1979, and the only state with an election of legislators this fall is VIRGINIA. A hopeless state anyway.

Hope was fading, and in another year she would write Benedick in despair, "It is too disgusting to contemplate that a handful of men keep millions of women from being constitutional citizens of this land."

A few days after Marguerite's birthday in October 1977, WEAL launched the Marguerite Rawalt Trust Fund to assist in precedent-setting sex discrimination cases. A month later, she arrived in Houston for the historic National Convention for International Women's Year. The Hyatt Regency's huge, sunlit lobby was overflowing with women, sitting on suitcases, standing in clusters, frantically calling around for rooms. There would be 14,000 of them before it was over, and many came without reservations. Marguerite would have been one of them if Martha Griffiths hadn't called a few days before and insisted on sharing the suite provided for her as a member of the IWY Commission.

Fourteen thousand activists. Marguerite remembered the handful of women who had started NOW over lunch in 1966, and the 300 who showed up for the organizing meeting in the spare Washington Skyline Motel. They wanted the same things they had wanted then, some of the same things women wanted at the first National Conference of Women in Seneca Falls, New York, almost fifty years before she was born.

But not all of them were on the same side, and Marguerite had to work hard to get pro-ERA women ready to battle Phyllis Schlafly and the "antis." The next morning, her ERA Ratification Council held a breakfast to brief pro-ERA organizations on the day's events. The rest of the day went to an ERA Ratification Assembly organized by Marguerite and sponsored by BPW. That night 3,000 women packed the Hyatt's Imperial Ballroom and contributed $100,000 to eat and drink and talk with the leaders of ERAmerica and First Ladies Lady Bird Johnson, Betty Ford, and Rosalynn Carter.

Despite the continued concern for ERA and her work on the board of directors of ERAmerica and as chairman once again of the ERA Ratification Council, Marguerite wasn't driving herself as hard as she once had. She put more of her time into writing, analyzing court cases, advising other women, and organizing her archives—a vast collection of documents, clippings, letters, and photographs spanning a century of change.

Nurturing the collection as it grew, making room for it in closets, under beds, in the kitchen, moving it from one apartment to another, she had wondered why she kept it all. Now her women's rights collection was probably the most comprehensive existing record of the American women's movement from 1945 through 1972.

Early in 1978, she began organizing her archives for the Arthur and Elizabeth Schlesinger Women's History Library at Radcliffe. Soon she was at work as well on interviews for the Oral History Project at Columbia University.

In July, she joined 100,000 women demonstrating before the White House on behalf of a three-year extension of time for ERA ratification, many of them wearing white as the suffragists had done before them. In high spirits, she described it to NAWL president, Alice Duffy, "the march was a huge success. . . the heat got to me and I mounted a trolley and rode to the Capitol where the NOW girls very cordially gave me a reserved seat in front of the platform. I heard all of the speeches, which were splendid."

When she and other women met with President Jimmy Carter in the White House in the spring of 1978 to discuss the legal needs of women, she described it to her niece, Sandra, in words that reflect her never-waning awe, pleasure, and amazement at life's adventures: "I must say I marvel that a man can carry such heavy responsibility on one shoulder, then walk into the East Room and address scores of women about their wishes as if that were the one and most important thing on his agenda." For her, the women's movement had begun in that room in 1944.

Early in 1980, she was surprised when the BPW Foundation Library became the Marguerite Rawalt Resource Center. In May, she joined Esther Peterson and civil rights activist Virginia Foster Durr in a series of lectures at Radcliffe's Schlesinger Library.

Asked to speak about herself as well as her work, she equivocated and described her reservations to another niece, "I never made a talk about *ME* before, and just shrink from it. It has me on edge. I can talk easily enough about the Equal Rights Amendment — or about someone else, but about myself is quite another thing."

When the day came, she spoke not about her personal life but about the influence of other people on her life and the continuous growth of her feminist consciousness: Lucy Moore, a rare example, superintendent of schools returning to law school in middle age; Pat Neff who said, "Here is your chance go to law school"; the terrible shock of being refused by Georgetown University; the influence of women lawyers and her accomplishments in organizations; the awakening and recommitment of the 1960s and 1970s. She was proud to have been part of it all.

By the time the Republicans nominated the ultra-conservative Ronald Reagan for president and retreated from the party's historic endorsement of ERA, the amendment's chances were slim indeed. Outraged, Marguerite wrote her nephew Wallace Rawalt.

> A candidate who could have let the ERA plank recognizing women as persons in this country stand as it was, but chose instead not only to remove it but to forcefully stand on ANTI-women will never have a vote of mine. He could have left the plank, which the Republicans were first to enact and which had been in the platform since 1940, stand. . .

When the extension expired in June 1982, ERA was still three states short of ratification. Already deeply engrossed cataloging her women's history archive for the Schlesinger Library, Marguerite took the defeat philosophically. There were, as she wrote her Secord relatives, "So many things to do before I leave this planet." Both her acceptance of the inevitable and her indignation show in a letter to a grandniece, "After 200 years of the constitution, a few key men are so antediluvian that they will not tolerate the idea of women being LEGALLY equal. This is something you will have to take over — where my generation has failed."

Later in the year, she wrote friends "It was a national disgrace to lose the ERA, but of course we will start, and have done so, all over again." An article she wrote for the *Women Lawyers' Journal* ends with a new slogan. "There is no deadline for equality in our society."

Now in 1985, when Marguerite stands with other women to say a prayer written especially for women who work together in organizations, there is a line she always omits: "Let us take time for all things; make us to grow calm, serene, gentle."

Until there is equality for all women, she can't afford serenity. No woman can. There is too much to be done.

Amid the labors and the setbacks, life had been for her a mounting spiral that moved upward, always upward, a cornucopia of experience. Serenity and passivity are luxuries she hasn't had. Life is seen as focus, drive, energy propelling her forward toward an undoubted destination — not always seen clearly, but always, amid the struggle, worth it.

Marguerite, Louis, Willis with Lee Shaner and Tom Stucker crossing the Texas pan-handle, summer 1907.

— Photograph by Viola Rawalt

Threshing season at Kingfisher, c. 1907.

[All photograghs not credited are from the personal collection of Marguerite Rawalt.]

Marguerite, c. 1909.   *Marguerite's high school graduation picture, 1913.*

Master Sergeant Jack Tindale, c. 1918.

Marguerite in El Paso, 1924.

Charles Rawalt, 1936.

Marguerite as a law student, 1930.

Harry Secord, c. 1937.
— Photograph by Harris & Ewing

Marguerite admitted to practice before the
Supreme Court, 1938.

Christmas at the Rawalt's in the 1940s. Willis, Harry Secord, Louis, Ruth, Anna,
Kenneth, Marguerite, Viola, Vi, Wallace.

Harry Secord, 1942.

— Photograph by Bachrach

Marguerite and Harry, Cherry Blossom Time, 1937.

Judge Justin Miller, Eleanor Roosevelt, and Marguerite at Federal Bar Luncheon, December 1, 1943.

Eleanor Roosevelt and Marguerite at Federal Bar Luncheon, December 1, 1943.

Marguerite and Viola in Corpus Christi during the 1940s.

Margie Neal, first woman in the Texas Senate, in Washington during the 1940s.

Marguerite and the only women holding federal judicial appointments in 1943, Judges Marion J. Harron, Florence Allen, Genevieve Cline, and Marguerite.

Marguerite, 1945.

Marguerite and Harry at Atlantic City, October, 1946.

Marguerite, 1950.

Marguerite tells President Eisenhower about ERA, April 1955.

Marguerite and Lady Bird Johnson, 1956.

Marguerite, Hazel Anderson, and Libby Sachar at the BPW headquarters sweep-stakes, 1956.

Esther Peterson at BPW national convention, July 1961.

Eleanor Roosevelt, Katherine Ellickson, Helen Hill Miller, Marguerite, and Dorothy Height at President's Commission meeting at Val-Kill, June 16, 1962.

The first President's Commission on the Status of Women presents its report to President Kennedy and Vice-President Johnson on October 11, 1963.

Marguerite and Vice-President Johnson signing the commission's report, "American Women," October 11, 1963.

Marguerite and Congresswoman Martha Griffiths in 1966. The women's movement begins.

Marguerite picketing the White House with NOW, May 1969.

Marguerite picketing the White House with NOW, May 1969.

Marguerite, Jeanne Wasile, Elizabeth Duncan Koontz, and Dr. Irmagene Holloway working for ERA in the 1970s.

Elizabeth Boyer, founder of Women's Equity Action League, c. 1975.

Journalist Sarah McClendon and Marguerite with Justice Sandra Day O'Connor, January 7, 1982.

Lorena Weeks at home in Wadley, Georgia, Christmas 1983.
— Photograph by Jayne M. Rushin

Marguerite and Judith Paterson at work on her biography, 1986.
— Photograph by Joan Delaney Grant

Marguerite at work at her desk, 1986.
— Photograph by Joan Delaney Grant

Endnotes

Chapter 1. SETTING OUT

1. Pete Daniel, *Breaking the Land: the Transformation of Cotton, Tobacco, and Rice Cultures since 1880* (Urbana and Chicago, 1985), 46–49.
2. Harriot Stanton Blatch, *Mobilizing Woman-Power* (New York, 1918), 124.

Chapter 3. FINDING A PLACE

1. Author's interview with Irene Scott, United States Tax Court, Washington, D.C., June 6, 1983.
2. Letter from Molly Dewson to Eleanor Roosevelt, October 29, 1935. Eleanor Roosevelt papers, Franklin Delano Roosevelt Library.

Chapter 4. GOING FORWARD

1. Author's interviews with Virginia Allan, George Washington University, June 8, 1983; Allan's home in Falls Church, Virginia, September 24, 1983.
2. India Edwards quoted by Kirsten Amundsen, *The Silenced Majority* (Englewood Cliffs, N.J., 1971), 83.
3. Amelia R. Fry, *Conversations with Alice Paul: Woman Suffrage and the Equal Rights Amendment* from a transcript, Regional Oral History Office, Bancroft Library, University of California (Berkeley, 1972–73), 518–530.
4. Author's interview with Libby Sachar, at Sachar's home in Plainfield, New Jersey, September 14, 1983.

Chapter 5. RISING TIDE

1. Author's interview with Grace Daniels at Daniels's home in Kingston, Pennsylvania, September 15, 1983.
2. Author's interview with Esther Peterson at Peterson's home in Washington, D.C., June 16, 1983.
3. Sachar interview.
4. Peterson interview.
5. Sachar interview.
6. Peterson interview.
7. Author's interview with Mary Eastwood at the American Cafe, Washington, D.C., June 22, 1983.

8. Author's interview with Catherine East at East's home in McLean, Virginia, August 11, 1983.

9. Author's emphasis.

10. Author's emphasis.

Chapter 6.　CRESTING

1. Carl M. Brauer, "Women Activists, Southern Conservatives, and the Prohibition of Sex Discrimination in Title VII of the 1964 Civil Rights Act," *Journal of Southern History* 49 (February 1983), 52. Brauer gives an intriguing report of Title VII's journey through Congress.

2. Author's interview with Betty Friedan at the Washington Hilton, Washington, D.C., October 1, 1983. Author's interview with Pauli Murray at Murray's home in Baltimore, Maryland, August 3, 1983.

3. East, Eastwood, and Friedan interviews.

4. Author's interview with Kathryn Clarenbach, Washington Hilton Hotel, Washington, D.C., October 1, 1983. Also Murray, Friedan, and Eastwood interviews.

5. Author's interview with Martha Griffiths at the National Women's Democratic Club, Washington, D.C., September 26, 1983. Also Clarenbach, Friedan, and Peterson interviews.

6. Letter from Pauli Murray to MR, August 9, 1966, MR Papers at the Schlesinger Library. Copy of letter from Betty Friedan to Anne Steinman, September 2, 1966, in MR Papers at the Schlesinger Library.

7. Clarenbach interview.

8. Copy of letter from Mary Eastwood to Kathryn Clarenbach, September 12, 1966, in MR Papers at the Schlesinger Library.

9. Author's interview with Elizabeth Boyer at Marguerite Rawalt's apartment in Arlington, Virginia, April 30, 1983.

10. Eastwood interview.

11. Letter from Betty Boyer to MR, August 31, 1967, in MR Papers in the Schlesinger Library.

12. Letter from Inka O'Hanrahan to MR, November 29, 1967, in MR Papers, Schlesinger Library.

13. See Eastwood's correspondence with political scientist Jo Freeman in Eastwood Papers at Schlesinger Library.

14. Author's interview with Lorena Weeks at Weeks's home in Wadley, Georgia. December 28, 1983. Assisted by Jayne M. Rushin.

15. Copy of letter from Betty Friedan to Faith Seidenberg, June 25, 1968, in MR Papers at Schlesinger Library.

16. Letter from Mary Eastwood to Pauli Murray, September 1, 1968, in Eastwood Papers at the Schlesinger Library.

Chapter 7.　CONTINUING

1. Author's interview with Elizabeth Koontz at the National Airport Cafe, November 15, 1983.

2. Allan interviews.

3. Griffiths interview.

4. Martha Griffiths in *Putting it Together: Goals for Contemporary Feminists* by Carol Atkins (published by Carol Atkins), ix.

5. Author's interview with Margaret Laurence, at Laurence's law office in Arlington, Virginia, April 11, 1985.

6. Letter from MR to Rita Mae Brown, October 16, 1969, in MR Papers at Schlesinger Library.

7. Fry interview with Paul, 540–550.

8. Author's interview with June Norris, Kenwood Country Club, Kensington, Maryland.

9. Norris interview.

Chapter 8.   IN THE MARKETPLACE

1. Murray interview.

Bibliography

Allen, Frederick Lewis. *Only Yesterday*. New York: Blue Ribbon Books, Inc., 1931.

Brown, Norman D. *Hood, Bonnet, and Little Brown Jug: Texas Politics, 1921–1928*. College Station: Texas A&M University Press, 1984.

Caro, Robert A. *The Years of Lyndon Johnson*. Alfred A. Knopf: New York, 1982.

Daniel, Pete. *Breaking the Land: The Transformation of Cotton, Tobacco, and Rice Cultures since 1880*. Urbana and Chicago: University of Illinois Press, 1985.

Freeman, Jo. *The Politics of Women's Liberation: A Case Study of an Emerging Social Movement and its Relation to the Policy Process*. New York: David McKay Company, Inc., 1975.

Friedan, Betty. *It Changed My Life: Writings on the Women's Movement*. New York: Random House, 1975.

Gammage, Judie Karen Walt. "Quest for Equality: An Historical Overview of Women's Rights Activism in Texas, 1890–1975." Ph.D. dissertation, North Texas State University, 1982.

Harrison, Cynthia Ellen. "Prelude to Feminism: Women's Organizations, the Federal Government and the Rise of the Women's Movement 1942 to 1968." Ph.D. dissertation, Columbia University, 1982.

Hole, Judith and Levine, Ellen. *Rebirth of Feminism*. New York: Quadrangle Books, 1971.

Lash, Joseph P. *Eleanor: The Years Alone*. New York: W. W. Norton & Company, Inc., 1972.

Lemons, J. Stanley. *The Woman Citizen: Social Feminism in the 1920s*. Urbana and Chicago: University of Illinois Press, 1975.

McGlen, Nancy E. and O'Connor, Karen. *Women's Rights: The Struggle for Equality in the 19th & 20th Centuries*. New York: Praeger Publishers, 1983.

Rawalt, Marguerite. *Descendants of Adam Flake*. 1969.

———. *Descendants of Captain John Rawalt (Rewalt)*. 1974.

———. *History of the National Federation of Business and Professional Women's Clubs, Inc., 1944–1960*. Washington, D.C.: The National Federation of Business and Professional Women's Clubs, Inc., 1969.

———. *History of the Business and Professional Women's Club of the District of Columbia, Inc.* Washington, D.C.: B&PW Club of the District of Columbia, Inc., 1927 through 1948, 1949.

———. "Constitutional Rights for Women — The Equal Rights Amendment," *The Study of Women: Enlarging Perspectives of Social Reality*, ed. Eloise C. Snyder. New York: Harper & Row, 1979.

————. "The Equal Rights Amendment," *Women in Washington*. Beverly Hills: Sage Publications, 1983.

U.S. Congress (1970) Senate Judiciary Committee Subcommittee on Constitutional Amendments. Hearings on S. J. Res. 61, 91 Cong., 2nd sess., May 5–7.

U.S. Congress (1970) Senate Judiciary Committee Subcommittee on Constitutional Amendments. Supplemental Hearings on S. J. Res. 61 and S. J. Res. 231, 91st Cong., 2nd sess., Sept. 9–15.

U.S. Congress (1971) House Judiciary Committee Subcommittee No. 4. Hearings on H. J. Res. 35, H. J. Res. 208 and H. R. 916 and related bills, 92nd Cong., 1st sess., March 24, 25, 31; April 1, 2, 3.

Ware, Susan. *Beyond Suffrage: Women in the New Deal*. Cambridge and London: Harvard University Press, 1981.

————. *Holding Their Own: American Women in the 1930s*. Boston: Twayne, 1982.

INDEX

A

Abell, Bess, 154
abortion, 177, 179, 181, 182, 183,
    186, 189, 210, 211
Abzug, Bella, 229
Adams, Jed, 46
Add Ran College, 15
AFL-CIO, 132, 205, 217
Agagnost, Catherine, 144
Agriculture Adjustment Act (AAA),
    47, 54
Alda, Alan, 234
Allan, Virginia, 92, 144, 150, 152,
    199, 201, 205, 206, 208, 226,
    227
Allen, Florence, 51, 61, 86, 142, 190
    Tess, 36, 38
Allred, Miss, 143
American Association of University
    Women (AAUW), 138, 220
American Bar Association (ABA),
    viii, ix, xiii, 2, 69, 70, 74, 78,
    89, 90, 91, 233
American Bar Association (ABA)
    House of Delegates, 66, 67,
    68, 69, 70
American Bar Association Founda-
    tion, 109
American Civil Liberties Union, 161,
    162
American Federation of Government
    Employees, 151
American Law and Lawyers, 77
American Legion, 97
American Medical Women's Associa-
    tion, 143
American Newspaper Publishers As-
sociation, 195, 199
American Nurses Association, 138,
    220
American Veterans Committee, 179
American Women, 147, 189
"Anacostia Flats," 43
Anderson, Hazel, 103, 109
    Mary, 51
Anthony, Susan B., 18, 112
armistice, 27
Arnold, Henry H. (Hap), 53
Arthur and Elizabeth Schlesinger
    Women's History Library at
    Radcliffe, 236–237
Assembly of Women's Organizations
    for National Security, 96
Atkinson, Ti-Grace, 179, 181, 182,
    190, 191, 194
Atlanta, Georgia, 67
Austin, Texas, 19, 22, 23, 30, 33, 90,
    93

B

Bachman, Lula, 82
Baker, Howard, 214
Baltimore Sun, 197
Banning, Margaret Culkin, 86
bar associations, minority involve-
    ment in, 69, 70, 75, 76, 77
Bardwell, C. M., 63, 64
    Myra, 20
Barkley, Alben, 99
Battles of Peace, The, 30
Bauerlein, Anne, 37, 52
Baughman, Wilbur, 72, 74, 77
Bayh, Birch, 202, 206, 212, 214, 215,
    216, 217, 218, 223, 225, 226,
    228